To
Anni and Brian
For their hospitality

PREFERENCES, INSTITUTIONS, AND
RATIONAL CHOICE

Preferences, Institutions, and Rational Choice

Edited by

KEITH DOWDING

and

DESMOND KING

CLARENDON PRESS · OXFORD

1995

Oxford University Press, Walton Street, Oxford OX2 6DP
Oxford New York
Athens Auckland Bangkok Bombay
Calcutta Cape Town Dar es Salaam Delhi
Florence Hong Kong Istanbul Karachi
Kuala Lumpur Madras Madrid Melbourne
Mexico City Nairobi Paris Singapore
Taipei Tokyo Toronto
and associated companies in
Berlin Ibadan

Oxford is a trade mark of Oxford University Press

Published in the United States
by Oxford University Press Inc., New York

British Library Cataloguing in Publication Data
Data available

Library of Congress Cataloging in Publication Data
Preferences, institutions, and rational choice / edited by
Keith Dowding and Desmond King.
'Most of the chapters were first delivered to meetings of the
Political Studies Association Specialist Subgroup on
Rational Choice Politics'—Pref.
Includes bibliographical references.
1. Rational choice theory.   2. Decision-making.
I. Dowding, Keith M.   II. King, Desmond S.
HB846.8.P743   1995   658.4'03—dc20   95-16133
ISBN 0-19-827895-0

1 3 5 7 9 10 8 6 4 2

Set by Hope Services (Abingdon) Ltd.
Printed in Great Britain
on acid-free paper by
Biddles Ltd
Guildford & King's Lynn

PREFACE

Rational choice is one of the leading approaches deployed at present by political scientists to a diverse range of topics. This diversity is apparent in the chapters collected in this volume. Most of the chapters were first delivered to meetings of the Political Studies Association Specialist Subgroup on Rational Choice Politics, which meets regularly in London at the home of Brian Barry and at the PSA annual conference. Regular meetings of this include researchers working on a variety of topics, from empirical political science to political philosophy, from international relations to local government; but each may learn from all given their shared methods. That is the strength of a common methodology.

Keith Dowding
Desmond King

Oxford
January 1995

CONTENTS

LIST OF FIGURES

LIST OF TABLES

LIST OF CONTRIBUTORS

EDITORS

KEITH DOWDING is Lecturer in Public Choice and Public Policy at the London School of Economics and Political Science. His recent publications include *Rational Choice and Political Power* (1991) and *The Civil Service* (1995).

DESMOND KING is Official Fellow and Tutor in Politics at St John's College, Oxford. His recent publications include *Actively Seeking Work? The Politics of Unemployment and Welfare Policy in Britain and the USA* (1995) and *Separate and Unequal: Black Americans and the US Federal Government* (1995).

CONTRIBUTORS

ANDREW BAILEY is Senior Manager in the Banking Department of the Bank of England. He completed a Ph.D. thesis on 'The Impact of the Napoleonic Wars on the Development of the Cotton Industry in Lancashire: A Study of the Structure and Behaviour of Firms during the Industrial Revolution' at the University of Cambridge in 1984.

ALAN CARLING is Lecturer in the Department of Interdisciplinary Human Studies at the University of Bradford. His recent publications include *Social Division* (1991).

PATRICK DUNLEAVY is Professor of Government at the London School of Economics and Political Science. His recent publications include *Democracy, Bureaucracy and Public Choice* (1990) and *Developments in British Politics 4* (1993).

IAIN MCLEAN is Official Fellow in Politics at Nuffield College, Oxford. His recent publications include *Public Choice* (1987) and articles in the *American Political Science Review* and *Public Administration*.

MOSHE MAOR is Lecturer at the European Institute of the London School of Economics and Political Science. His recent publications include *Political Parties: Comparative Approaches and the British Experience* (1995).

HELEN MARGETTS is Lecturer in Public Policy at Birkbeck College, University of London. Her recent publications include the co-edited *Turning Japanese* (1994) and articles in *Political Studies*, *West European Politics*, and *Public Administration*.

MICHAEL NICHOLSON is Professor of International Relations in the School of Social Sciences, University of Sussex. His recent publications include *Rationality and the Analysis of International Conflict* (1992).

CHERYL SCHONHARDT-BAILEY is Lecturer in Government at the London School of Economics and Political Science. She has published articles in the *American Political Science Review*, *World Politics*, and *Parliamentary History*, and completed a Ph.D. thesis on 'A Model of Trade Policy Liberalization: Looking Inside the British "Hegemon" of the Nineteenth Century' at the University of California, Los Angeles in 1991.

HUGH WARD is Senior Lecturer in Government at the University of Essex. He has published widely in many academic journals including *Political Studies* and *British Journal of Political Science*.

MARK WICKHAM-JONES is Lecturer in Politics at the University of Bristol. His publications include articles in the *British Journal of Political Science*, *Political Quarterly*, and *Twentieth Century British History*. He completed a Ph.D. thesis on 'The Labour Party's Alternative Economic Policy' at the University of Manchester in 1994.

1

Introduction

KEITH DOWDING AND DESMOND KING

1. INSTITUTIONAL RATIONAL CHOICE

The title of this book conveys the two important aspects of rational-choice methods in social science: preferences provide the motivation of individual action; institutions provide the context allowing causal explanation. Rational choice, we argue, offers causal explanation of any political outcome only where the reasons for individual action are specified, and the structural conditions under which those reasons for action have been modelled are explained. More often, rational choice provides a specification of the general conditions under which actors (including individuals, organizations, or groups) behave, thereby facilitating comparative structural analysis.

The underlying assumption of this approach is, of course, the rationality assumption. It assumes that the behaviour of actors can be explained by imputing rationality to them. 'Rationality' here is a transparent concept. It may involve only the minimal amount of validity or internal consistency and may include beliefs and desires which the analyst may not be able to imagine holding personally. It is what Jon Elster terms 'thin rationality'.[1]

This method of ascribing beliefs and desires to an individual is simplified for models involving a group of individuals. Rather than assuming a complex set of beliefs and desires for each individual, the group members are assumed to share a set of preferences. In rational choice this usually takes one of two forms. 'First principles rational choice' uses simplified models often with no obvious practical application to real world situations.[2] They are generated to specify the rationality assumption, to explain how rational actors operate under constrained conditions, and to examine the paradoxical results that may emerge. Often first-principles rational choice theorists presume no particular set of preferences, but rather aim to deduce what will happen under any possible combination of preferences. Such 'preference-open' models are assumed, for example, in social-choice theory. Arrow's General Impossibility theorem demonstrates that there is no universally applicable method of generating a coherent social preference ordering for groups larger than two. If we allow that individual preferences for a choice set of three or more items may be ordered in any way, and we assume that each individual's ordering is equally valid, the social ordering may be inconsistent.[3] Similarly, models of the power of individuals within a committee system, and the coalition theory based upon such models, assume that any set of preferences is possible. Such models are truly generalizable across all logically possible worlds, illuminating certain general problems and paradoxes within political theory because they constrain what is logically possible. They are less illuminating for empirical political science, however, since empirical explanation also crucially relies upon what actually is.

Preference-open models need to be replaced with 'preference-constrained' models which specify precisely what the actors desire. This can be done within a first-principles exercise by assuming a set of preferences for the actors whose behaviour is being modelled. These assumptions generate abstract models which may be illustrative, but are rarely fully explanatory, of any given social situation.[4] More interestingly, however, we may examine how preferences are generated by the institutions and social structure in which actors find themselves situated. Much of what is to be explained in social science requires the institutional component, because institutions both constrain what is possible and 'structurally suggest' individual interests.[5] Institutions do this in two ways. First, by constraining what is possible, indeed what is probable, they shape interests. Individual interests cannot include that which is not possible—desiring the impossible is a form of wishful thinking,[6] and requires a calculation of the probabilities associated with the outcomes of different actions. Secondly, the interests of any given individual are given by her relationship to others, that is her position within the social structure. Whilst the rationality assumption itself may assume that I desire, say, material wealth, my attitude towards the rate of inflation may vary depending on my relationship to regular trade. Subsistence farmers, for example, are scarcely troubled by high inflation; someone with high debts and fixed interest payments may positively welcome it. But even one's attitude towards material wealth may be affected by the sort of society one inhabits. The Buddhist monk who can be assured of his next meal because others will feed him before themselves finds immaterialism easier than the secular contract worker.

In this volume the term 'institutional rational choice' denotes the application of rational-choice methods to substantive political and social problems rather than engagement with the a priori assumptions of first-principles theorists. Interest in institutional rational choice developed partly in response to certain problems which emerged through the abstract formulations generated by first-principles social choice. Richard McKelvey demonstrated that unless preferences are symmetrical around a median, a global cycle around all possible choices may result.[7] Norman Schofield similarly proved that multi-dimensional voting games typically have an empty core and again, in consequence, a global cycling of bundles of possible policies emerges.[8] These results suggest that there is inherent instability in politics: any possible bundle of policies proposed by some party can be beaten in a binary vote by some other bundle. General instability results from the constant cycling around rival policy sets. The problem for empirical rational choice is that such instability is not often manifest. One reason for this pattern is that institutions create stability. That is, the setting in which individuals find themselves helps to generate, or 'structurally to suggest', both their preferences and actions to realize their interests. Institutions—variously defined—channel preferences, slow the cycling process, and foster stability. For example, the simple institution of a rule stating that decisions reached cannot be challenged for three years ensures at least three years of stability. Institutions typically create stability and since political scientists are concerned with the results of the political process—stable outcomes—they are interested in the institutions which generate them.[9] But politics is also about change, and so both stability and change are important.

The dynamics of politics is manifested in numerous ways. Riker has written about the 'heresthetics' of change.[10] This is the art of manipulating political situations to increase the probability of winning the political game. Riker examines the actions of leading politicians to alter previously stable situations by discovering and

exploiting latent cleavages in existing coalitions. By dissolving
existing coalitions and forming new ones, politicians are able to
gain and then retain power.[11] In effect the heresthetic politician
introduces a new conflict, z, to terminate a winning coalition
around y, to achieve x. It is agenda manipulation based around the
failure of the condition of 'the independence of irrelevant alternatives' employed by Arrow when creating modern social-choice
theory.[12] This process of breaking up extant coalitions and then
controlling the political agenda may lead politicians to work within
already existing institutional structures. Another way is to break
previous institutional structures and create new ones. The new
institutional structure may then lead to a new equilibrium, stabi-
lizing expectations and creating new coalition groups with common
interests. These revolutionary changes may occur by changing the
voting rules—for example, modifying the structure of property
rights and entitlements, or reforming the local units of administration. New institutional arrangements create new equilibria and new
stability. Such changes may help to cement groups by reinforcing
common interests, or they may create new common interests
through 'preference shaping'.[13] For example, by creating a new
class of property-owners a government may alter attitudes towards
taxation (and strengthen their own electoral support). A new
health structure may alter attitudes towards public or private
health provision. These institutional changes create new interests
and shape old ones.

This process may occur deliberately, as Riker's 'heresthetics' or
the 'art of manipulation' suggests. But it may also occur uninten-
tionally through a process of natural selection of issues. One set of
institutional arrangements may favour one group over another. As
the losing group comes to recognize this fact it eventually mobi-
lizes to defend its interests, the mobilization process itself shaping
and cementing common interests. No one may have intended that
that institutional system would lead to the mobilization of any
group, even though in retrospect it may appear an obvious outcome. Often a change in the institutions leads to changes in other
institutions unanticipated by the architects of the first change.
Institutional rational choice examines these institutional changes.
It studies their causes and the consequences, intended and unin-
tended, of such adjustments.

2. PREFERENCES AND PREFERENCE FORMATION

It is a conventional criticism of rational-choice theorists that they pay insufficient attention to the formation of actors' preferences. Thelen and Steinmo use this trait most saliently to differentiate their approach from rational-choice theory: 'the core difference between rational choice institutionalism and historical institutionalism lies in the question of preference formation, whether treated as exogenous (rational choice) or endogenous (historical institutionalism) . . . [Historical institutionalists] argue that not just the strategies but also the goals actors pursue are shaped by the institutional context.'[14] The charge that institutional rational-choice theorists neglect the way in which context informs preference is misplaced, however. Imputing rationality to individuals' behaviour is compatible with delineating a complex range of influences upon individuals in their preference formation. What rational choice may do is to assume that preferences are exogeneous in one model and use another, complementary model to explain how the preferences were formed in the first place.

The contributions by Alan Carling, Patrick Dunleavy and Helen Margetts, Iain McLean, Mike Nicholson, and Mark Wickham-Jones all to some extent consider the preference side of the equation and its relationship to institutional form. In Chapter 2, Carling reconsiders the problem of the rationality of voting, which has plagued rational choice from the outset. Why should a rational individual bother to vote when the probability of her vote making a difference to the outcome is negligible? Many scholars have asked that if rational-choice methods cannot even explain as simple a political act as this, what hope have they of helping us to understand deeper political problems? Carling uses an institutional account to answer this problem. Dismantling traditional formulations of, and solutions to, the problem he argues that to understand why people vote we need to look at the history of voting. The right to vote was not some distant divine given but a privilege that was fought for. Carling advances an evolutionary-historical account to explain the rationality of voting. In his view, the most plausible candidate for explanation of the institutional structure which makes voting rational is one which suggests that democratic procedures were socially selected.

Dunleavy and Margetts pose a fundamental challenge to the some problem of voting in Chapter 4. As their starting-point they examine an argument from Brennan and Lomasky which contrasts the rationality of market decisions for private goods with political decisions for collective goods.[15] Dunleavy and Margetts argue that decisions for private goods are more inter-dependent than Brennan and Lomasky appreciate, whilst rational-choice analysis of decision for collective goods has concentrated disproportionately on efficacy measured by pivotality. By attacking the distinction between market decisions for private goods and political decisions for collective goods from both sides Dunleavy and Margetts demonstrate that there are not two distinct types of decision-making in the two arenas, and produce a model for rational voting.

McLean uses the introduction of railway regulation to test alternative theoretical explanations of policy choices including rational choice. In Chapter 7, he finds that self-interest is not a sufficient explanation for all the actors and groups affected by railway regulation. For instance, the Prime Minister, Gladstone, was motivated by a conception of the public interest. Wealth maximization explains the railway interest. Members of Parliament were also motivated by the public interest, but non-trivial relative differences in MPs' views reflected their constituency. Overall, public-interest motivations best explain the final legislation. His study is a fascinating example of the use of rational-choice methods in historical explanation and demonstrates how the nature of political institutions affects the behaviour of the relevant actors, in this case legislators and railway interests, but also how dominant ideas about the economic and social consequences of different acts affects ideas about legislation. Mike Nicholson's chapter (Chapter 8) also examines the individual decision-maker. In times of crisis, decisions may not appear rational to outside observers, as decision-makers make brisk decisions based upon faulty or partial analysis. Nicholson demonstrates the rationality of excluding certain sorts of information and even sources of information during a crisis, as the requirements of rapid decision-making demand that the members of a group harmonize their disparate positions to produce coherent strategies. In Chapter 11 Mark Wickham-Jones tackles the well-established problem of collective action as it operates in revolutionary situations. He argues that complex understanding of actor preferences and the differing structures of revolutionary situations can help us to understand the historical proliferation of revolution.

3. STRUCTURES AND INSTITUTIONS

The development of institutional rational choice has mirrored a revived interest in institutions amongst political scientists more generally. The latter is a reaction to the behaviouralism which dominated political methodology for so long. In common with rational choice, behaviouralists explain politics by looking for uniformities in the behaviour of actors engaged in politics—be they voters, parties, or groups. Institutionalists have suggested, however, that concentrating upon actions and actors, decisions and interests, neglects how many political outcomes arise from institutional processes,[16] and how these structure the context of politics. Institutional context is both formal—rules such as constitutional arrangements and laws; and informal—such as co-operative and reciprocated norms that develop between groups and individuals within a social system. Peter Hall, for example, argues that different policy outcomes in France and Britain can be explained, not by the fact that the British and French have different interests, but that the institutions in those nations are so distinct. He defines institutions very broadly as the 'formal rules, compliance procedures, and standards operating in practices that structure the relationship between individuals in various units of the polity and economy.'[17] The contrast between institutionalism versus behaviouralism and first-principles rational choice versus institutional rational choice is analogous to that drawn between behavioural (as manifest in preferences, beliefs, and interests) and institutional explanations of politics.

To a certain degree the contrast is otiose; both interests and institutions are important. It would be impossible to explain political behaviour and political outcomes without attending to the role each plays. But it is easy to see that, generally speaking, the institutions of politics provide a larger part of the explanation than do preferences. This is something acknowledged even by political scientists who eschew rational-choice assumptions. For instance, in their presentation of the historical institutionalist framework, Thelen and Steinmo declare that the 'idea that institutions provide the context in which political actors define their strategies and pursue their interests is unproblematical.'[18] We can begin to see the importance of institutions even in a first-principles exercise. Consider the following matrix:

		Actor j	
		C	D
Actor i	C	R,R	S,T
	D	T,S	P,P

Given this matrix, how will actors i and j behave? We cannot say without further information about the preference orderings of the two players. Preferences are crucial to understanding their behaviour in this case. There are twenty-four possible combinations of preference orderings of the two players. Consider just the following six combinations shared by each player:

$$T > R > P > S \text{ (PD)}$$
$$T > R > S > P \text{ (Chicken)}$$
$$T > P > R > P$$
$$P > T > R > S$$
$$P > R > S > T$$
$$P > S > T > S$$

Given our rationality assumptions we must assume that we can predict the outcome of this simple game under each combination. Tsebelis makes a similar point: under rational choice

individual action is assumed to be optimal adaptation to an institutional environment, and the interaction between individuals is assumed to be an optimal response to each other. Therefore, the prevailing institutions (the rules of the game) determine the behavior of the actors, which in turn produces political or social outcomes.[19]

The two named combinations above—Prisoners' Dilemma (PD) and Chicken—have an extensive literature over which there is now general agreement upon rational strategies. There is also little controversy in the analysis of Assurance games. The key aspect to note, however, is that the form of the game in which the actors are engaged is given by the relationship between the players who are defined by their preference orderings alone. If we apply this simple game to any social situation we are concluding that that situation has the structure of this game, say, Chicken. To the extent that the game is explanatory of that situation it is explanatory because of its structure. The relationship of the preferences always determines the nature of the game and therefore the analysis of the situation to which it is applied. As Carling remarks:

What constrains each individual is . . . a combination of what every individual possesses and what every *other* individual *does*. The game theoretic concept of equilibrium then corresponds to a certain meshing of everyone's social structures: no actor has any incentive to act differently at equilibrium, which means that there is no tendency to structural alteration.[20]

Thus even first-principles rational choice provides structural explanation. The theorems of McKelvey and Schofield are explanatory of any situation to the extent that it is structured to generate global cycles. It is the relationship of preference orderings and the decision rules which generate such cycles. In this case it is generated for preferences which are assumed to be 'preference open'—that is any preference ordering is possible; and the decision process is that the simple majority wins. Institutionalists believe that preferences, which are usually exogenously assumed in rational modelling, are formed, to a significant extent, by the institutions through which we identify actors (and through which they identify themselves). Thus the institutional rational-choice perspective expands the structural component of first-principles rational choice by according institutional arrangements a central place in analytic frameworks. In Chapter 3, Keith Dowding examines the consequences of a non-structural causal interpretation of coalition theory. He argues that the traditional causal understanding of coalition theory creates unfulfilled expectations about its potential to explain observable coalitions. To explain variation in coalition formation, a structural interpretation enables analysts to compare institutions cross-nationally. Generalizations about coalition theory therefore need to be predicated upon institutional form rather than upon theorems derived from a first-principles approach. These theorems form the basis of the method, rather than its conclusion.

4. DEFINING INSTITUTIONS

It is difficult to give a definition of institutions which is not so broad as to be unilluminating. For instance, Elinor Ostrom defines institutions as:

the sets of working rules that are used to determine who is eligible to make decisions in some arena, what actions are allowed or constrained, what aggregation rules will be used, what procedures must be followed, what information must or must not be provided, and what payoffs will be assigned to individuals dependent on their actions.[21]

There is a danger here of making institutionalism trivially true. Its importance derives, however, from the unpacking of such statements and from disaggregating institutions into their component forms. For example, a person is unlikely to be affected in the same way by some forms of institutional rules as by others. Breaking a law is not comparable to breaking a convention; doing as the law demands may result from very different motivations to doing as we believe is normal. We react to different sorts of institutions in different ways and the internal causal story (or 'reasons for action') of behaviour is different with distinct types of institution.

Institutional rational-choice theorists have proved adept at explaining the operation of preferences within fixed environments, such as the committee structure of the US Congress and other legislatures.[22] In the US Congress, political scientists have imputed stable interests to members, deduced from the structure and rules of the legislature, and derived hypotheses about how members are likely to behave given these interests.

The assignation of property rights and the form those rights take are a key aspect of institutionalist analysis.[23] Chapter 9, by Cheryl Schonhardt-Bailey and Andrew Bailey, considers the effects upon principal-agent problems of large firms with different types of asset-holding. They demonstrate how the asset holdings of large firms create incentives for shareholders to act collectively. They explain the processes by which shareholders' interests form, concentrating in particular upon the incentives deriving from national financial institutional frameworks and government policy in both the United States and Germany.

Other chapters consider the structural and institutional relations between different types of actor. In Chapter 6, Moshe Maor examines the effects that interlinked political markets have upon each other. He borrows from George Tsebelis's account of 'nested games': in such games individuals or groups appear to pursue suboptimal behaviour but are in fact pursuing aims in different contexts or spheres.[24] Maor shows how the characteristics of national party systems become altered through the operation of another electoral game at the European level. Chapter 10, by Hugh Ward, tests Mancur Olson's well-known claim that the development of interest-group organizations stultifies the political process by causing economic stagnation through rent-seeking activities.[25] Borrowing a balance-of-power argument from international relations, Ward demonstrates that the leaders of distributive coalitions within societies engage in zero-sum games to maximize the security of their political leadership and of their power. Under this framework, political institutions and coalitions which arise for strategic reasons prove harmful to economic prosperity by, for instance, delaying the response to economic growth opportunities. Ward's empirical analysis corroborates his own model. In their analysis of the adoption of punitive work-welfare regimes in Chapter 5, Desmond King and Hugh Ward explain how conservative administrations in Britain and the United States wished to exclude undeserving recipients of welfare from public benefits. Each government designed programmes to achieve this end, whereby the benefit of discouraging undeserving applicants was judged greater than the cost of excluding some deserving cases. These five chapters all illustrate the importance of institutional factors in determining political outcomes.

5. EPISTEMOLOGICAL CHALLENGES TO RATIONAL CHOICE

Rational-choice actors need not necessarily be people but may include organizations (though usually analysts assume that the actions of organizations can be causally explained by considering the decision-making individuals comprising the organization). Rational-choice theorists are often accused of being too individualistic, but we have demonstrated that even first-principles rational choice provides structural explanation. The longstanding holist–methodological individualist debate has been challenged by a recognition that individualist methods in social science have always identified individuals by their social roles.[26] It is as role-bearers that individuals are shown to be causally efficacious. Identifying people as role-bearers necessarily provides a structural basis for social explanation because roles define individuals by their relationship to others.

It is true that rational choice relies upon an egotistical self, that is one which views the world from its own perspective. It is sometimes claimed that this view depends upon a Kantian tradition which upholds an unproblematic conception of the self, an atomistic conception summarized by Rawls in his statement that the 'self is prior to the ends which are affirmed by it.'[27] This view is challenged by communitarians and feminists. The former reject the Kantian self because 'it ignores the fact that the self is embedded or situated in existing social practices, that we cannot always stand back and opt out of them. Our social roles and relationships, or at least some of them, must be taken as givens for the purposes of personal deliberation.'[28] In a formal sense the Kantian view is surely correct. In order to identify a being across logically possible worlds one must have some form of signifier, whether it be a letter standing for a variable defined in some way, say, the genetic imprint of a person. But the letter as a signifier is identified by the variable and can only be said to have interests once it is placed in some context, and few would dispute that a genetically identical individual placed in two completely different contexts may develop different interests and preferences, even if some psychological and behavioural responses are genetically encoded. It is surely true that any given genetic being could take on another role if the world he or she occupied had a different type of society and culture. However, taking the Kantian self as a formally correct description of people in this sense should not trouble communitarians. They are perfectly correct, in that the very different interests that a genetically distinct person may develop are formulated through that person's own history, including the social role he occupies within a society and the society in which that role is occupied,[29] a point long acknowledged by Amartya Sen.[30] However, once the structural component of rational-choice explanation is identified there is nothing in this communitarian claim that need trouble the rational-choice analyst.[31] Indeed rational choice may take a leading role in explaining how different cultures operate given different sets of resources and interests which individuals formulate. It may also take a leading role, using an evolutionary form, in explaining how different cultures develop.

Some feminists attack the liberal tradition for different reasons. They charge that the way in which this tradition conceives of the individual is unduly male-biased, and that consequently the issues with which rational-choice theorists are concerned are male-oriented.[32] Certainly, the rational-choice tradition tends to use the notion of an agent who is both egoistical and egotistical. Though most writers merely defend or transcend the egoistical or self-interest assumption, the egotistical or self-centred assumption may be more problematic. The self-interest assumption is used more for theoretical convenience than theoretical correctness and is, in a fairly straightforward fashion, false. It is used, however, for its effectiveness in generating models which seem to go a long way towards explaining the social world, and bringing in to sharp focus the questions that need asking where the models fail. Carling has utilized fairly simple rational-choice models to elucidate gender-based exploitation in the household.[33] He uses Chicken games to suggest how, in societies where average male income is higher, some individuals (women) become locked into providing the household collective goods while others (men) go out to work. Similarly, he uses Chicken games to suggest that female exploitation in the household may be based upon differential socialization by gender leading to differential aptitudes to pre-commit either to aggressive or to acquiescent responses to conflict.[34] In Carling's argument the socialization process is seen as a form of institution creating differential aptitudes to respond to situations. The pure model of Chicken is the explanatory tool which explains how this apparently moderate and innocuous institution may lead to exploitation: 'we might think of the rational choice mechanism as responsible for an *amplification of socialization*. People are led by marginal differences of initial socialization into patterns of behaviour which leave them trapped, with the wish perhaps but no incentive to escape.'[35] Carling maps this process through the generations, thus helping to explain socialization as well as using it as the explanans in his initial model. Such an exercise succinctly exposes the mechanisms and processes facilitating and perpetuating unattractive household relations, and suggests apposite solutions to ameliorate such arrangements. A comparable analysis of Britain's indifferent industrial and vocational training framework is developed by Finegold and Soskice by reference to the idea of a low skills equilibrium.[36] In outlining the development of this equilibrium—based on the expectations of employers, workers, and the state—Finegold and Soskice also explain why improving training programmes in Britain is so difficult. The two very different applications of similar models aptly demonstrate the range of rational-choice methods.

Formally speaking, self-interest is not required for rational choice; utility maximization can suffice. Utility can be defined across any set of aims and objectives to encompass any set of principled beliefs. As long as we can identify a fairly determinate set of actions based upon these principled beliefs we can test for consistency, as Iain McLean demonstrates in Chapter 7.[37] The much less discussed and criticized egotistical assumption of rational choice may be harder to defend against a feminist critique. The rational actor is self-centred, which means that the world is viewed from the perspective of the individual decision-maker rather than from an essentially social viewpoint. This egotistical assumption trades upon the Kantian assumption of the genetic self as the seat of denotation and the 'window upon the world' by which each individual gains her or his perspective.[38] The egotistical viewpoint is a necessary aspect of rational choice and it is not one which can be easily transcended. Indeed it is hard to explain a non-egotistical position without it being parasitic upon the self-centred one. The very idea of empathetic understanding of others requires the recognition of 'others' with which to empathize. It is noticeable how, despite all the claims of the importance of the community as opposed to the atomistic individual, communitarians are unable to refrain from individual denotation. Here the truth in the Kantian self as the bearer of a proper name seems manifest.

6. RATIONAL CHOICE AND POLITICAL SCIENCE

Rational-choice theory is a rival form of explanation to many others. Brian Barry long ago contrasted it with functional (or what he called 'sociological') explanation.[39] There are various rival interpretations of the rational-choice method. One causal view, juxtaposed to functionalism, is that of Harsanyi.[40] His version attempts to provide a causal explanation of social behaviour, and in the attempt to produce fully determined explanations Harsanyi's method becomes hell-bent on producing equilibrium solutions to any problem. For the empirical researcher such equilibrium models merely bring frustration, for it is not always empirically obvious quite what constitutes an equilibrium solution unless it is a given structure or institution. Other contending models are concerned with rival models based on different motivational assumptions. McLean considers some of these rivals in his chapter and finds that different motivations underlie different sets of actors. Though McLean does not suggest that structure is important, we can interpret the different motivations he identifies partly in terms of the situation of the actors concerned. We might suggest that the role that actors take on is connected to the motivations they display. Maximizing behaviour is displayed in all aspects of social life, and the rational-choice method has no area beyond its jurisdiction, though beyond the market-place it becomes less like egoistic maximization. We see empirically in Chapter 7 and theoretically in Chapter 11 how important other motivations are. As marketization expands into new areas, then market motivations may assume greater precedence outside ordinary economic markets. How would Gladstone's actions have changed if spin-doctors had been interpreting his speeches? This prompts some observers to complain that rational choice is an ideological programme in the sense that it tends to suggest that egoistical maximizing is rational and pervasive, thereby encouraging such behaviour.[41] That may well be, but rather than dismissing the approach—which has proved so explanatorily powerful—we need to probe beyond myopic models to broader motivational assumptions. This also requires much more widespread recognition of the deeply normative nature of much of public choice, which paradoxically is so often interpreted positivistically.[42] The truly deep division in the rational-choice method concerns the controversial and profoundly normative concept of 'efficiency' or 'Pareto-efficiency' which has taken such a hold upon modern political economy or public choice. Banishment of the concept is difficult given its role in so many equilibrium models. Greater care in its interpretation and the use of models which do not attempt to provide equilibrium conditions may overcome some of these difficulties.

Rational choice should not be seen as a method which is rival to all other methods. It is not the be-all and end-all of social science. Rational choice may be used in conjunction with more descriptive methods and the strict assumptions of the simplest models may be relaxed, as Mark Wickham-Jones demonstrates, yet still provide illumination of some of the hardest problems in social science.

McLean uses rational choice together with historical data to illuminate the history of railway regulation in nineteenth-century Britain. Hugh Ward uses cross-national statistical data to test rival rational-choice models. In his chapter, Keith Dowding turns the focus on to rational-choice methods to consider the nature of rational-choice explanation itself. Rational-choice theorists strive for parsimonious explanation, and to simplify rather than complicate in order to explain. For example, using only the simplest models of firms in competitive and monopolistic situations, Gambetta manages to explain a wide variety of criminal behaviour amongst mafia and similar bodies of 'organized crime'.[43] His book elucidates many aspects of behaviour which previously received scant attention or were reduced to being explained by culture or other such vague and unhelpful concepts. Rational choice has no thematic limitations, as evidenced by the diverse nature of the subject-matter in the chapters of this book. It provides a coherent methodology which allows researchers in different fields to have a common purpose and common research agenda to facilitate dialogue across diverse fields.

NOTES

1. J. Elster, *Sour Grapes* (Cambridge: Cambridge University Press, 1983), ch. 1.
2. P. Dunleavy, *Democracy, Bureaucracy and Public Choice* (Hemel Hempstead: Harvester Wheatsheaf, 1991).
3. K. J. Arrow, *Social Choice and Individual Values* (New York: John Wiley, rev. edn., 1963).
4. Keith Dowding's contribution to this volume discusses preference-open modelling in more detail.
5. See K. Dowding, *Rational Choice and Political Power* (Aldershot: Edward Elgar, 1991) for the idea of 'structural suggestion'.
6. See J. Elster, *Ulysses and the Sirens* (Cambridge: Cambridge University Press, 1979), 174–5 and id., *Sour Grapes* for a discussion of wishful thinking.
7. R. D. McKelvey, 'Intransitivities in Multidimensional Voting Models and some Implications for Agenda Control', *Journal of Economic Theory*, 12 (1976), 472–82, and id., 'General Conditions for Global Intransitivities in Formal Voting Models', *Econometrica*, 47 (1979), 1085–111.

8. N. Schofield, 'Instability of Simple Dynamic Games', *Review of Economic Studies*, 45 (1978), 575–94 and id., 'Generic Instability of Majority Rule', *Review of Economic Studies*, 50 (1983), 695–705.

9. Not all have taken the institutionalist line and there are attempts to explain stability in other ways; for example, N. R. Miller, 'A New Solution Set for Tournaments and Majority Voting: Further Graph-Theoretical Approaches to the Theory of Voting', *American Journal of Political Science*, 24 (1980), 68–96; id., B. Grofman, and S. L. Field, 'The Geometry of Majority Rule', *Journal of Theoretical Politics*, 1 (1989), 379–406; R. D. McKelvey, 'Covering, Dominance, and Institution-Free Properties of Social Choice', *American Journal of Political Science*, 30 (1986), 283–314; G. W. Cox, 'The Uncovered Set and the Core', *American Journal of Political Science*, 31 (1987), 408–22; R. G. Niemi, 'Why So Much Stability? Another Opinion', *Public Choice*, 41 (1983), 361–70; S. L. Field and B. Grofman, 'Partial Single-Peakedness: An Extension and Clarification', *Public Choice*, 51 (1986), 71–80. Some of these solutions include restricting the domain of preferences without explaining why. It would be hard to give a non-institutional account of such restrictions.

10. W. H. Riker, *Liberalism Against Populism* (San Francisco: W. H. Freeman, 1982); id., 'Political Theory and the Art of Heresthetics', in A. W. Finifter (ed.), *Political Science: The State of the Discipline* (Washington, DC: American Political Science Association, 1983); id., 'The Heresthetics of Constitution-Making: The Presidency in 1787, with Comments on Determinism and Rational Choice', *American Political Science Review*, 78 (1984), 1–16; *The Art of Political Manipulation* (New Haven, Conn.: Yale University Press, 1986).

11. A good example of such a story is found in J. H. Nagel 'Populism, Heresthetics and Political Stability: Richard Seddon and the Art of Majority Rule', *British Journal of Political Science*, 23 (1993), 139–74.

12. Arrow, *Social Choice*.

13. Dunleavy, *Bureaucracy*.

14. K. Thelen and S. Steinmo, 'Historical Institutionalism in Comparative Politics' in S. Steinmo, K. Thelen and F. Longstreth (eds.), *Structuring Politics: Historical Institutionalism in Comparative Analysis* (Cambridge: Cambridge University Press, 1992), 9, 8.

15. G. Brennan and L. Lomasky, *Democracy and Decision: The Pure Theory of Electoral Preference* (Cambridge: Cambridge University Press, 1993).

16. For an argument that these are complementary approaches see K. Dowding, 'The Compatibility of Behaviouralism, Rational Choice and "New Institutionalism" ', *Journal of Theoretical Politics*, 6 (1994) 105–17.

17. P. Hall, *Governing the Economy* (New York: Oxford University Press, 1986), 19. See also the essays in S. Steinmo, K. Thelen, and F. Longstreth (eds.), *Structuring Politics: Historical Institutionalism in Comparative Analysis* (Cambridge: Cambridge University Press, 1992); J. March and J. Olsen, 'The New Institutionalism: Organizational Factors in Political Life', *American Political Science Review*, 78 (1984), 734–49.

18. Thelen and Steinmo, 'Historical Institutionalism', 7.

19. G. Tsebelis, *Nested Games: Rational Choice in Comparative Politics* (Berkeley, Calif.: University of California Press, 1990), 40.

20. A. Carling, *Social Division* (London: Verso, 1991), 276.

21. E. Ostrom, *Governing the Commons* (Cambridge: Cambridge University Press, 1990), 51.

22. K. A. Shepsle, 'Institutional Foundations of Committee Power', *American Political Science Review*, 81 (1987), 85–104; id. and B. R. Weingast, 'Structure-Induced Equilibrium and Legislative Choice', *Public Choice*, 37 (1981), 503–19; id., 'Political Preferences for the Pork Barrel: A Generalization', *American Journal of Political Science*, 25 (1981), 96–111; R. L. Hall, 'Participation and Purpose in Committee Decision Making', *American Political Science Review*, 81 (1987), 105–28: and essays in M. D. McCubbins and T. Sullivan (eds.), *Congress: Structure and Policy* (Cambridge: Cambridge University Press, 1987).

23. D. W. Bromley, *Economic Interests and Institutions* (Oxford: Blackwell, 1989); T. Eggertsson, *Economic Behaviour and Institutions* (Cambridge: Cambridge University Press, 1990).

24. Tsebelis, *Nested Games*.

25. M. Olson, *The Rise and Decline of Nations* (New Haven, Conn.: Yale University Press, 1982).

26. See Dowding, *Rational Choice*, ch. 1.

27. J. Rawls, *A Theory of Justice* (Oxford: Oxford University Press, 1971), 560.

28. W. Kymlicka, *Contemporary Political Philosophy* (Oxford: Oxford University Press, 1990), 207.

29. See E. Frazer and N. Lacey, *The Politics of Community* (Brighton: Harvester Wheatsheaf, 1993).

30. See essays in A. Sen, *Choice, Welfare and Measurement* (Oxford: Blackwell, 1982), and the useful discussion by A. B. Atkinson, 'Original Sen', *New York Review of Books*, 22 Oct. 1987.

31. Quite what this truth means for universalizing principles of social justice need not detain us here. That battle is over the modal status attainable by any proposition propounded by a person who is necessarily situated in a particular social position in a particular society.

32. See, for example, the arguments advanced in C. MacKinnon, *Feminism Unmodified: Discourse on Life and Law* (Cambridge, Mass.: Harvard University Press, 1987); S. Okin, *Justice, Gender and the Family* (New York: Basic, 1989); I. Young, 'Polity and Group Difference: A Critique of the Ideal of Universal Citizenship', *Ethics*, 99 (1989), 250–74.
33. Carling, *Social Division*.
34. Ibid. 265–71.
35. Ibid. 266.
36. D. Finegold and D. Soskice, 'The Failure of Training Policy in Britain: Analysis and Prescription', *Oxford Review of Economic Policy*, 4 (1988), 21–53.
37. See also, for example, chapters in J. E. Alt and K. A. Shepsle (eds.), *Perspectives on Positive Political Economy* (Cambridge: Cambridge University Press, 1990).
38. Some feminists complain that this misspecifies the female viewpoint. They suggest that women do not have such a constrained perspective but rather see the world through the vista of others as much as through themselves. Women, they claim, empathize with others in a non-egotistical manner. This view does not, of course, apply to all feminists: see M. E. Hawksworth, *Beyond Oppression: Feminist Theory and Political Strategy* (New York: Continuum, 1990) for a feminist argument with institutionalist bite.
39. B. Barry, *Sociologists, Economists and Democracy* (Chicago: University of Chicago Press, 2nd edn., 1978).
40. J. C. Harsanyi, 'Individualistic vs. Functionalistic Explanation in the Light of Game Theory', in I. Lakatos (ed.) *Problems in the Philosophy of Science* (Amsterdam: Cambridge University Press, 1968).
41. See D. S. King, *The New Right: Politics, Markets and Citizenship* (London: Macmillan, 1987).
42. W. H. Riker and P. C. Ordeshook, *Introduction to Positive Political Theory* (Englewood Cliffs, NJ: Prentice-Hall, 1973); P. C. Ordeshook, *A Political Theory Primer* (London: Routledge, 1992).
43. D. Gambetta, *The Sicilian Mafia: The Business of Protection* (Cambridge, Mass.: Harvard University Press, 1993). For a rather older but not dissimilar analysis of urban machines in the United States see R. K. Merton, *Social Theory and Social Structure* (New York: Free Press, 1957), 70–82.

2

The Paradox of Voting and
the Theory of Social Evolution

ALAN CARLING

Things economic and social move by their own momentum
and the ensuing situations compel individuals and groups to
behave in certain ways whatever they may wish to do—not
indeed by destroying their freedom of choice but by shaping
the choosing mentalities and by narrowing the list of possibilities from which to choose. If this is the quintessence of
Marxism then we all of us have got to be Marxists.[1]

1. THE ALLEGED PARADOX OF VOTING

The paradox of voting is less paradoxical than is commonly
assumed because it is more paradoxical than is usually thought:
this is its paradox. Assume that members of an electorate are
instrumental and rational in their orientation to the act of casting
a vote. The fact that they are instrumental means that they are in
it for what they can get out of the result. The fact that they are
rational means, in this context, that they vote or not according to
whether their benefit from the act of voting does or does not exceed
the cost incurred in performing the act. But the chance of any one
vote affecting the outcome of the election in the voter's favour is
so tiny (in any electorate of reasonable size) that the potential gain
from the act is bound to be outweighed by the costs of the act, even
if the voter stands to gain a great deal from a favourable outcome
to the election and the costs of voting are very low. So rational
instrumental voters will not vote. But voters do vote, as a matter
of observation. Hence the (alleged) paradox of voting, as it is commonly understood.

I notice, first, that the alleged paradox deploys the term 'paradox' in a novel, unconventional sense, to mean a theoretical prediction unsupported by the facts. Perhaps it is so called because if it sailed under its true colours as 'the false theory of voting', it would appear less well qualified to discharge its time-honoured function of bemusing generations of undergraduate students. Perhaps its true labelling would also cause an uncomfortable increase in the pressure on political scientists to abandon a theory so contradicted by the evidence, a move that scientists are nearly always reluctant to make.

One can appreciate why such a move would be especially tricky in the current case. If voters do not behave in the way that rational instrumental persons should behave, and voting is the characteristic practice of a democratic society, then there seems to be a fundamental incompatibility between democracy and rational instrumentalism. Yet Western democratic institutions are importantly legitimized by the notions first, that they exist to further the electorate's interests (which ratifies an instrumental outlook), and second, that the electorate is both the best judge of its own interests (which justifies individualism) and of the optimal means to attain them (which implies rationality).[2] Rational instrumentality thus lies deep within the liberal conception of a defensible polity, and it is not surprising that when a tension appears to exist between democratic institutions and their liberal justifications, the liberal theorist dignifies the tension by the name of paradox, which effectively postpones the moment of choice between a desired set of institutions and its cherished rationale, neither of which the theorist wishes to abandon. Treating the alleged paradox as paradoxical is, in every sense of the word, an ideological manœuvre.

2. THE TRUE PARADOX OF VOTING

The manœuvre described above, which inappropriately raises a refutation to the status of a paradox, nevertheless turns out to be otiose, since the refutation which is wrongly named as paradox is wrongly deduced from the theory, so no contest in fact arises between the theory and the practice of voting behaviour.

The fault in the deduction lies in the inconsistent use it makes of parametric analysis. What parametric analysis does is to create in thought experiment a fixed environment of choice, against the background of which a given (rational) actor optimizes his or her decision. It is as if the social landscape, including other actors, is momentarily frozen, so that one actor alone appears to move within it. Thus it is asked, in the present case, if a particular constituent will vote, given that a number of fellow constituents have voted or will vote in the relevant election. This is to treat the votes, or the voting intentions, of other constituents as part of the fixed environment of choice against the background of which the given constituent is asked to make a decision. And the answer will be, according to the standard discussion, that the chances of any individual voter's vote being decisive is so low that no individual votes. But it is clear that the premiss of this deduction (that many people have voted or will vote) is not independent of its conclusion (that no one votes) and that one cannot therefore properly treat as a fixed part of the analysis that which is subject to variation according to the outcome of the analysis.

To see this, consider particular voters Arthur, Barbara, Colin, etc. The parametric analysis proceeds by taking each such voter in turn, and scrutinizing each voter's decision as if all the other voters were momentarily paralysed. There is nothing inconsistent about this from the point of view of any single voter considered just by herself—there is nothing inconsistent in Arthur, for example, taking Barbara's decision process as given for the purposes of working out his own parametric response. But there is something inconsistent in the theorist taking Barbara's decision as given for the purposes of working out Arthur's response and as not given for the purposes of working out Barbara's own response. So parametric analysis is inappropriately applied to the case of predicting the voting behaviour of a whole electorate.[3]

The alternative is to use a strategic analysis, in which each voter takes into account what every other voter is liable to decide. Here it is: suppose a voter concludes, on the basis of the initial assumption that everyone else will vote, that it is not rational to vote. Then no one will vote, so it is rational to vote (since the one voter can decide the election for him or herself, with massive potential gains, for example if I nominate that Poll Tax be reintroduced, with all the proceeds going to me). But if everyone votes, it is as we have seen not rational to vote, so no one votes. So do voters vote or don't they vote? We can't tell, which means that the theory makes no prediction about voter behaviour.

Formally, and in the standard notation, let p, B, and C stand respectively for the probability of a person's vote being decisive (p), the voter's gain from a favourable electoral outcome (B), and the (real and/or opportunity) cost of voting (C).[4] Strictly speaking, different values of p, B, and C need to be specified for each voter, but the argument works on orders of magnitude rather than precise quantities, and we may therefore attribute the same variable to each voter (up to orders of magnitude). p, for example, may be of the order of 1/1,000,000 (in a large electorate most of whom decide to vote); B is of the order of £10,000, and C is of the order of £1.[5]

Then the voter will vote or not according as:

$$pB > C \quad \text{Vote}$$

or

$$pB < C \quad \text{Don't Vote}$$

But, I have argued, the value of p is not independent of the value of ($pB - C$). In particular, if one assumes that p is very small (say, 1/1,000,000), because many people vote, then ($pB - C$) is less than zero, since the expected gain is measured in pennies when the cost is measured in pounds. So no one votes, and p is equal to 1.0, contrary to hypothesis. But if $p = 1.0$, then ($pB - C$) is positive, and everyone votes, contrary to hypothesis. The arithmetical conclusions are:

(1) If p is very small, then p is not very small.
(2) If p is not very small, then p is very small.

and the corresponding behavioural conclusions are

(1) Everyone votes if no one votes.
(2) No one votes if everyone votes.

The theory, in short, is self-contradictory, and is therefore unable to make any prediction about voter behaviour. But if it makes no prediction about voter behaviour, then the theory cannot be falsified by any empirical observation of voter behaviour—either voting or abstaining. There is, consequently, no paradox of voting, not even in the degenerate, ideological sense identified above. Nor is the theory of voting false, rather it is vacuous. The real paradox of voting lies in the failure of a strategic analysis to predict an outcome, but this failure relieves the theory of any possible contradiction with experience, and therefore resolves what many people wrongly believe is the paradox of voting.

3. THE IMPORTANCE OF A STRATEGIC APPROACH

The strategic approach to the analysis of the voting decision, and its attendant instability, has haunted the discussion from its beginning in Downs's work, but without being granted the prominence that in my view it deserves. Downs was very clear about the existence of the strategic difficulty, even though its discussion occurs at the very end of his pioneering book, and he finally swerves away from its implications. His key paragraph reads:

Each citizen is . . . trapped in a maze of conjectural variation. The importance of his own vote depends upon how important other people think their votes are, which in turn depends on how important he thinks his vote is. He can conclude either that (1) since so many others are going to vote, his ballot is not worth casting or (2) since most others reason this way, they will abstain and therefore he should vote. If everyone arrives at the first conclusion, no one votes; whereas if everyone arrives at the second conclusion, every citizen votes unless [the party differential B is zero].

Thus if we assume all men think alike, democracy seems unable to function rationally. What rule can we posit within the framework of our model to show how rational men can arrive at different conclusions though viewing the same situation?[6]

Notice the logic which leads to this conclusion. If the model doesn't work when we assume that people think the same, then we can either (*a*) retain the assumption that people think the same, and abandon the model or (*b*) retain the model, and abandon the assumption that people think the same. One might think that (*a*) would be the scientific reaction to this dilemma, facing squarely the indeterminacy that Downs has pin-pointed in his preceding remarks, but he opts instead in his culminating sentence for (*b*). This is despite the fact that there is no particular reason to think that members of the electorate facing the same initial data will come to different conclusions upon it, except for the need to dig the theory out of a hole in which it has found itself enmired.

Judging by two of the most influential current textbook treatments, digging still proceeds apace. McLean, for example, is aware of the strategic analysis, which he calls the 'what if everyone thought like that?' argument.[7] His question is a good one, more serious than he seems to believe. He comments briskly that Downs's 'maze of conjectural variation' 'is not exactly Hampton Court', because 'an easy way out is to assume that on average half the population will flip on one side and half will flop on the other. So the expected value of my vote' according to his argument, doubles under the flip-flop assumption, since the expected turnout halves to 50 per cent, with a corresponding increase in the probability that 'my' vote will determine the result. As McLean concludes, 'This does not get us very far'. Indeed it doesn't. It seems to divide the electorate into two parts acting on different bases; the two parts consist of one individual ('me') and the remaining $(N - 1)$ members of the electorate. In this scenario, it appears that I decide not to vote after taking a parametric decision based on my expectations about the behaviour of the rest of the electorate, who, however, all decide whether or not to vote by tossing a coin, or some analogous random procedure.[8]

Now it is true that if voters decided to vote by tossing a coin, one would have a correspondingly good, and completely unparadoxical, theory of turnout based on the probabilistic distribution of outcomes to coin tosses. But in the absence of independent evidence for the existence of such a decision procedure (surreptitious pocketings of loose change around the polling booth, and so on) the hypothetical random model underlying the behaviour merely redescribes the fact that various people have voted, and cannot therefore be part of the explanation we are seeking for why they did or didn't vote.[9]

Mueller calls the strategic analysis 'voting as a game of cat and mouse', and concludes his very brief discussion with the comment that 'this effort to rescue the rational voter hypothesis by resorting to game theory does not succeed'.[10] I take it from the context that this means that the strategic analysis ultimately fails to show what at one moment it promises to show—namely, that voting may be rational after all, contrary to the implications of the standard (misnamed) paradox.

The way in which both McLean and Mueller have approached the strategic analysis is symptomatic. First, they both seem to regard it as one option among many from the theoretical point of view, and as a potential way out of the (alleged) rational voter paradox. My view, as I have argued it in the previous section, is that the standard, parametric analysis rests on inconsistent theoretical premisses, and is therefore inadmissible as a piece of rational-choice theory. If you want a rational-choice theory of the voting act, what Mueller calls 'the resort to Game Theory'—i.e., the strategic approach—is not just one option theoretically speaking, but is mandated by the terms of the problem as set. Yet the conclusion of an appropriately conceived rational-choice theory of voting is disappointing, since the theory fails to make any prediction about whether voters will vote.

Does this offer a way out of the original (alleged) paradox? It all depends what sort of way out you require. McLean and Mueller, for example, seem to want a way out which shows unproblematically that voting can sometimes be a rational act. This is why McLean remarks that his (misguided) flip-flop model 'doesn't get us very far', since, according to his argument, it doesn't transform the pay-off structure sufficiently to make voting a rational act (a mere doubling of p will not be nearly enough, when it would have to increase by at least a hundredfold to make much of a difference). The strategic analysis does not offer a way out in this sense either, since, although it disperses the original paradox of voting, it cannot supply a rational-choice explanation of the vote, and tends to show that such an explanation will not be forthcoming within the terms of the problem as originally set. I now argue that the way in which to alter the terms of the problem takes us inevitably in the direction of institutional rational choice, if we are going to continue to adhere to rational choice. This involves a 'reorientation of the theoretical object' with important implications for the nature of the social explanations it is possible to give.

4. THE RELEVANCE OF DUTY

Theorists who stick with rational choice face essentially two alternatives for transforming the terms of the voting problem in order to render it more tractable:

(1) stay with the three variables p, B, and C, but make B enormously greater, so that pB outweighs C, even if p remains very small.

(2) add another, positive, variable—usually labelled D—to the

equation, to overcome the negative effect of the cost variable C without necessarily changing either p or B.

The first result is achieved by positing altruistic interests. If, instead of contemplating only my own benefit, I somehow focus on the returns of a favourable election result to millions of my fellow citizens, then my view of the expected benefit expands a million-fold, sufficient to outweigh the million-to-one shot that the casting of my vote still is.

This explanation is not vulnerable to strategic instability, since my voting is predicated on p remaining very small, and is therefore consistent with my altruistic fellow citizens coming to similar conclusions as myself, and also voting, which leads of course to a very small value for p. (It is also consistent with my non-altruistic fellow citizens not voting (on account of p being very small), in their consistent knowledge that large numbers of their altruistic fellow citizens, such as me, will vote.) Everyone can therefore act rationally (and also instrumentally), turn-out being predicted by the distribution of altruistic versus non-altruistic preferences in the electorate.[11]

I am sure the general drift of this argument is sound, but I have my doubts about its portrayal of human psychology. There is a scene in Star Trek in which Spock is visibly shaken by the news of the destruction of a Vulcan starship. Captain Kirk teases him for showing any emotion, and Spock delivers a magisterial rebuke: 'You humans are strange creatures', he says 'the death of one child can move you to tears, and yet the death of millions leaves you cold. We Vulcans are different. For us, the impact of suffering is multiplied by the numbers who suffer.'[12] I don't know what the mental operation could feel like to take on board the utilities of millions, far less to balance this in the imagination against an unimaginably tiny probability, as the altruistic voter is supposed to do. I have no problem with altruism *per se*, but I am not convinced that this application of it describes a feasible mental performance.

The other alternative is to posit a variable D which captures a hitherto-neglected aspect of the voting situation—a non-instrumental benefit which can by itself outweigh the cost C. Here the act of voting is given an intrinsic value, as the expression of a commitment or the fulfilment of a duty, so that the calculus of decision reduces to the comparison of D for Duty versus C for Cost, with the troublesome pB term effectively dropping out of the analysis.[13] And it is precisely because the C term is relatively modest that it is not necessary to posit a very well-developed sense of obligation to vote in order to make the act of voting a rational decision. Voting is not, at least not usually, like fighting a war, where it must be explained how a sense of duty manages to prevail over a high probability of losing one's life. Indeed, it was part of the general air of paradox surrounding the turn-out decision that instrumental considerations could not overcome costs of voting measured merely in pounds.

At this point, the original paradox has fizzled out rather ingloriously. 'You mean to tell me' an unsympathetic critic might respond, 'that people vote because they experience a mild sense of obligation to vote. And you're presenting this as some kind of new and insightful analysis?' Indeed, this manner of resolving the turn-out problem reads into an easy general indictment of rational choice, which can be placed in the mouth of the same hypothetical critic as follows:

You rational-choice types begin by assuming a parsimonious description of agents' motivations, backed by a handful of strict behavioural axioms. When that doesn't work out, you pull in various more or less implausible auxiliary hypotheses, so as to preserve the contention of rational action, no matter what. For example, you say that this duty variable exists, which you hadn't bothered to notice before. And how strong is this duty effect? Oh, I see, just strong enough, is it, to outweigh the cost of casting a vote? How very convenient for you. You have turned the initial promise of rational explanation of behaviour into *post hoc* rationalization of behaviour.

I think that this fairly standard critique of rational choice is fair comment, but only up to a point. The lesson I draw from it is not that rational choice should be abandoned, but that it always needs to be situated socially: set in a context in which agents' preferences and values are also subject to explanation.[14] It is true that this is going to shift the burden of explanation significantly, and perhaps also change its character. For example, it is true that once you have explained the existence of a duty to vote, or indeed, the occurrence of altruistic preferences in a given electorate, you have done most of the explanatory work, since the inference of rational behaviour on the basis of those values or preferences becomes almost a trivial matter. And you may have broadened the conception of what counts as rational action, for example by allowing expressive as well as instrumental behaviour to count as rational. ('what wouldn't count as rational if all this does?' says the critic. 'At least some things' is one reply.) The prospects of a highly general, axiomatic, deductive theory may also have been dented in the process, taking with it part of the appeal of rational-choice theory over its rivals. But I don't consider that this limitation of its scope and reach destroys its utility. Rather it relocates and redirects it, in a manner I now address.

5. THE INSTITUTIONAL TURN

Consider the context in which voting takes place. There must already be a democratic, or at least a representative, polity: a set of institutions with a history of development, with particular habits and meanings, rules and procedures, customs and rituals, means of supervision and enforcement, and so on. Individuals don't participate in these institutions naked, so to speak. They come pre-formed, moulded to a certain extent to the requirements of the institution. But even this way of putting it sets up too great a distance between the institution and its participants. The institution only exists to the extent that individuals also exist who are capable of transacting its business; the history of the development of the institution is also the history of the creation of the kinds of individuals whose own preferences, tastes, and values will cohere with what the institution will demand of them. The reproduction of the institution is the reproduction of the conditions of existence for that type of individual.

The picture I have in mind is roughly this: individuals behave according to their values, preferences and beliefs, aims and ambitions. They don't necessarily all behave in the same way, since they may have different values, preferences and beliefs, aims and ambitions. Their different orientations to action may lead them to behave in complementary ways which define distinct roles in a given institution—in a typical contemporary election, there's little alternative to voting for a politician (the only alternative in the recent by-election in the Christchurch constituency, was a candidate dressed as a large chicken). This set of behaviours, taken as an interacting whole, generates certain consequences, and these consequences feed back sufficiently on to the pre-conditions of the behaviours to ensure the repetition of the behaviours, and thus the endurance of the institution that the behaviours comprise.

Voters vote for politicians, some of whom are thus enabled to
form a government. Because the government is (regarded as) legitimate, it can raise taxes to finance elections, and otherwise sustain
the integrity of the electoral process, including the defence of the
geo-social terrain over which the election takes place; it can advertise its operations remorselessly, so as to generate a sense of its own
importance, to reinforce the identification of its constituency with
its actions, and thus enhance its own legitimacy; it can take more
direct measures—educational and ideological—to instil in the
electorate the values of and commitment to the democratic process
which will have to be mobilized at the time of the next election.[15]

It is only if all the requirements like these continue to mesh that
one should speak of the existence of institutions—in this case, electoral institutions; but the meshing of requirements like these is
what enables the theorist to identify an institutional complex—
such as an electoral complex—within the undifferentiated flux of
human activity that presents itself to first sight.

6. INSTITUTIONAL RATIONALITY

The previous paragraphs sketch an institutional approach to theory, but is it also a rational-choice approach? The sketch seems to
require explanations to be provided in three roughly distinct areas.
First, there must be an explanation of the inner workings of the
institution—of how and why certain characteristic behaviours of
the institution are elicited on the basis of given aims, beliefs, and
values. Second, there must be an explanation of the feedback
process from the behaviours to their pre-conditioning aims, beliefs,
and values. Taken together, these two kinds of explanation will
show, if successful, how and why the institution is able to repro-
duce itself—how and why it is sustainable, within some given social
and/or geo-physical environment. But there is a third, and most
fundamental, type of explanation which concerns the origins and
the subsequent fate of an institution—its propensity to change: to
come into existence, to spread, to grow, or to decay. To ask
whether the theory is a rational-choice theory is therefore to ask
whether any or all of these types of explanation are likely to be
rational-choice explanations. I will consider each type in turn.

The Inner Workings of an Institution

First, I think the rationality postulate is indispensable for explanations of the inner workings of the institution, to bridge the gap between beliefs and behaviours. That is to say, I think we ought to, perhaps must, proceed on the assumption that behaviour is locally rational: rational in the immediate context of its occurrence.[16] This excludes behaviourist and psychoanalytic explanations, but it is a more delicate question what it does include. Action must certainly be regarded as meaningful to its participants, and therefore 'social' in Weber's sense. But this is probably compatible with explanations couched in terms of, say, cognitive-dissonance theory as well as rational-choice theory. There is in any case a doubt about how far the notion of rational choice should be stretched: can it go so far, for example, as to encompass expressive as well as instrumental action?

But these partly definitional issues are ultimately less important than the substantive issues. The so-called paradox of voting arises as a query about the inner workings of democracy—why doesn't it collapse spontaneously through non-participation? I don't see that there is any special mystery, let alone a paradox, about the voting act. People vote out of a sense of responsibility to, or identification with, a constituency, a cause, a candidate, a party, or a polity. Part of the identification may involve the conviction that a particular cause, candidate, or party stands for an interest or a policy that will benefit the would-be voter, either as an individual, or as a member of some social category to which the voter belongs and the policy ostensibly caters.

But it is not this interest that motivates the act of voting itself. Rather, it is a combination of an internal push and an external pull: the internal push is the sense of duty which is the psychological reflection of the social identification (to identify is, in this conception, to feel the push); the external pull is the (imagined or experienced) social sanction consequent upon abstention. What sustains the act is the thought of the omission: the feeling that one will have let the side down, the knowledge that others may know it, and the apprehension that they will say it. Without the (informal or formal) external sanction, the internal value might be insufficient to motivate costly value-oriented behaviour, especially over the longer run; but without the internal value, the external sanction would enjoy no leverage over behaviour. The existence of the value and the possibility of sanction must therefore be considered together—as aspects of a single social mechanism that constitutes the voter as already a member of a political community, open to its opportunities and subject to its constraints.[17]

This kind of mechanism is not unique to voting. As the epigraph from Schumpeter which heads this chapter implies, it is an instance of a ubiquitous phenomenon. I take it to be the principal means of resolving the problem of social order in a large public; something like it being necessary, for example, to underpin the paradigmatic instance of instrumental activity—free-market exchange.[18] And there are plenty of examples of expressive behaviour whose rationality no one would surely dispute. Is it irrational to attend a funeral? The action can hardly be instrumental, when it's too late by then to influence the will.[19]

Institutional Feedback

If rational explanation, though perhaps not always rational-choice explanation, may be applied to the inner workings of institutions, how does it fare on the feedback from action to belief? To some limited, and maybe not inconsiderable, extent beliefs, aims, preferences, norms, and so on are acquired and modified by processes of rational deliberation and persuasion (though not by rational decision, exactly).[20] But they probably arise more commonly from processes of habituation, assimilation, imitation, conscious training, role-modelling, and the like.

How are we to incorporate an understanding of these processes into the theory? In general, the answer is clear. One must look to the conditions under which a supply of recruits to the institution's major roles is forthcoming: how and where their commitments and beliefs are created, enabled, and sustained, partly from sources external to the institution and partly through the operation of the institution itself. At best, we should expect explanatory regularities in this process—a certain characteristic balance for any institution regarding the sources of its personnel and their modes of socialization and reward—but it is doubtful that this is going to generate persuasive general theory, especially axiomatic general theory. The possible combinations appear too various and unpredictable.

Take two contrasting examples. It would be tempting to impose as a general rule, say, that an institution in order to survive must offer its participants some kind of satisfaction of the values for the sake of which they participate in the institution. But consider early professional medicine: patients no doubt went to doctors in the sincere belief that they might be cured by a blood-letting, but they couldn't in fact have been cured, since leeches don't cure anything. Yet this did not apparently prevent the medical profession from prospering, nor stem the flow of patients (far from it). In the long run, the practice of scientific medicine eventually caught up to some extent with the promise, and doctors became able to cure many painful conditions by accurate causal interventions. In the early stages however, the medical myth was able to survive massive—presumably almost universal—evidence against its own claims for success, even though this was empirical evidence of the very kind with which the new scientistic medicine sought to justify its operations.[21]

This example suggests that institutions which are sufficiently entrenched around a set of material interests can gull the public indefinitely, possessing an almost infinite resource in rationalizing their performance. But how then can we explain the collapse of the Soviet states? It is clear that at some point their reproduction conditions were ruptured, leading to an unimaginably rapid unravelling of their institutional structure. A key moment was undoubtedly the awareness that the Soviet Union would not intervene militarily to maintain the dependent condition of Eastern Europe, but to what extent did this decision reflect a judgement by the Soviet élite that its legitimacy was already so much undermined that military intervention would be either impossible or hopelessly counterproductive? Again, which element(s) in the ordinary chain of state reproduction had snapped so comprehensively in the Soviet Union itself that the release of Eastern Europe—which in other circumstances might have been seen as a noble, liberal, or at least a timely, gesture—destabilized the metropolitan regime? It is not going to be an easy matter to detail the general means by which a set of institutions holds itself together.

Suppose, however, that this composite explanation is forthcoming. We then have a plausible picture of a unit of social interaction which recurrently duplicates itself, by reproducing in its operations its own conditions of existence. Even though this would be more of an explanation than is commonly provided in social science, it is in some ways only a prelude to the real explanation: the explanation of how and why this particular unit of social interaction, with its characteristic internal configuration, comes to exist in the form that it does. Here we require a theory of origins and a theory of growth and spread, to complement the theory of survival (i.e. reproduction) that is implicit in the previous discussion.

Origins and Destinations

A theory of origins is essentially a theory of variation: of how social elements differentiate themselves and then recombine in novel permutations, such that a new entity crystallizes, or gels. (Mineral metaphors seem inescapable at this point.) Thus, new religions typically draw on precursors within a generic tradition—one monotheistic religion branches out from another, and so on; the Renaissance is conceived as rebirth (though its significance lay precisely in the fact that it was not tied to the social conditions which generated its classical forerunner); capitalism assembles new relations of production from the recurrent debris of a feudal economy.[22] This process is probably predictable only within certain quite narrow limits, where the initial conditions are quite closely specified in terms of the ingredients in the primordial social soup from which new varieties may emerge. The process is genetic in the general sense of building in new ways with existing elements, but it evidently lacks the precision of biological genetics, since among other features there does not appear to exist a universal mechanism of genetic transmission for social entities. At any rate, even if it does exist, no one has cracked the DNA of social structure.

There are then two general approaches to the growth or decay, and therefore the existence, of social entities, both evolutionary (at least in a loose sense of the term). The approaches revolve respectively around design and selection as alternatives for the main principle of explanation. It might be said that these are respectively the Lamarckian and Darwinian approaches to the theory of social evolution, but care is required with this analogy, on two counts. First, the distinction between these two approaches to biological evolution rests on the distinction between the genotype and the phenotype, and the associated Darwinian inference that lifetime modifications of the phenotype cannot be transmitted to the next generation. Hence biological evolution must be explained by mutation and selection rather than by learning or acquisition. A parallel inference does not get off the ground in the case of social evolution precisely because the underlying distinction between phenotype and genotype cannot be made (or, at least, has yet to be made). Thus, there is nothing in principle to prevent an institutional complex being reformed from within, and the reforms passed on to the next generation of participants because their socialization experience has also been modified to take account of the reforms. Institutional design and institutional selection— Lamarck and Darwin—are from this point of view equally serious general contenders in the case of social organization.

The second difficulty concerns the role of intention and reason in the process of social evolution. It is certainly not true that reason and intention are present in the one case—design—and absent in the other—selection. We are dealing, after all, with intentional beings, and I have committed myself to explanations of the inner workings of institutions which respect the rationality of those involved. The question is rather the scope and efficacy of intentional and rational action: whether it is by and large within the grasp of (collective) action to establish institutions by design, or whether institutions will typically escape the attempt.

Much here will depend on the identification of the boundaries of the relevant unit of analysis. It is a comment on the state of social theory that we lack a word to designate the discrete nexus of social relationships which is subject to evolutionary change—the nexus that hangs, and therefore falls, together. 'Institution' itself is usable, though potentially misleading; Elias's 'figuration' and Runciman's 'systact' are in the field, though neither has established itself as favourite.[23] I have used inexact terms like 'entity' and 'nexus' in a similar sense. The need for a special terminology arises because of the desire not to prejudge the outcome of the enquiry with respect to common-sense perceptions of the boundaries of social interaction, since the location of the boundaries in fact depends both on the reproduction conditions of social formations and their related evolutionary fates, neither of which may be available to common-sense perceptions. There is a chronic problem in social science in distinguishing the growing plant from the soil in which it grows.[24] Is democracy, for example, to be considered an independent entity which may or may not flourish on the ground provided by capitalism, or one organ of a more comprehensive entity—'capitalist democracy'—which can be understood only as an interrelated whole? I cannot consider the substance of this complex historical question on this occasion; here I only wish to suggest that the answer will always depend on the findings of the analysis itself—on whether a democratic form of state favours the reproduction of an undemocratic form of economic life, or is strictly neutral to it.

This point has implications for which of the two types of theory is most plausible. It is no doubt possible to establish institutions, or at least to replicate them, by deliberate action—to set up hospitals, monasteries, trading companies, universities, and even states, but probably not nations, by conscious design. If one can take for granted a certain background of socio-cultural conditions—conceived as the soil in which these new offshoots are planted—their reproduction conditions may be guaranteed. But the wider the circle of explanation needs to be drawn, the less likely it is that all the concomitant reproduction conditions can be the subject of one rational will; the less likely therefore that the process as a whole can be the subject of conscious direction and control.[25]

It seems to me, then, that the more integrated social systems become, and the more dependent on ramified and specialized values for their operation, the more it is likely that a selectionist explanation will be appropriate. It will only be under very special conditions that preferences and values can be divorced sufficiently from behaviour to license a pure rational-choice explanation. This marks the limit of a purely economic explanation, as this is usually understood within economic theory itself, or in some recent applications of the economic approach to sociological questions.[26] Rationality will still enter as a local moment of most explanations of social phenomena, related to each institution's inner workings. But rationality has a more restricted role in the explanation of the institutional complex itself. In some cases there may be elements of a conscious design, in other cases there may be a pattern of development for an institutional complex—a 'law of motion'—which is the tangential outcome of the interaction of locally rational choices, in yet other, perhaps most, cases there may be a fortuitous combination which happens to embody a reproductive advantage in an environment composed of competing, parasitic, or symbiotic social entities. But the example of Darwinism shows, *pace* Popper, that such a state of affairs is potentially theorizable.

In summary, then, we should not look to the level of individual decision to find a solution to the paradox of voting, where it is either not a paradox, or not solvable. The solution of the paradox emerges as a footnote to a larger and more daunting enquiry: the evolution of democratic institutions.

NOTES

1. J. A. Schumpeter, *Capitalism, Socialism, and Democracy* (London, George Allen & Unwin, 1976), 129–30.
2. On instrumentality, cf. Thomas Jefferson: 'The only orthodox object of the institution of government is to secure the greatest degree of happiness possible to those associated under it'; cited in D. Mueller, *Public Choice II* (Cambridge: Cambridge University Press, 1989), 384.
3. There is a line of argument against this conclusion, which, though superficially attractive, is I believe ultimately untenable, and is therefore confined to this note. It runs as follows. I have convicted the would-be parametric theorist of inconsistency, for assuming as given in one part of his or her analysis that which is the subject of explanation in another part of the same analysis. But perhaps the inconsistency can be resolved by distributing the trouble-making assumptions among the actors themselves, whom we do not lay under the same types of constraints as the theorist. Suppose, in particular, that A believes (1) that the actions of B, C, D, etc. are already fixed, but (2) that A's own action has yet to be determined by parametric calculation. Then B can believe (1) that the actions of A, C, D, etc. are similarly fixed, while (2) that B's own action is similarly variable, and so on for the beliefs of C, the beliefs of D, etc. There is no logical inconsistency within either A's or B's sets of beliefs (or within C's or D's, etc.). There is incompatibility between the various sets of beliefs, it is true, but this does no damage because the beliefs are now attributed to different agents. Thus, it might be argued, we can resume the parametric analysis without fear of inconsistency.

   I have two responses. First, while none of our hypothetical actors is labouring under internally inconsistent beliefs, they are all labouring under a systematically erroneous belief, since they all believe something about each of the others which is false, namely, that each of the other's decisions is fixed (when none of them is in fact fixed). It is not clear that it is sociologically plausible to assume this degree of mutual ignorance among agents, nor proper to regard as 'rational' overall a decision process which depends on this level of disjunction between an actor's beliefs and what one might call his or her surrounding social reality. These actors have certainly failed to absorb their lessons from Kant, and are loath to universalize their axioms of behaviour.

Second, even if we accept for theoretical purposes the stability of the relevant web of partly true and mostly false beliefs about the fixedness of voting intentions, the problem is still not solved, because we don't know on what basis each actor attributes the content of every other's voting intention, for example, why A assumes that B will vote (if A does assume that B will vote), and so on. Thus A must, in effect, hold some theory about B, and about C, and D, etc., but we do not know what this is, and in the absence of this knowledge, A (and therefore the theorist on A's behalf) cannot attribute particular voting intentions to others. But without attributing a distribution of others' voting intentions, A cannot perform the parametric calculation on which his or her own voting decision depends. This superficially attractive line of argument thus winds up with an unconvincing description of a social world which is as much in need of explanation as the world from which it was designed to escape: out of the frying-pan, into the fire.

4. For the origin of the standard notation in Riker and Ordeshook, see Mueller, *Public Choice II*, 351.

5. These estimates are designed to be conservative in each case, i.e. favourable to the conclusion that voting is rational. In particular, p is set fairly high—I. McLean, *Public Choice: An Introduction* (Oxford, Basil Blackwell, 1987), 46 gives $p=1/15,000,000$. It is also worth noting that Mueller, *Public Choice II*, 350 gives the extremely misleading figure of $p=1/16,666$ as the probability of a tie-break in a US presidential election. This arises from computing the value of p from the exponential approximation to the binomial formula, assuming that the expected probability of voting for each of two parties is exactly 0.5. In this case, of course, the value of p will be a maximum, but the steepness of the gradient of the function around this maximum is indicated by the fact that if the expected probability of the vote for one of the two parties in the US electorate were to equal 0.499 instead of 0.500, then p would fall from 1/16,666 to approximately 1/1,000,0 . . . 83 zeros . . . 0,000! (McLean, *Public Choice*).

6. A. Downs, *An Economic Theory of Democracy* (New York: Harper and Row, 1957), 267.

7. McLean, *Public Choice*, 46–47. I have taken McLean and Mueller as representative accounts for this purpose.

8. If we assume instead that each member of the electorate believes (wrongly) that every other member of the electorate decides by coin-tossing, we have a special case of the situation covered in n. 3. If McLean's 'easy way out' via probability theory simply reflects a confession of ignorance about whether and why people vote, we are back at square one rather than out of the maze.

9. The best *post hoc* estimate for the prior probability of voting for each party (assumed constant) would simply be the proportions of the electorate voting for each party (i.e. the actual turn-outs for each party). This shows that the random model envisaged in passing by McLean adds nothing of explanatory value to the bare facts of any given electoral outcome.

10. Mueller, *Public Choice II*, 351–2.

11. Actions are instrumental when they are consequence-regarding, no matter whose interests are served by the consequences. So altruistic action can easily be instrumental action, compatible for example with the Jeffersonian view of government cited in n. 1.

12. This is quoted from rather distant memory. About a fortnight after this paragraph was written, the injured five-year-old Irma Hadzimuratovic was plucked from the carnage of Sarajevo by the British Government and taken to Great Ormond Street Hospital amid enormous publicity, leaving behind her thousands of children and countless more adults in a similar plight. Yet the perception of her suffering served also to mobilize feeling momentarily on behalf of the others, not least because it enabled observers to comment on the hypocrisy of the political manœuvres in her case. Human altruism seems to work by processes of symbolization and metonymy rather than straightforward aggregation.

13. Commentators' resolutions, part I: McLean goes for altruism, although some of his remarks admit the role of duty, too, as 'participation altruism'; Downs's resolution is in effect to rely on duty, in the form of a commitment to democratic process entitled 'long-run participation value'. Critics have not been slow to point out that this resolution is inconsistent with Downs's general rational-choice approach (McLean, *Public Choice*, 47; B. Barry, *Sociologists, Economists and Democracy* (London: Macmillan, 1970), 20). The other point is that Downs introduces 'long-run participation value' in answer to his question cited above why some members of the electorate think differently from others. He fails to see, however, that the introduction of this new variable changes the model which gave rise to his motivating question, and it does so in a way which makes the question no longer a pertinent one, since the positive impact of a sense of duty on voting behaviour does not depend on voters having different senses of duty. As I have suggested, strategic instability lapses once duty can outweigh cost. Elster also plumps for commitment: 'Voting does seem to be a case in which the action itself, rather than the outcome it can be expected to produce, is what matters': J. Elster (ed.), *Rational Choice* (Oxford: Blackwell, 1986), 24.

14. Commentators' resolutions, part II: Mueller takes a very curious but quite interesting line. He recognizes the role of the duty variable, and

despairs of the theory as a result: 'it provides the end for a story about voting, not the beginning of a behavioural theory of voting' (*Public Choice II*, 362). He does not think that duty can be explained rationalistically, and he explores behaviourist explanations for both the existence of 'ethical voters' and for the decline in turn-out for US presidential elections (according to which the voters' voting actions decay because they have not been reinforced over the last few Presidencies by the performance of their favoured candidates in office). The curiosity here is the speed with which Mueller junks the rationality assumption in a book otherwise devoted entirely to the political applications of rational choice. No wonder the students are confused!

15. I discovered on rereading it after many years that a general conception similar to this was put forward by Brian Barry, *Sociologists, Economists and Democracy*, 92–8. It is as well to remember, amidst all the criticism directed at it, from what rational choice delivered us: Almond and Verba, Eckstein, and Parsons, as subjected to Barry's caustic intelligence in chs. 3–4 of his wonderful book.

16. Cf. 'To understand other people, we must assume that, by and large, they have consistent desires and beliefs and act consistently upon them.': Elster, *Rational Choice*, 27, paraphrasing Donald Davidson.

17. Explanations have traditionally emphasized one of these elements to the virtual exclusion of the other; either the Parsonian stress on values or the Hobbesian stress on external incentives (Barry tended to pose the question in this way). In fact, sociology and economics each need the other. This conception also seems consistent with the empirical findings that (*a*) commitment is an important explanatory variable and (*b*) turn-out is correlated with indices of membership of the political community, which is why, I hazard, that years of education emerges as an important empirical factor (see Mueller, *Public Choice II*, 354–66 for a summary of the evidence).

18. See A. Carling, *Social Division* (London: Verso, 1991), ch. 8.

19. After the analogy between voting and attending a funeral had occurred to me, I wondered whether the idea was subconsciously inspired by my experiences over the years of supporting the Labour Party in Britain.

20. Elementary considerations in the distinction between 'thin' rational choice and 'thicker' rationality in the general sense of action or belief in conformity with reason include the following: to say that a belief arises from rational decision in the thin sense, for example, is to say that the belief is chosen because holding that belief offers a better payoff than holding any other belief. This prescinds entirely from the requirement that a belief be held because it is true: belief is reduced in effect to ideology pure and simple. To say that a preference arises from rational decision seems a contradiction in terms, since what makes a

decision thin-rational is its optimum satisfaction of some (necessarily pre-existing) preference—optimization principles cannot be applied to that in respect of which optimization takes place. But if a preference is referred to some preference structure, this conclusion is not so obvious, and it may make sense to apply rational deliberation among the preferences. For example, an actor might be in a position to infer a lower-level preference (e.g. it is best to refuse this cigarette) by a rational process from a higher-level one (e.g. a desire to give up smoking, especially I suppose if it's a burning desire). So it is difficult to make hard-and-fast judgements about the appropriate scope and reference of either rational explanation or rational-choice explanation.

21. I am less confident than Schumpeter, *Capitalism*, that 'no magic device can survive an unbroken sequence of failures'.

22. On the latter, see A. Carling, 'Analytical Marxism and Historical Materialism: The Debate on Social Evolution', *Science and Society*, 57/1 (1993), 31–66, as well as id., *Social Division*, ch. 3.

23. N. Elias, *What is Sociology?* (London: Hutchinson, 1978) and W. G. Runciman, *A Treatise on Social Theory*, ii. *Substantive Social Theory* (Cambridge: Cambridge University Press, 1989).

24. This problem underlies the distinction made in P. Van Parijs, *Evolutionary Explanation in the Social Sciences: An Emerging Paradigm* (Totowa, NJ: Rowman and Littlefield, 1981) between external 'natural selection' and internal 'reinforcement' of social entities, since what counts as external and internal will depend on where the boundaries of social entities are drawn. The distinction was modified in Van Parijs, 'The Evolutionary Explanation of Beliefs', in W. Callebaut and R. Pinxton (eds.), *Evolutionary Epistemology* (Boston: W. Reidel, 1987) to take account of his new views on the evolution of beliefs, but Van Parijs still tends to treat the evolution of beliefs in a different department to the evolution of practices. In my view, they must be treated together, in terms of the evolution of a combined belief–action nexus.

25. This is the basis for the argument in Carling, 'Analytical Marxism' in favour of what I call Competitive Primacy (of the Productive Forces) over what I call Intentional Primacy as a potential explanation of historical development.

26. Thus J. Roemer, ' "Rational Choice" Marxism', in J. Roemer (ed.), *Analytical Marxism* (Cambridge: Cambridge University Press, 1986) considers the problem of explaining preferences, but he still divorces the preference-forming process from the action process, in order that the two may be explained separately. In fact, they are explained sequentially: preferences explain an equilibrium of action, then the equilibrium causes new preferences to be formed, and so on. In my view, the equilibrium should be seen as a simultaneous equilibrium of

both recurrent action and reproducible preference-formation. Cf. the comment on Van Parijs in the previous note. See also the general discussion in I. Steedman, *From Exploitation to Altruism* (Cambridge: Polity Press, 1989) on the history of preference-explanation in neoclassical economic thought.

3

Interpreting Formal Coalition Theory

KEITH DOWDING

We should not expect too much from the confrontation
between theories that deal with coalition formation and the
formation of real government coalitions in Western Europe.
Such a confrontation is far more productive if it is seen as a
heuristic exercise rather than a scientific test.

Michael Laver and Norman Schofield,
Multiparty Government

All too often analysts describe their methods as 'heuristically useful'. What is this supposed to mean? How much should we expect
from formal coalition theory? If we cannot test rival coalition theories against empirical evidence how are we to adjudicate between
them? I hope to answer these questions in this chapter. I argue that
to understand why actual coalitions have formed we need to examine the preferences of the actors and the negotiations which took
place. Explanation comes close to description, and the possibility
of some general theory of coalition-formation recedes. To defend
the use of formalized theorizing about coalition-formation we need
to understand that such general theories are not capable of producing causal explanations of each, or indeed any, actual coalition.
Rather they are only capable of modelling the general structures,
or institutions, under which each coalition forms. Formal models
enter into causal explanations of coalition-formation only by highlighting the structural conditions under which the prime actors
negotiated. I argue here that formal theorists should direct their
work towards (*a*) denoting important institutional features which

I would like to thank Anne Gelling and Desmond King for their editorial sugges-
tions. The final draft of this paper was completed whilst the author was enjoying a
Hallsworth Fellowship in the Department of Government, Manchester University.

structurally condition political actors, and (*b*) generating a set of questions to be asked about actual coalition-formation.

1. THE RIVAL THEORIES

There are many rival coalition theories. Riker's early work set the scene for later formal theories. His simple theory, based upon the Shapley–Shubik power index, argues that government coalitions will be created from minimum-winning coalitions of parties.[1] Riker imputed exiguous motivational assumptions to his actors. Party leaders sought as big a slice of the winnings—office—as possible. Later analysts suggested that this motivation was too simplistic and if parties were stimulated by ideology—i.e. they sought to make policy—then minimum-connected winning coalitions would result.[2] Axelrod's argument depended upon lowering conflict in coalition-formation, whereas other theorists analysed agreements over policy. Most of the empirical evidence comparing the predictions of the office-seeking and the policy-seeking models supported Riker.[3] Laver and Schofield demonstrate that out of 196 minority situations in Europe between 1945 and 1987, fifty-three were both connected and minimal-winning, twenty-four were just minimal-winning, whilst only nine were connected without being minimal-winning.[4] This result shows the superiority of models that predict minimal-winning coalitions over other simple models but they still only predict the outcomes of 40 per cent of minority situations. This may not seem much of a success rate, although it does better than mere contingency. The most predictive models are also the most inefficient. That is, whilst they suffer from fewer counter-examples, they also predict a greater number of possible coalitions. Since the minimal-winning criterion often does not produce unique predictions, less than 1/15 of its predictions are correct. These numbers imply that the models are not producing causal explanations of coalition-formation, though they may be highlighting features which structurally suggest action to party leaders.[5]

Despite the greater predictive success of office-seeking models, some analysts argue that ideology cannot be ignored. Dodd, for example, believes that ideology plays a role in the duration of coalition governments.[6] He argues that party systems with moderate fragmentation tend to have long-lived minimal-winning coalitions, whilst higher fragmentation results in minority government or surplus coalitions, depending upon the degree of ideological conflict. Dodd's work can be compared with studies which construct typologies of political systems in terms of their party fragmentation and duration of coalition government. The properties of systems most correlated with cabinet duration seem to be fragmentation of the party system and the polarization of the opposition.[7] Features of the coalition itself also seem to provide predictors for duration. Not surprisingly, majority cabinets are more stable than minority ones; and minimal-winning cabinets tend to last longer than others, including those with surplus majorities.

The measurement of such tendencies needs to be handled carefully. One cabinet is not necessarily more stable than another merely because it lasts longer. The stability of any government lies in its capacity to prevent contingencies from forcing its non-survival.[8] Its duration is therefore also related to the contingencies which arise to threaten it. The 'events approach' to cabinet durability takes account of this problem.[9]

In the events approach it is assumed that governments collapse as a result of random contingencies. This must of course be true: something must happen to cause the collapse of a government, since the cause of all events is other events. The events approach assumes that such destabilizing contingencies are equally probable throughout the natural lifetime of a government. Therefore the duration of cabinets in any system, taking all cabinets together, will conform to a particular mathematical distribution: the negative exponential distribution. Browne and colleagues note that governments of four countries (Belgium, Finland, Italy, and Israel) conform to the distribution expected, and argue that other nations which are more stable obviously have factors which induce greater stability.

A more general typology categorizes party systems as unipolar, bipolar, multipolar, and fragmented. In unipolar systems one large party dominates a system of three or four parties, usually forming a government in coalition or as a minority with tacit support. In bipolar systems, with two large parties and one or two smaller ones, most coalition governments are minimal-winning. Multipolar systems have two large parties and numerous smaller ones, and again minimal-winning coalitions are the norm. Fragmented systems are not dominated by larger parties and have many parties. Here coalitions tend to form around one of the larger parties, though they tend to be short-lived.[10] So it appears that there are indeed structural relationships between party systems and coalition-formation. Coalition models attempt to capture these relationships in different ways. Typologies are useful for ordering systems and setting out what is to be explained, though of themselves they are not explanatory. Recent work by Schofield attempts to provide a game-theoretic model which may causally explain the pattern of coalition politics in terms of the fragmentation and characteristics of the party systems contained in earlier typologies and models.[11]

Schofield concentrates upon a competitive two-dimensional model of ideological position. Parties choose their positions on the ideological spectrum with regard to their electoral consequences and the basis of their future coalition bargaining. Schofield proposes the concept of a political heart consisting of the set of possible coalition outcomes. It is either the core of a bargaining game or is determined by the party positions when no core obtains. He uses selected factors—the configuration of the party positions, the relative number of votes they receive, and the long-term dominance of certain core parties—to explain standard typologies of party systems and to account for the occurrence of minority, minimal-winning, and surplus coalitions. Whilst Schofield's argument is illustrated by examples from European nations in the post-war period, his account, using standard rationality assumptions, is largely theoretical. Nevertheless his bargaining model does suggest which systems are most likely to be destabilized by changes in the environment, and predicts quite accurately the results obtained from the events approach.

Most recent work on coalition theory consists of modifying the 'pure' models of Riker and resource-bargaining models of Schofield to introduce institutional factors which affect the bargaining position of parties. In only 40 per cent of all minority situations are minimal-winning coalitions formed. This failure of Riker's model requires explanation. Riker's model assumes that in order to win, a coalition must command a majority of the seats in a legislature. Often this is simply not true. Governments can survive despite controlling only a minority of the seats. Particular institutional features of different systems are often crucially important to the nature of coalition-building. These can only be captured by making the models more descriptively accurate.

Minority governments may form simply as 'caretaker administrations' to await the next general election.[12] However, some systems seem to have structural features which allow minority administrations to form regularly. Two important features are the requirement of investiture votes and the ability of a government to make votes on specific legislative proposals votes of confidence (or the ability after losing such a vote to call for a vote of confidence). Viable minority governments may form though they prove ineffectual.[13] Other parties may have little incentive to bring down a government even if they are able so to do. Parties in the legislature may be pivotal though they can see little to gain by being in the government itself. In part this depends upon the ability of opposition parties to affect legislation. Where policies can be effectively pursued outside government the rewards of office immediately diminish. This capacity varies from system to system, so that institutional rules across systems are very important to understanding the variation of governing coalitions across nations. The willingness to remain outside government so long as the party can affect legislation is used as theoretical support for policy-seeking models rather than office-seeking ones. In one sense this is obviously true. But office-seeking is hardly a motivation in itself: people rarely desire power for power's sake; rather what they desire is power in order to effect some aim.[14]

Laver and Schofield use the notion of policy-seeking to account for all instances of surplus majority coalitions. If government policy is a collective good then parties have nothing to lose if additional members are added to a cabinet as long as they do not demand different policies. Therefore a coalition will not suffer from additional members if they are in the middle of the policy spectrum represented by the other, necessary, members of the coalition. Luebbert argues that where there is one dominant party with many more members than its rivals, yet which does not constitute a majority on its own, it will prefer to form a coalition with excess members to ensure that none of its coalition partners is pivotal.[15] Luebbert also believes that in any coalition the dominant party is going to ensure that it holds the central position on the policy spectrum to preclude its partners acting together against it. Laver and Schofield write: 'It may seem rather surprising that

Luebbert predicts surplus majority governments on the basis of more or less the same argument that the notion of policy viability predicts single-party minority governments';[16] but, as they also recognize, predicting whether minority or surplus majority governments will form at any given time also depends upon other institutional features of the system, for example the ability of a party from outside the governing coalition to affect policy.

Luebbert's model of coalitional politics is based upon assumptions regarding party leaders. He assumes that party leaders are motivated by the desire to retain their position and must therefore satisfy the different factions within their party. In negotiations they must ensure that the positions adopted are sufficiently detailed to attract broad party support but sufficiently vague to avoid creating internal splits. Luebbert suggests that party leaders therefore concentrate upon particular issues on which to base coalition negotiations. These sticking-points are ones which command widespread support within the party and become the basis upon which the coalition must be built. In Luebbert's view, coalition negotiations are not really about the desires of party élites but about leaders' needs to satisfy their followers: 'Most negotiation in cases of protracted government formation takes place between leaders and their followers and among rival factions within parties.'[17]

This is a generalized model which Luebbert applies to particular examples, and as a dynamic model it can help to explain why some potential minimal-winning coalitions cannot be formed if general agreement over the sticking-points is lacking. As Laver and Schofield acknowledge, Luebbert's theory can explain both minority and surplus majority coalitions where Riker's theory falls down. But it would be a mistake to dismiss Riker's theory on those grounds, or to believe that a combined Riker–Luebbert model would be superior to both. Such a model may merely fail to produce deterministic solutions or produce trivial results when it explains an outcome by utilizing assumptions which have been established as fact by other means.

2. INTERPRETING THEIR FINDINGS

Several factors have been introduced to accommodate the purported exceptions to the generalizations which can be made about coalition-formation. The danger of complicating theory in this way is familiar. The more complicated the model grows, to include all the variations from the simple generalization, the less it resembles a true generalization. Rather, it resembles a description of all possibilities. However, there are important logical differences between the models, particularly with regard to their assumptions. To highlight these divergences I want to note some important differences in the nature of formal explanation I have introduced elsewhere.[18]

Part of the failure of the more simple structural coalition models such as Riker's rests on their derivation from the index approach to political power, which measures voting resources, not power.[19] More complex bargaining models of coalition-formation are able more accurately to compute the full set of resources which underlie true power ascriptions. Even the most complex bargaining model of power still attempts to measure power, which is an inherently counteractual and dispositional concept. This means that even when the bargaining model accurately reflects the power-holding of the participants it may not accurately predict their actions. They may choose not to use the power they hold. This may occur for epistemological reasons: that is, actors misperceive the bargaining situations and so misuse their resources (they have imperfect knowledge). Or it may occur for ideological reasons: that is, they see the expected gains as trivial.

Formal theories can be divided into two different classes, each of which can be further subdivided into two groups. The first two classes I will call, for reasons which will emerge later, the 'parametric' and the 'strategic'; the second two the 'structural' and the 'causal'. In order to explain these classes I wish to introduce a further distinction: the type and token distinction. A 'token' is a specific example of a general class. A 'type' is the general class, composed of many token examples. Each token may belong to many different classes and each type may have many different token examples. Desmond O'Malley is therefore a token example of 'Irish politicians' and of 'party leaders', Bettino Craxi a token example of 'Italian politicians' and 'party leaders'. If we wish to produce some general proposition which helps to explain the behaviour of 'party leaders' then it must apply to both Craxi and O'Malley. In both cases, however, the proposition may be subject to revision if it conflicts with other general propositions held to obtain in the case of other types such as 'Irish politicians' and

'Italian politicians'. This is type explanation and is the paradigm application of formal theory—both structural and strategic. Explanations of the behaviour of the tokens 'O'Malley' and 'Craxi' take a very different style.

To develop a full explanation of the behaviour of token individuals we require a more detailed and complex set of propositions. We need to understand the actual dispositions which motivate Craxi and O'Malley: their beliefs, desires, preference orderings, psychological propensities, and so on. Crudely, we need to understand their real history. This form of explanation is that in which biographers, historians, and journalists standardly engage. But it is also the sort of explanation von Mises calls 'praxeological', in which psychologists in their different ways engage, and the sort recommended by Jon Elster as the basis of rational choice—the Davidson method.[20]

It is my contention that the mixing of type and token explanations in formal coalition theory, without the recognition that they are very different ways of explaining the world, is the reason for disappointment with formalism. The four types of explanation (all of which can be formalized) can be represented in a two-by-two table (Table 3.1).

Box 1 explanations are straightforward causal explanations of what has happened in non-strategic situations. A simple example of this is an explanation of an individual voting in an election with only two candidates. (Non-strategic voting often occurs, of course, but necessarily takes place when there are only two candidates.) If we wish to explain why one candidate won in an election we can

TABLE 3.1. *Modes of explanation*

	Causal (Token)	Structural (Type)
Parametric	*Box* 1 'actual' 'preference discovered' e.g. non-strategic voting	*Box* 2 'logically possible' 'preference open' e.g. S–S power index
Strategic	*Box* 3 'actual' token game theory e.g. Maastricht bargaining	*Box* 4 'logically expected' type game theory e.g. *n*- person Chicken

give a causal explanation of all the actual votes. A simple causal explanation will include the rules under which the election was held and the number of votes received by each candidate. A more thoroughgoing explanation will look deeper into the reasons why each person voted for the candidate he or she supported. It will give a complete causal account of each vote, thereby giving a complete causal explanation of the overall pattern of voting. Following Davidson in assuming that reasons are causes, we can causally explain the result by examining the reasons that each voter had for voting as she or he did.[21] Again, following Davidson, this will involve explaining the beliefs and desires of each voter. Very rarely, if ever, in social science do we attempt to give such a complete causal explanation of some election. Rather, when we try to explain why one candidate beat another, we look at some general reasons why voters chose one candidate rather than the other. We discover from poll data the salient issues of the election and why the policies (or personality) of one candidate appealed to a greater number of people. But once we start to look for the more general reasons we are moving away from straightforward causal explanation and into structural or type explanation.

Non-strategic voting is not the only example of parametric causal explanation in political science, though generally the very nature of politics means that most political explanations take on a strategic form. Box 3 explanations, therefore, are more general. The example given in Box 3 is the full causal explanation of the bargaining that created the Maastricht Treaty. This would require a detailed understanding of the beliefs, preferences, and aims of all the treaty negotiators, their knowledge of the beliefs and objects of one another, and the structural factors, time constraints, and so on which led to the eventual outcome. Again a full causal explanation of the final treaty requires specifying the actual bargaining moves made by each of the negotiators. In such a case we can still utilize the findings of type models. For example, the formal result that temporal cut-off points in extended bargaining games produce 'arbitrary' outcomes will be very useful in explaining the final form of the Maastricht Treaty.[22] Such a bargaining situation can be represented by formal game theory with realistic assumptions about the beliefs and desires of all the constituent players. It does make general assumptions about player motivation, but it also incorporates the actual beliefs and preferences of each genetic individual.

In describing such a situation we can give a full causal explanation of the outcome.

Box 3 and Box 4 explanations are rather different. These are structural explanations in which the assumptions are often unrealistic and assumptions about preferences may be kept broad. In Box 2 we have parametric models from which strategic considerations have been left out. The example given in the matrix is the Shapley–Shubik power index upon which Riker's formal coalition theory is built. This simple example illustrates the complex nature of the structural features of more complicated coalition theories.

Shapley and Shubik recognized that the power of each individual voter is some function of the number of voters in the electorate and the voting rules under which the result is determined.[23] They argued that the power of each member of a committee can be ascertained by the number of times that that member's vote is pivotal. The pivotal vote is the vote which secures the passage of a motion under sequential voting. By calculating how many times some voter could be pivotal under all possible sequences of votes and preference orderings we can calculate the voting power of each individual voter. Given equality of voting their index provides the trivial result that in a committee of nine people each voter has the power of 1/9. However, their index proves less trivial when it reveals that under weighted voting a member with a lesser weight (i.e. fewer votes) may be just as powerful as a member with a greater weight if each is pivotal the same number of times. In other words the crucial factor is not the number of votes one commands, but rather how many times one is pivotal. Riker applied this principle to national legislatures, and demonstrated that when no party has an overall majority, parties may command the same amount of Shapley–Shubik voting power despite the fact that they command vastly different votes in the legislature.[24] He added to the Shapley–Shubik result two further assumptions: first, that political rewards are zero-sum; and second, that these rewards will be handed out to winning parties in proportion to the percentage of votes each party brings to the coalition. This gave him his minimum-winning coalition theory.

What is important here is the manner in which the Shapley–Shubik index produces its results about power distribution, for their method fits parametric structural explanation perfectly. This is because it is 'preference open'—a complete set of the logically possible preferences and the complete set of the power resources, i.e. 'votes' of each player. It leaves no room for individual action—all possible actions are combined in the index result. Riker's theory, in so far as it is based upon the Shapley–Shubik index, also produces parametric structural explanation. A full causal explanation of, for example, any actual coalition must utilize strategic causal explanation. The Shapley–Shubik index suggests the 'background conditions' against which the bargaining occurs. It constitutes (a part of) the structure. Because Riker's index cannot produce causal explanation I term such models 'structural'.[25] Some of the rival coalition theories are explicitly game-theoretic: that is, they are strategic structural explanations. Therefore these different theories (or, as I would prefer to term them, models) are not all on a par, and should be treated differently. We cannot expect the same sorts of results from each of these formal models of coalition theory, and should not therefore pit them against each other in some sort of competitive scientific test. Rather, we should see what we can learn from each of these different models of coalition-formation which can help us to understand more fully (1) the institutions and structures which affect the nature of coalition-formation, and (2) how these structures and institutions affect the formation of actual individual coalitions.

This type of generalized bargaining model with standard rationality assumptions and realistic assumptions about the preferences of the actors fits into the Box 4 strategic-structural explanations. It suggests the sorts of outcomes we can expect from different types of bargaining situation. From the point of view of testing these models, the problem is that the more realistic the assumptions about preferences and the greater the number of resources utilized within the framework of the bargaining game, the more likely it is that multiple equilibria will emerge and hence produce non-deterministic solutions. The model becomes less predictive, harder to test, and less useful as an explanatory device.

The cause of any particular coalition is the actual negotiations which took place, which can be explained by the actual resources the actors have at their disposal and the use they make of these resources. This is Box 3 explanation. It does not follow that we cannot learn about the progress of negotiations within such bargains by use of the models which conform to Box 2 and 4 explanations. The lessons to be learned from these types of explanations are (1) the nature of the resources available and (2) the conditions under which actual bargains take place. They teach us about the structural constraints and opportunities within which actual bargains are struck, for, as we saw with the Shapley–Shubik power index, the structural conditions constitute resources for the actors. Similarly, Schofield's game-theoretic explanation is not a full causal explanation, for it only tells us what to expect if parties outside the core—if no core exists, outside the 'heart'—of the game attempt to form a coalition. The structure of the game determines the core and hence the background conditions under which any actual coalition may form. It is not entirely structural in the manner of the Shapley–Shubik power index, since the set of individual preferences is constrained by ideological considerations generated by the 'manifesto group's' classification of all European parties on the basis of twenty dimensions.[26] Despite its more complex form, Schofield's game-theoretic explanation is still, broadly, a specification of the structure of coalition-bargaining. The structure includes not only the voting resources of each party, but also their relationship in terms of their preferences. We can only say broadly structural, however, since these preferences are assumed to reflect reality and lead the actors to choose one set of partners rather than another.[27] The strength of Schofield's theory is its specification of the background conditions against which we can expect the bargaining which will create the coalitions to take place. In so far as it helps us to explain coalition formation it does so by specifying the structure of politics. 'Structural explanation' seems a reasonable name for it.

Formal coalition theory needs careful interpretation. Some forms of coalition theory simply provide the parametric structural conditions under which coalition bargaining takes place. The Shapley–Shubik power index demonstrates that the voting-power resources of the parties are not simply the number of votes they command but also include their pivotal position. Riker built on this with his minimum-winning model by assuming that politics was zero-sum and that all that mattered to the parties was forming a winning coalition. Given that even this model makes some assumptions about preferences, it goes beyond simple structural constraints upon bargaining. Both of these assumptions are not generally true. Parties have wider aims than simply forming government. They also have policy commitments—which destroys the zero-sum element of Riker's model. But its predictive robustness demonstrates that there is enough truth in the assumptions to help explain coalition outcomes. This is so since policy-seeking is, to some extent, office-driven. To the extent that one can only get one's policies enacted through being in office, policy-seeking parties must also seek office. Laver and Schofield write that if politicians are motivated.

only by a desire to affect policy in and of itself, then coalitions should be connected regardless of whether all parties within the ideological range of the coalition are needed for a legislative majority; 'surplus' majority coalitions should not carry passengers. There will be a tendency for coalitions to drop non-essential members even if this means that they cease to be ideologically connected.[28]

Independent tests of the conflict within connected and unconnected coalitions does not suggest that the latter are more conflict-ridden.[29] But, other things being equal, the greater the number of parties in a coalition the greater the tendency towards shorter periods of government durability. It appears that carrying passengers increases conflict.

3. MODEL NON-RIVALNESS

This account of the logic of explanation inherent in different types of models of the political process reflects upon other issues often raised by writers in these fields: for example, the relative worth of models which assume that parties are single actors and those which see them as collections of actors. Both sets of models may be useful in different contexts, depending upon the problematic addressed.

Utilizing policy or ideological dimensions is now standard in political science, though there is no agreement on the number of dimensions to be considered, nor the precise scale for measuring ideological distance. Those who use two ideological dimensions use Euclidean space, those who utilize more dimensions have a greater variety of options from which to choose. Laver and Hunt suggest that the appropriate measure is an empirical issue to be based upon the preference structures of political actors.[30] However, the issue may not be that straightforward. A model which is driven by its structural form may make assumptions about ideological distances without actually claiming that those distances would be measured in that way by any of the actors to which the model is applied. A game-theoretic model purporting to explain the actual moves of bargainers in some coalition game would require a measure of and the number of dimensions as seen by the actors themselves.

Real actors will utilize a small number of dimensions. The advantage of the Euclidean measure is that it is easy to visualize. Once we proceed into higher numbers of dimensions the more general Minkowski measure can be used to calculate ideological space. It is hard for the analyst to visualize the dimensions of the mathematics; it is even harder for the non-mathematicians being studied. A greater number of dimensions may be theoretically plausible, and indeed may give accurate predictions for a complex interaction of players (though in general the operation of the McKelvey–Schofield Chaos Theorem defies unique predictions), but they are unlikely to represent the actual views of real players, for they will not be able to visualize n-dimensions any more than the analyst. Perhaps this is the reason why a small number of dimensions seems to work so well, even though the salience of issues across dimensions may vary through time.

Most coalition theories treat parties as unitary actors. The number of votes commanded in the legislature by a party gives that party its Shapley–Shubik power resource. Even critics of formal coalition theory recognize that, whilst there may be a great deal of intra-party conflict which can explain the strategies adopted in coalition negotiations, parties can be considered as unitary actors in models of those negotiations.[31] Factionalism within parties is often the cause of the break-up of coalitions, and so parties as unitary actors may not be satisfactory as a means of explaining why coalitions fail. This fact has led Laver and Schofield to suggest that 'When a genuinely more dynamic approach to the analysis of coalition bargaining is developed, the splitting potential of such parties must become an integral part of the account of the politics of coalition.'[32] And they describe the development of a dynamic game-theoretic account as 'the outstanding task facing coalition theorists'.[33] *Pace* these remarks, the different explanatory logic of the dynamic game-theoretic models and the parametric structural ones should be understood. If we wish to explain through game theory the fractious politics of coalition in Italy during 1986–8 we will be using the logic of the token explanation—causal strategic explanation in which the actual beliefs and desires of the actors must be known in order for the model to predict correctly the actions of the leading actors. Whilst such a token model will utilize insights from more general bargaining models it will not itself tell us much about comparative bargaining across Europe. The insights of the Shapley–Shubik power index will also be useful, but only as an element in the belief-set of the leading negotiators. Such token modelling of actual situations may prove useful, though personally I am sceptical of its utility. It requires such detailed knowledge of the actors in order to produce a model which provides accurate predictions that everything the model could teach us must already be known. Such formalism in token cases is likely to be a chimera producing nothing more than a complex but ultimately trivial explanation. Rather, the insights of more generalized game-theoretical models can be applied to particular cases in order to denote the structural constraints under which the negotiators operate.

I think, therefore, that Laver and Schofield are mistaken if they believe that, as coalition theory develops along game-theoretical lines, the assumption of parties as single actors will have to be dropped. It may continue to prove useful to many static generalized models, but will be omitted from some generalized game-theoretical ones. These different models do not need to be seen as rivals to be pitted against one another in scientific tests. Rather they are complementary, and the different models can teach us about different aspects of the structures and institutions under which coalition negotiations are conducted. Models which have a different explanatory logic, and even produce different predictions, may not be rivals as such if it is recognized that as models they do not take a truth-value: that is, they are not to be considered as true or false. Rather they are useful in highlighting an aspect or complexion of a complex reality. Different models may highlight different aspects of the structures which ultimately suggest action to the leading players. What we must not expect is one general model which is applicable to all countries at all times and is capable of producing the explanation of all coalitions. To expect this much from formal coalition theory is to court disappointment.

NOTES

1. A minimal winning coalition is one where if any party leaves, the coalition ceases to control a majority of seats in the legislature. A minimum-winning coalition is the subset of minimal winning coalitions which controls the lowest majority of seats in the legislature. W. H. Riker, *The Theory of Political Coalitions* (New Haven, Conn.: Yale University Press, 1962) based on L. S. Shapley and M. Shubik, 'A Method for Evaluating the Distribution of Power in a Committee System', in R. Bell, D. V. Edwards, and R. H. Wagner (eds.), *Political Power: A Reader* (London: Collier-Macmillan, 1969).

2. A minimum-connected coalition is a coalition where the parties are connected in policy space: R. Axelrod, *Conflict of Interest* (Chicago: Markham, 1970).

3. M. Taylor and M. Laver, 'Government Coalitions in Western Europe', *European Journal of Political Research*, 1 (1973), 205–48; M. Laver, 'Dynamic Factors in Government Coalition Formation', *European Journal of Political Research*, 2 (1974), 259–70.

4. Laver and Schofield, *Multiparty Government*, 100.

5. See K. Dowding, *Rational Choice and Political Power* (Aldershot: Edward Elgar, 1991) for the conception of structural suggestion.

6. L. C. Dodd, 'Party Coalitions in Multiparty Parliaments: A Game Theoretic Analysis', *American Political Science Review*, 68 (1974), 1093–117; id., *Coalitions in Parliamentary Governments* (Princeton, NJ: Princeton University Press, 1976).

7. Laver and Schofield, *Multiparty Government*, 149–50.

8. K. Dowding and R. Kimber, 'The Meaning and Use of "Political Stability" ', *European Journal of Political Research*, 11 (1983), 229–43.

9. E. Browne, J. Frendeis, and D. Gleiber, 'An Events Approach to the Problem of Cabinet Stability', *Comparative Political Studies*, 17 (1984), 167–97; id., 'The Process of Cabinet Dissolution: An Exponential Model of Duration and Stability in Western Democracies', *American Journal of Political Science*, 30 (1986), 625–50; id., 'Contending Models of Cabinet Stability: A Rejoinder', *American Political Science Review*, 82 (1988) 939–41; E. Browne, D. Gleiber, and C. Mashoba, 'Evaluating Conflict of Interest Theory: Western European Cabinet Coalitions, 1945–80', *British Journal of Political Science*, 14 (1984), 1–32.

10. N. Schofield, 'Stability of Coalition Governments in Western Europe: 1945–86', *European Journal of Political Economy*, 3 (1987), 555–91.

11. N. Schofield, 'Political Competition and Multiparty Coalition Government', *European Journal of Political Research*, 23 (1993), 1–33.

12. V. Herman and J. Pope, 'Minority Governments in Western

Democracies', *British Journal of Political Science*, 3 (1973), 191–212.
13. K. Strom, *Minority Government and Majority Rule* (Cambridge: Cambridge University Press, 1990).
14. Dowding, *Rational Choice*.
15. G. Luebbert, *Comparative Democracy: Policy Making and Governing Coalitions in Europe and Israel* (New York: Columbia University Press, 1986).
16. Laver and Schofield, *Multiparty Government*, 88.
17. Luebbert, *Comparative Democracy*, 52.
18. K. Dowding, 'The Compatibility of Behaviouralism, Rational Choice and "New Institutionalism" ', *Journal of Theoretical Politics*, 6 (1994), 105–17.
19. Dowding, *Rational Choice*.
20. L. von Mises, *Human Action: A Treatise on Economics* (London: William Hodge, 1949); J. Elster, 'Introduction' in id. (ed.) *Rational Choice* (Oxford: Blackwell, 1986); D. Davidson, *Essays on Actions and Events* (Oxford: Clarendon Press, 1980).
21. Davidson, *Actions and Events*.
22. See D. Kreps, *Game Theory and Economic Modelling* (Oxford: Clarendon Press, 1990) for an informal discussion of this feature of bargaining games.
23. Shapley and Shubik, 'Method for Evaluating'.
24. Riker, *Political Coalitions*.
25. Dowding, *Rational Choice*; id., 'Compatibility of Behaviouralism'.
26. M. Laver and W. B. Hunt, *Policy and Party Competition* (London: Routledge, 1992).
27. Given that the account of causation underlying the specification of causal models in Table 3.1 is generated by Davidson's account of 'reasons as causes', the nature of preferences leading to choice must be accounted for on the 'cause' rather than the 'structure' side of the distinction I have elucidated.
28. Laver and Schofield, *Multiparty Government*, 99.
29. Browne *et al.*, 'Contending Models'.
30. Laver and Hunt, *Policy and Party Competition*.
31. K. von Beyme, *Political Parties in Western Europe* (Aldershot: Gower, 1983).
32. Laver and Schofield, *Multiparty Politics*, 27.
33. Ibid. 28.

4

The Rational Basis for Belief in the Democratic Myth

PATRICK DUNLEAVY AND
HELEN MARGETTS

In a rational-choice perspective the problem of explaining why people vote has proved resistant to plausible explanation. While public-choice theorists insist that individual voters cannot objectively influence outcomes, large majorities of the eligible population continue to vote in most liberal democracies, except in the United States. In their responses to surveys, the voters of these countries regularly demonstrate their belief in the 'democratic myth', denying that their votes can make no difference, and affirming that the vote gives ordinary people influence over politicians and power over public policy.

This chapter explores the reasons for the disjuncture between academic analysis and mass beliefs. We take as our starting-point the recent treatment of voting choice as a game played by each citizen against all others in Brennan and Lomasky's *Democracy and Decision*.[1] Their theme is that the problems which most public-choice theorists have long accepted as a fact of life in explaining the decision to vote or not, also extend to cover how people choose whom to vote for—a choice heretofore treated as a largely unproblematic instrumental choice. Drawing a contrast between voting and a classical view of market decision-making, Brennan and Lomasky argue that political choices are conditioned principally (or even exclusively) by the structure of people's expressive utilities in the choice process. If accepted, their thesis has some powerful empirical lessons and unfortunate normative implications for our understanding of democracy.

We would like to thank Won-taek Kang, Sheila Dunleavy, and Albert Weale for stimulating some of the ideas included here.

Against their analysis, we argue that:

(i) Individual decision-making in real markets is more determined by other people's reactions than they acknowledge. The chances of an individual consumer being able to control fully the benefits of their choices can be as remote as in the political realm.

(ii) In modelling elections it is inconsistent to formulate and deploy the concept of 'expressive benefits' while retaining the hard-line rational-choice assumption that elections deliver solely public-goods outcomes, about which voters are assumed to be perfectly informed. A consistent approach requires that we acknowledge that voters operate on subjective perceptions, and that they choose parties by forming a 'party identity' (defined as the partisan equivalent of a group identity, the recognition of a self-interest shared with others). Hence when people vote they will come subjectively to 'own' outcomes differently, depending on the choice they make.

(iii) Without party identities and ownership of outcomes it is otherwise impossible satisfactorily to explain why anyone votes in elections where a single individual can never be decisive in determining objective outcomes—that is in competitions which yield either clear majorities or no-overall-control situations, but no possibility of a tied outcome. No-overall-control situations occur in virtually all elections under proportional representation, and in many plurality systems.

(iv) In most liberal democracies, there are elections for national governments, state or regional governments, and for local authorities. In many countries there are also separate elections for legislative chambers and of executive officials. Such multi-level and multi-component arrangements strongly encourage participation if voters in some degree own the outcomes of their choices and are indifferent about being objectively decisive. By contrast, if voters were perfectly informed and paid attention only to objective outcomes, these institutional arrangements would be disincentives to vote. We use empirical data to show how the study of different levels of election can illuminate the continued high levels of turnout and patterns of partisan change in British elections.

(v) Combining these arguments, we can reconstruct a public-choice account of voting by recognizing that citizens define appropriate aspiration levels for their influence as an integral part of the electoral process. Most people's aspiration levels will bear little similarity to the classic public-choice focus on individual pivotality, which is anyway an almost impossible goal of action, whether in mass political behaviour or in complex product markets.

1. EXPRESSIVE AND INSTRUMENTAL BENEFITS IN MARKETS AND POLITICS

In *Democracy and Decision*, Brennan and Lomasky argue that the choice facing consumers in market contexts can be pictured as a game of each against all, with pay-offs consisting of instrumental benefits flowing from the consumer's choice, and expressive benefits inherent in making the choice (Table 4.1). In a pure market, other people's decisions will not affect the benefits of an individual's choices, and everyone's expected utilities will therefore be insensitive to others' behaviour. We write E_A for the expressive benefit of choosing A, Y_A for the instrumental benefits of A, p_a for the probability that a majority of others will choose A, and U_A for the expected utility of choosing A. A simple alteration of the subscripts denotes the same things respectively for B. The expected utility of choosing A rather than B will simply be the expressive and instrumental benefits of A minus the expressive and instrumental benefits of B.

Brennan and Lomasky argue that in an election, the flow of instrumental benefits to an individual voter will be conditioned completely by the majority decision, except in the remote possibility that the votes of all others are tied, in which case the individual's single vote would be decisive in determining the election

TABLE 4.1. *The choice situation of an individual consumer in a 'pure' market*

Each	All others		
	Majority choose A	Majority choose B	Tied result
Choose A	$E_A + Y_A$	$E_A + Y_A$	$E_A + Y_A$
Choose B	$E_B + Y_B$	$E_B + Y_B$	$E_B + Y_B$
Expected utility of choosing A (U_A)	$p_a(E_A+Y_A$ $- E_B-Y_B)$	$+ \; p_b(E_A+Y_A$ $- E_B-Y_B)$	$+ \; 1-p_a-p_b(E_A+Y_A$ $- E_B-Y_B)$

TABLE 4.2. *The choice situation of an individual voter in an election*

Each	All others		
	Majority choose A	Majority choose B	Tied result
Choose A	$E_A + Y_A$	$E_A + Y_B$	$E_A + Y_A$
Choose B	$E_B + Y_B$	$E_B + Y_B$	$E_B + Y_B$
Expected utility of choosing A (U_A)	$p_a(E_A - E_B)$ +	$p_b (E_A - E_B)$ +	$1 - p_a - p_b (E_A + Y_A - E_B - Y_B)$

outcome (Table 4.2). If a majority of other voters support A, then the instrumental benefits the individual voter will receive are Y_A, irrespective of whether the individual voter chooses A or B. It follows that the only difference which the voter can take into account in deciding how to vote is the expressive benefits she receives from choosing A or B. The same thing applies if most other voters choose B. Only if the election would otherwise be tied will a rational individual take instrumental benefits into account in deciding how to vote. But the probability of a tied result is very low, approaching zero for any substantial electorate, and hence will be discounted in determining the expected utility the individual receives from voting A rather than B. Political decisions will be determined by the expressive benefits people receive from voting one way rather than another, and not by instrumental considerations at all.

If there are some circumstances in which people's expressive and instrumental preferences diverge, this stark contrast between market and political choice situations has important implications. Brennan and Lomasky argue that political choices should not be assigned the same normative significance as people's choices in markets, because the logic set out above implies that political choices reflect only expressive benefits and not the distribution of more important (because larger) instrumental utilities. They also point out that if instrumental and expressive benefits diverge, people making political choices may easily act against their own interests. For example, in a foreign policy crisis which could degenerate into military conflict, voters who derive expressive benefits from advocating or voting for a tough stance would do so, even if their interests are badly damaged by the advent of war. Similarly people may derive expressive benefits from voting for redistributive social policies, even though their interests would be better served by no redistribution. The consequence of political choices being based entirely on expressive benefits (except for tied outcomes) is to undermine any connection between people's overall interests and their political choices, and thus to impugn the validity of the collective choice process.

2. RE-MODELLING MARKET DECISION-MAKING

Although Brennan and Lomasky acknowledge that their picture of market decision-making is an idealized one, and hence that there would actually be a continuum between the situations in Tables 4.1 and 4.2, they provide no indications of what more realistic market choices might be like. However, if the benefits which flow from individual choices depend on the choices made by other consumers, then the stark contrast between market processes revealing people's interests and political choices reflecting only expressive benefits is eroded.

One starting-point in achieving more realism is to partition instrumental benefits into two components:

- Q_A, the default level of instrumental benefits which the individual consumer will receive from their choice of option A, irrespective of the choices/decisions made by others; and
- C_A, conditional instrumental benefits, an addition which the individual consumer will receive from opting for A if a majority of other consumers do likewise.

In very simple choice situations Q_A will be overwhelmingly important and C_A will be zero or negligible. But with more complex product choices C_A becomes increasingly important.

Consider, for example, someone choosing a new personal computer and confronting the decision between going for an Apple or for an IBM-compatible PC. The default value of their choice will cover the functionality of the equipment and software for their immediate needs. The additional benefits dependent on other people's choices would include such things as transferring disks and files to other computers, and receiving disks and files back, accessing the full range of software, updating software, the resale value of the equipment, and so on.

A second change is to recognize that in market conditions where people are making important or large-scale product choices of this kind, expressive benefits are likely to play a more important part in the choice process than in simpler choices. 'Expressive benefits' is in itself a complex notion, worth unpacking into two parts:

- T_A, autonomous expressive benefits, those which the person receives from making a choice reflecting her own personality, character, or dispositions; and
- X_A, exogenously set expressive benefits, which are conditioned by how a wider society or social sub-group regards outcome choices as reflecting the character, moral standing, or fundamental orientation of the chooser.

The X_A category reflects the fact that product choices acquire associations (such as Apples with imaginative or creative people, and IBMs with solidity or business values). So people are likely to make backward inferences from product choices to personal characteristics, especially since product choices are often very public and durable over a long period. In the IBM/Apple case, autonomous expressive benefits would reflect how the consumer sees the choice as consistent with her overall approach to life. Whereas all the brand-name conditioning effects developed by PC companies' advertising, and all the customary evaluations which people might make on the basis of someone's choice of a PC, would fall under exogenously set expressive benefits. (Of course, these two are inter-related.)

In fact, large parts of X_A might just be disguised instrumental benefits. For example, if someone chooses an Apple PC for their office in order to impress clients with their creativity, or opts for a company car of a certain opulence to convey an impression of financial stability, these choices are not really expressive at all: they are just rather intangible or hard to quantify instrumental benefits, because they are slightly masked from an external observer, and possibly even from the consumer herself.

There is a form of continuum, then, between autonomous expressive benefits at one pole and default instrumental benefits at the other (Figure 4.1). If we now model a complex product choice in these terms, the matrix in Table 4.3 looks very different from that in Table 4.1. Consumers always receive the autonomous expressive benefits (T_A or T_B) and the default instrumental benefits (Q_A or Q_B) associated with their product choices. If a majority of consumers choose in line with the individual consumer, that person also receives the full exogenously set expressive benefits (X_A or X_B) and the conditional instrumental benefits (C_A or C_B) associated with that choice. But where a majority of consumers choose differently from the individual's decision, then he or she simply does not receive any conditional instrumental benefits. And the individual's exogenously set expressive benefits are discounted by a factor k (where $0<k<1$) because the relative unpopularity of her choice adversely affects other people's evaluation of that decision.

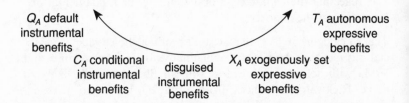

Q_A default instrumental benefits

C_A conditional instrumental benefits

disguised instrumental benefits

X_A exogenously set expressive benefits

T_A autonomous expressive benefits

Fig. 4.1 The continuum between autonomous expressive benefits and default instrumental benefits

If a decision is tied in a complex product market, then consumers make no clear-cut or predominant choice between alternatives. Hence it seems likely that people in general receive lower exogenously set expressive benefits whether they choose A or B in Table 4.3. Because no clear product winner emerges, because the choice remains contested, every choice now has drawbacks as well as advantages in expressive terms: we assume that both X_A and X_B are discounted by k in this case.[2] A tied outcome also reduces the extent to which conditional instrumental benefits are available by a factor r (where $0 < r < 1$). If the product market is evenly divided then consumers still receive some proportion of C_A or C_B depending on their choice, but not what they would have gained had their choice turned out to dominate the market. (In the IBM/Apple example, where C stands for connectivity and full software availability, a divided market implies problems for both groups of PC

TABLE 4.3. *The choice situation of an individual consumer in a complex product market*

Each	All others Majority choose A	Majority choose B	Tied result
Choose A	$T_A+X_A+C_A+Q_A$	$T_A+kX_A+Q_A$	$T_A+kX_A+rC_A+Q_A$
Choose B	$T_B+kX_B+Q_B$	$T_B+X_B+C_B+Q_B$	$T_B+kX_B+rC_B+Q_B$
U_A	$p_a(C_A+T_A-T_B+$ $Q_A-Q_B+X_A-kX_B)$	$+\ p_b(-C_B+T_A-T_B+$ $Q_A-Q_B+kX_A-X_B)$	$+\ 1-p_a-p_b(T_A-T_B+$ $Q_A-Q_B+kX_A-kX_B$ $+rC_A-rC_B)$

users.) Note the contrast here with Table 4.1, where in a tied market consumers received full levels of utility, dependent only on their own choices.

Looking at the expected utility (U_A) row in Table 4.3, the importance of other people's choices in influencing the individual's decisions is clear. Suppose that the individual prefers A to B on all components (Q, C, X, and T). If a majority are going to opt for A, then the reasons for choosing A would be strong because $X_A > kX_B$, $Q_A > Q_B$, and $T_A > T_B$, while C_A would weigh in the scales for A on its own. If a majority were going to opt for B, however, it is perfectly conceivable that:

$$C_B > T_A - T_B + Q_A - Q_B + kX_A - X_B$$

That is, so long as the conditional instrumental benefits C_B outweigh the better performance of A on autonomous expressive benefits, default instrumental benefits, and exogenously set expressive benefits (where kX_A may anyway be smaller than X_B), then a rational individual who unambiguously prefers A but knew that most other consumers would choose B should also choose B. By contrast, in the case of a tie (so long as the k factors applying to X_A and X_B are the same) a rational consumer who prefers A on all counts will clearly choose A.[3] If p_B is very high then the result in this column may decisively colour the U_A calculation as a whole.

Overall, the consumer's expected utility calculation will probably be sensitive to the probabilities of different outcomes occurring. To appreciate this it may be useful to look at a numerical example. We assume the following values:

$$T_A = 10 \quad X_A = 15 \quad C_A = 40 \quad Q_A = 80 \quad p_a = 0.2 \quad k = 0.7$$
$$T_B = 5 \quad X_B = 10 \quad C_B = 35 \quad Q_B = 75 \quad p_b = 0.7 \quad r = 0.5$$

(These values are arbitrarily chosen, except that one might make a case for $r=0.5$ on the grounds that in an evenly divided product market each choice yields around half of the conditional benefits which would have obtained had one product become dominant.)

In terms of all four components the consumer clearly prefers A to B. Yet if we feed these values into Table 4.3 the matrix generated in Table 4.4 is one where the consumer should choose B, because the probability of a majority of other consumers choosing B is so high. The negative U_A score of 17.2 more than offsets the positive scores in the other two columns. We conclude that in complex product markets, with disaggregated expressive and instrumental benefits, it is perfectly feasible for rational consumers to choose outcomes which run against the underlying structure of their preferences. In this important sense, the contrast which Brennan and Lomasky draw between market choice and electoral choice is inaccurate and over-polarized. Consumers' 'revealed preferences' do not have the unambiguous normative significance attributed to them by mainstream economists.

3. REMODELLING ELECTIONS: HOW VOTERS 'OWN' OUTCOMES

Voters' choices in elections are much more similar to those of consumers in complex product markets than Brennan and Lomasky's

TABLE 4.4. *Numerical example for the choice situation of an individual consumer in a complex product market*

Each	All others		
	Majority choose A	Majority choose B	Tied result
Choose A	145	100.5	120.5
Choose B	87	125	104.5
U_A	+11.6	−17.2	+1.6 = − 4.0

dichotomy acknowledges. For voters as well as consumers we can distinguish the four kinds of benefits discussed above:

- T_A, the autonomous expressive benefits of voting, denotes the voter's purely personal utilities from voting for party or candidate A, those which are received even when the voting decision is known (or guessed) only by the individual concerned;

- X_A, the exogenously set expressive benefits of voting, includes all those utilities from voting for party or candidate A which follow from the social approval or distinction or simply characterization of one as an individual which this choice confers;

- Q_A denotes the default instrumental benefits of choosing party or candidate A, the party outcome benefit, irrespective of whether they win or lose. Thus it covers all the hard-edged, near-pecuniary utilities which flow to the voter as a result of party A existing in the political arena. As in choosing personal computers, the whole point of Q_A is that it is unaffected by other people's behaviour (subject of course to the party continuing to exist and a background *ceteris paribus* clause that the basic political and constitutional system remains unchanged);

- C_A is again the conditional instrumental benefit of choosing party A if it succeeds in winning a majority and becoming the government until the next election. Thus C_A is the governmental outcome benefit which flows to the voter as a result of party A controlling state power and altering public policy to favour (or adversely affect) the voter's interests.

It is important to stress that in political contexts C_A, Q_A, and X_A can all be negative. Whereas in market contexts a consumer choosing between competing products will usually derive some positive utility from each of them, electoral choices may often involve comparing net benefits from some choices with severe losses from others; or even making a Hobson's choice between competitors each of which is unattractive or involves net losses.

To see how the disaggregated expressive and instrumental benefits operate in electoral choices we need to consider two rather different possible situations, where:

- elections produce strictly public-goods outcomes in terms of instrumental benefits, which are standardized across all voters; or

- elections produce standardized governmental outcomes only, but people also 'own' the party outcomes of their choices, so that instrumental benefits are differentiated depending on how a majority of other voters decide.

To simplify the analysis we also assume temporarily that there is no likelihood of an election producing any other outcome except either a majority for party A, or a majority for party B, (so that $p_A + p_B = 1$). We relax this assumption in the next section.

The public-goods view of elections is captured in Table 4.5, a more articulated version of the first two columns of Table 4.2. The C and Q benefits depend only on how a majority of voters decide (exactly as in Table 4.2), but the introduction of exogenously set expressive benefits introduces a difference. As in Table 4.3 we assume that a discount factor k applies to exogenously set expressive benefits when the chosen party is unsuccessful: supporting a loser delivers a reduced level of expressive benefits compared with backing a winner. The argument here draws strength from evidence for bandwagon effects: neatly captured by the 1987 British Tory tabloid headline boasting 'The Sun: The Paper with the BIG Majority', or the same paper's 1992 claim about Major's victory: 'It Woz the Sun Wot Won It!'. In addition, Noelle-Neumann argues that there are diminishing exogenously set expressive returns for the supporters of losing parties.[4] Declining popularity for party A can lead to a progressive reduction in the visibility of that alignment, as supporters become more reluctant publicly to affirm an unpopular allegiance.

Hence we write in kX_A (where $0<k<1$) if the individual votes for

TABLE 4.5. *The choice situation of an individual voter in an election delivering public-goods outcomes*

| Each | All others | |
	Majority choose A	Majority choose B
Choose A	$T_A+X_A+C_A+Q_A$	$T_A+kX_A+C_B+Q_B$
Choose B	$T_B+kX_B+C_A+Q_A$	$T_B+X_B+C_B+Q_B$
U_A	$p_a(T_A-T_B+ \quad\quad +$ $X_A-kX_B)$	$p_b(T_A-T_B+$ $kX_A-X_B)$

A but party *B* gains the majority. It seems likely that *k* is almost always appreciably less than 1, and that it gets smaller the more convincingly or comprehensively a party or candidate looks like being beaten. The discounting of exogenously set expressive benefits involved in voting for a no-hope party or candidate (such as Labour in the 1983 British election, or Dukakis in the 1988 US Presidential race) is likely to be especially severe.

The effects of variations in *k* in Table 4.5 of course depend on the probable size of X_A or X_B in the first place, compared with autonomous expressive benefits (*T*). If *X* benefits are trivial influences on choice compared with *T* benefits, even low values for *k* will not much influence voters' decisions. Yet it seems clear that *X* benefits will be significant, especially when compared with autonomous expressive benefits. Brennan and Lomasky's account of expressive benefits predominantly discusses exogenously set benefits, many of which seem almost disguised instrumental benefits.[5] 'Momentum' effects in the campaign period also operate primarily through large *X* benefits.

Examining the expected utility of voting *A*, Table 4.5 introduces new complexities compared with Table 4.2. Although voters' choices are still conditioned only by expressive benefits, and not by instrumental benefits at all, we cannot assume *a priori* that an individual voter's alignment will not be conditioned extensively by other people's behaviour. Where the *X* benefits are large relative to *T* benefits, variations in the *k* discount factor, together with variations in p_A and p_B affecting the expected utility calculation, both introduce a possibility that even if $T_A > T_B$ and $X_A > X_B$ for an individual voter then the voter may still vote for *B*. Consequently the stark contrast between market and political processes drawn by Brennan and Lomasky is further blurred.

Turning to the second possibility, that voters 'own' some instrumental benefits of their choices, and that only governmental outcome benefits are standardized, Table 4.6 shows the pay-offs which result. The key difference from Table 4.5 is that differences in the party benefits of voting for *A* or *B* now enter into the expected utility calculation as well as the two kinds of expressive benefits. Voters' instrumental benefits flowing from governmental policy are standardized depending on the election outcome, but their initial choice still determines the instrumental benefits they receive from their chosen party advocating their interests (whether the party

TABLE 4.6. *The choice situation of an individual voter in an election where voters own some instrumental outcomes*

Each	All others	
	Majority choose A	Majority choose B
Choose A	$T_A+X_A+C_A+Q_A$	$T_A+kX_A+C_B+Q_A$
Choose B	$T_B+kX_B+C_A+Q_B$	$T_B+X_B+C_B+Q_B$
U_A	$p_a(T_A-T_B+X_A-kX_B$ $+Q_A-Q_B)$ +	$p_b(T_A-T_B+kX_A-X_B$ $+Q_A-Q_B)$

wins or loses). Acknowledging an identity (recognizing an interest shared with others of similar alignment) opens the way for people to experience losses as well as benefits. Once a decision has been made and significantly incorporated into someone's life choices, social intercourse, and so on, it can only be changed at some cost. Our analysis supposes, then, that if, say, a middle-class person votes Conservative, but their party loses and a Labour government is installed instead, the voter now suffers from policy-induced changes adversely affecting her interests. But she continues to receive instrumental benefits from the Conservatives' presence in Parliament and their opposition to government policies. Default or party benefits are likely to be substantial in comparison with both kinds of expressive benefits, especially in polarized situations where political alignments are adversarial or are closely associated with different social locations (for example, social class or ethnicity).

A numerical example can help to illustrate the differences between Tables 4.5 and 4.6. We assume the following arbitrary values:

	T	X	C	Q	p	
A	10	20	−10	−10	0.5	$k = 0.5$
B	5	10	10	15	0.5	

In turn these yield the following pay-offs under the two different schema:

	Public goods elections		'Owned' party outcomes	
	Majority *A*	Majority *B*	Majority *A*	Majority *B*
Vote *A*	10	45	10	20
Vote *B*	−10	40	15	40
U_A	0.5(20+5) = +12.5		0.5(−5−20) = −12.5	

Following Brennan and Lomasky's key argument, we assume a voter who derives most expressive benefits from voting for party *A*, while her instrumental benefits are best served by voting for *B*. If, in instrumental terms, elections deliver only public goods, then the balance of expressive benefits is in most cases decisive, and in this case the expected value of voting for *A* is clearly positive.[6] By contrast, in the 'owned-outcome' scenario the expected utility calculation equally clearly indicates that the voter should choose *B*. Writing *B* for a majority for party *B* and *b* for the individual's choice of party *B*, the rank order of the cells in the two matrices is:

Public-goods outcomes: *Ba > Bb > Aa > Ab*
Owned outcomes: *Bb > Ba > Ab > Aa*

The inclusion of the party benefit associated with the individual's actual vote changes the pay-offs only in those cells of the matrix (*Ba* and *Ab*) where the individual and majority choices diverge.

In the owned-outcome scenario the individual always benefits from the vote going her way, while in the public-good scenario she is assumed to be better off by being on the losing side. This result looks highly implausible for the public-goods scenario, implying an unrealistic level of strategic calculation. Of course, our example follows Brennan and Lomasky's argument in assuming that voters have expressive and instrumental interests which diverge. It might be objected that only a small proportion of people fall into this category, and hence that the incidence of this problem is trivial. The objection may be empirically correct, but if so it also directly contradicts Brennan and Lomasky's argument that this kind of divergence will commonly arise.

Once we disaggregate expressive and instrumental benefits, there is in fact no a priori way of determining which factors will be decisive for voters in choosing which party or candidate to support. In our view, the public-goods view of elections was previously made to look plausible as a general assumption in rational-choice work only by implicitly bundling up party benefits from elections with the governmental consequences, and then smuggling in the implicit assumption that governmental benefits must somehow swamp party benefits. But it may also be true that some voters do decide in the way that Brennan and Lomasky envisage, especially those voters who form no strong identification with the party or candidate they support, and who take great care to keep their electoral choices completely private, for example, by never taking part in political discussions. In fact we might envisage the following four types of voter, with cell entries here showing which benefits they take account of in voting:

	Voters whose alignment is:	
	Kept private	Overt
Voters who are:		
Not identifiers	T and C only	T, C, and X
Identifiers	T, C, and Q,	T, C, X, and Q

Brennan and Lomasky's model works well for the privatized or socially isolated voters in the top left cell, whose utilities are shaped only by autonomous expressive benefits and governmental impact on instrumental benefits. But our hunch is that such voters are a small minority in liberal democracies. A much larger group are the politically involved voters in the bottom right cell, who form firm identifications with their chosen party and whose political alignments are closely interwoven with the fabric of their social life. One key reason for this hypothesis is that the electoral arrangements of liberal democracies are designed to generate this involvement, as we show in Section 5. But first, we need to remedy the limiting assumption made at the outset of this section that a clear majority for either party A or party B would exhaust the possible electoral outcomes.

4. THE PROBLEM OF NO OVERALL CONTROL

Since its earliest days, public-choice theory has been obsessed by the idea that it is irrational for an individual to participate in action which might secure a collective good unless her choices could be decisive. While non-excludable outcomes constitute one powerful disincentive against participation, the other key influence has been the negligibility of one person's action, their individual irrelevance to supply. Hence, for there to be rational action the individual must have a potential to be pivotal.

Transposing this link from the study of committees or small-group contexts to the analysis of mass behaviour has always seemed problematic to critics of public choice. But for adepts the fine calculation of orders of negligibility has seemed a perfectly proper activity. For example, Brennan and Lomasky devote an entire chapter to computing the chances of an American voter being decisive in the choice of US President (abstractly conceived as being the swing voter in a single national constituency with the election being directly decided by the popular vote).[7] Other serious analysts have suggested that voting participation in any election can be explained as a 'minimax regret' strategy, a kind of insurance against the chance (1 in 12,500 for US Presidential elections according to Brennan and Lomasky, or 0.00008) that the individual's vote would have been decisive but that she had in fact stayed at home. Both examples illustrate the bizarre lengths to which conventional public choice takes its orientation with pivotality.

The source of this obsession is a simple confusion between analytic and empirical significance. Analytically the potential existence of a tied outcome where the individual's choice is decisive is important in defining a situation where it would be feasible to assign clear values to the T, X, C, and Q components of utility. Both in market and in political outcomes, an outcome where the individual is pivotal is the only opportunity (hypothetically) to contrast a full slate of benefits for choice A (that is $T_A + X_A + C_A + Q_A$) with a full slate of benefits for choice B (that is $T_B + X_B + C_B + Q_B$). But there is no empirical possibility of tied outcomes and individual pivotality occurring, either in complex product markets or in mass political behaviour.

While such an outcome is logically possible, it is highly unlikely. The requirement that the choices of others in the market or the election be finely balanced is inconsistent with the idea that one choice can be decisive: if the choices of many others are finely balanced, then an individual decision one way or another is simply a negligible figure on one balance or another.[8] We noted above in Table 4.3 that if the number of people buying IBM-type PCs and Apples is exactly equal, my decision to choose one or the other does not change anything: the PC market remains as evenly divided after my choice as it was before. Hence the conditional benefits of either choice have to be heavily discounted by factor r, reflecting the fact that there will be connectivity and incompatibility problems with all kinds of PC, which would not have occurred had one outcome been dominant.

In almost all large-scale institutional elections the same situation exists. If the votes for party A and party B are evenly balanced, an individual's vote will not decisively tip the balance, creating a winner-take-all situation. Rather, the fact of the even balance automatically generates a no-overall-control ultimate outcome. In parliamentary systems, an individual voter can be decisive in securing an intermediate outcome, the election of one MP rather than another (about which more in Section 5), but she can never be decisive in securing a strong majority government. For if the number of MPs is finely balanced for rival parties then a single extra MP one way or another cannot deliver a secure working majority for either party: party A can perhaps monopolize ministerial office, but a no-overall-control situation must result, with the governing party's ability to legislate or to survive by-election losses severely curtailed. Even in the US presidential elections it is very unlikely that an individual voter could be decisive in determining who wins, rather than the election being thrown into the electoral college process.[9]

Consequently, it is systematically misleading for public-choice accounts to make reference to 'tied outcomes' or individual pivotality, as Table 4.2 does. In no mass political process is there the slightest chance of an individual voter being decisive on macro-outcomes. Rather we should focus instead on understanding how to assess the utility pay-offs under no-overall-control situations. As in Section 3, there are two possible resolutions, depending on whether elections produce purely public-goods outcomes or owned outcomes depending partly on the voter's initial choice.

With public-goods elections voters will receive their autonomous expressive benefits, and a discounted level of their exogenously set expressive benefits (discounted by k because their party has not gained a governing majority). They will also receive instrumental benefits averaged across the two parties' benefits, and then discounted by a factor r (where $0 < r < 0.5$) to reflect the fact that neither party will be able to legislate its programme. (With two parties the value of r will have to be below 0.5 to include the averaging-out across the instrumental benefits from party A and party B.) Thus the third column to be added to Table 4.5 would be:

All others

No overall control

Each

Choose A $T_A + kX_A + r(C_A + Q_A + C_B + Q_B)$

Choose B $T_B + kX_B + r(C_A + Q_A + C_B + Q_B)$

U_A ... $+ 1 - p_a - p_b(T_A - T_B + kX_A - kX_B)$

Again voters' expressive benefits are decisive in determining the expected utility consequences, because the instrumental consequences are standardized.

If voters can own the party outcome benefits from their individual choices, then the averaging and discounting by r applies solely to the governmental outcome benefits (C_A and C_B), with voters receiving Q_A or Q_B depending on their choice. Since their expressive benefits are the same, the extra column to be added to Table 4.6 becomes:

All others

No overall control

Each

Choose A $T_A + kX_A + r(C_A + C_B) + Q_A$

Choose B $T_B + kX_B + r(C_A + C_B) + Q_B$

U_A ... $+ 1 - p_a - p_b(T_A - T_B + kX_A - kX_B + Q_A - Q_B)$

Here the difference in party instrumental benefits enters into the expected utility calculation as well as expressive benefits. Returning to the numerical example discussed above on p. 68, we change both p_A and p_B to 0.4, creating a no-overall-control probability of 0.2, and also add in a value for r of 0.4. With the extra column for no overall control, the contrast between the two possible ways of characterizing elections remains clear-cut:

	Public-goods elections			Owned party outcomes		
	Maj A	Maj B	NOC	Maj A	Maj B	NOC
Vote A	10	45	22	10	20	10
Vote B	−10	40	12	15	40	25
U_A	$0.4(20+5)+0.2(10)=+12$			$0.4(-5-20)+0.2(-15)=-13$		

With the voter's expressive benefits favouring party *A* and her instrumental benefits greater with party *B* in our example, public-goods elections suggest an *A* vote whereas owned party outcomes push the calculus equally strongly towards a vote for *B*.

So far we have gone along with the Brennan and Lomasky assumption that political elections involve some simple form of plurality-rule voting with a winner-take-all result likely to predominate. However, we need to recognize that most liberal democratic parliamentary systems in the contemporary world rely instead on proportional representation methods, where no-overall-control outcomes are much more likely to occur. In some systems they may well be the predominant outcome, with absolute majorities for any party virtually infeasible.

From its earliest days, the public-choice analysis of PR elections has been extraordinarily weak. Downs devoted a whole chapter of *An Economic Theory of Democracy* to what he obviously felt was the mystery of why anyone at all ever votes in a PR system where coalitional government outcomes are effectively certain:

Once voters realize they will be governed by a coalition, a feedback effect occurs and changes the nature of voting. Rational voters no longer simply vote for the party they prefer as a sole government; instead they take into account the use of coalitions, which is itself made necessary by the scattered distribution of other people's votes. In short, every rational voter's decision depends upon how he thinks other men are going to vote.[10]

The problem here, however, is that the likelihood of any individual voter being pivotal in terms of 'choosing a government directly' becomes vanishingly small, indeed almost mythical in a system such as the Netherlands. Downs repeatedly verges on declaring voting in such systems 'irrational', always moderating his judgements with uneasy caveats:

When we call such behaviour irrational, we do not mean that it is unintelligent or not in the best interest of the voters. In fact, it may be the most rational thing for them to do as individuals. The only sense in which it is irrational is from the point of view of elections as direct government selectors. Obviously, if a large fraction of the electorate regards elections as a means of selecting a legislature via preference polls, they are no longer rational devices for the selection of governments by the people.[11]

This twisting and turning reflects the fact that in PR elections the probability of a 'hung Parliament' result may be so great that

Tables 4.5 and 4.6 above would reduce to the single no-overall-control column described earlier in this section.

If elections generate public-goods outcomes and also yield permanent coalition governments, then with instrumental benefits standardized, and with exogeneously set expressive benefits (X_A etc.) continuously discounted by k, however the individual votes, autonomous expressive benefits (T_A etc.) presumably become proportionately more important in influencing voters' choices compared with plurality systems. However, if voters own the party outcomes of their choices, then the Q element of instrumental benefits will also be more important in shaping people's decisions under PR systems with permanent coalition governments.

5. THE IMPACT OF MULTI-LEVEL ELECTIONS

In a recent paper Brams and colleagues took the public-choice obsession with pivotality a stage further by asking what proportion of people get the compound outcome they voted for in multi-level or multi-component elections.[12] They demonstrated, for example, that the proportion of US voters who live in districts where the outcome of the House, Senate, or Presidential races matched the national outcome varies sharply from election to election—higher in years of a Democrat clean sweep federally, and lowest in years producing divided government, such as 1980. Another example focused on Californian referenda, where the permutations of options from up to 80 propositions being simultaneously voted on are very numerous, and the likelihood of any voter having her individual preferences exactly reflected in the overall outcome is negligible. For the conventional picture of a rational voter preoccupied with pivotality, these results have some serious implications. The main unit of costs is the trip to the voting station (rather than the pressing of a lever or marking of an individual ballot), and per trip the chances of efficacious action decrease further while information costs rise. Thus multi-level or multi-component elections constitute disincentives to rational participation if elections generate only public-goods outcomes.

However, if voters own some instrumental outcomes of their choices, in particular receiving the party benefits of their choices, we can reconceptualize multi-level and multi-component elections as devices to maximize participation. We take the simplest and most pervasive example of parliamentary elections where a single vote helps decide a local constituency outcome, and where the local success of one party's candidate or another in turn contributes to determining which government takes power. We can adapt the concepts developed so far to apply to this situation by:

(1) adding an extra superscript to p_A (and p_B etc.) to denote national and local probabilities of winning respectively, p_A^N and p_A^L;

(2) adding a probability denoting no overall control nationally p_O^N, (where $p_O^N = 1 - p_A^N - p_B^N$), and a probability denoting an otherwise tied local result p_T^L, (where $p_T^L = 1 - p_A^L - p_B^L$);

(3) adding an extra subscript to k to denote different levels of discounting when the party chosen is unsuccessful nationally k_n, or locally k_l, with k retained to denote situations where the party loses at both levels;

(4) adding an extra superscript to C_A (and C_B etc.) to denote the governmental outcome benefits/costs of a party winning nationally C_A^N, and the constituency service outcomes of having an MP of that party representing the constituency C_A^L locally.

With these additional elements in place Table 4.7 shows the choice situation of a voter in a multi-level election. With two parties and two levels (national and local constituencies) there are nine possible outcomes, including no overall control at the national level and a tied result amongst other voters at constituency level. At first sight Table 4.7 seems extremely complex. However, the expected utility line shows a much simpler picture. Across all outcomes the voter needs to know the balance of her autonomous expressive benefits between the parties, and the balance of the party outcome benefits: this information is standardized. The finer grain information which varies with each outcome has only two elements. The first concerns the level of discounting of exogenously set expressive benefits, depending on whether each party is successful or loses nationally or locally. And the second concerns the probabilities of each party winning nationally or locally, and combinations of these probabilities.

The remarkable thing about the expected utility line in Table 4.7,

TABLE 4.7. *The choice situation of an individual voter in a multi-level election where voters own some instrumental outcomes*

Each	All others				
	Nat A Loc A	Nat A Loc B	Nat B Loc A	Nat B Loc B	Nat NOC Loc A
Choose A	$T_A+X_A+Q_A$ $+C_A^N+C_B^L$	$T_A+k_jX_A+Q_A$ $+C_A^N+C_B^L$	$T_A+k_nX_A+Q_A$ $+C_B^N+C_A^L$	$T_A+kX_A+Q_A$ $+C_B^N+C_B^L$	$T_A+k_nX_A+Q_A$ $+C_o^N+C_A^L$
Choose B	$T_B+kX_B+Q_B$ $+C_A^N+C_A^L$	$T_B+k_nX_B+Q_B$ $+C_A^N+C_B^L$	$T_B+k_jX_B+Q_B$ $+C_B^N+C_A^L$	$T_B+X_B+Q_B$ $+C_B^N+C_B^L$	$T_B+kX_B+Q_B$ $+C_o^N+C_A^L$
U_A	$+$ $(T_A-T_B$ $+Q_A-Q_B$ $+X_A-kX_B)$ $(p_A{}^N*p_A^L)$	$(T_A-T_B$ $+Q_A-Q_B$ $+k_jX_A-k_nX_B)$ $(p_A{}^N*p_B^L)$	$(T_A-T_B$ $+Q_A-Q_B$ $+k_nX_A-k_jX_B)$ $(p_B{}^N*p_A^L)$	$+$ $(T_A-T_B$ $+Q_A-Q_B$ $+kX_A-X_B)$ $(p_B{}^N*p_B^L)$	$+$ $(T_A-T_B$ $+Q_A-Q_B$ $+k_nX_A-kX_B)$ $(p_o{}^N*p_A^L)$

Each	All others			
	Nat NOC Loc B	Nat A Loc Tie	Nat B Loc Tie	Nat NOC Loc Tie
Choose A	$T_A+kX_A+Q_A$ $+C_o^N+C_B^L$	$T_A+X_A+Q_A$ $+C_A^N+C_A^L$	$T_A+k_nX_A+Q_A$ $+C_B^N+C_A^L$	$T_A+k_nX_A+Q_A$ $+C_o^N+C_A^L$
Choose B	$T_B+k_nX_B+Q_B$ $+C_o^N+C_B^L$	$T_B+k_nX_B+Q_B$ $+C_A^N+C_B^L$	$T_B+X_B+Q_B$ $+C_B^N+C_B^L$	$T_B+k_nX_B+Q_B$ $+C_o^N+C_B^L$
U_A	$+$ $(T_A-T_B$ $+Q_A-Q_B$ $+kX_A-k_nX_B)$ $(p_o{}^N*p_B^L)$	$+$ $(T_A-T_B$ $+Q_A-Q_B$ $+X_A-k_nX_B)$ $(p_A{}^N*p_T^L)$	$(T_A-T_B$ $+Q_A-Q_B$ $+k_nX_A-X_B)$ $(p_B{}^N*p_T^L)$	$+$ $(T_A-T_B$ $+Q_A-Q_B$ $+k_nX_A-k_nX_B)$ $(p_o{}^N*p_T^L)$

is that it fits closely with a great many existing research findings about the key influences on voters' behaviour. The importance of 'party identification' is consistent with the factors which recur in the U_A calculation (autonomous expressive benefits and party instrumental benefits). The importance of probabilities in influencing voting behaviour is well attested in phenomena such as bandwagon and spiral-of-silence effects and in tactical voting. And the variations in exogenously set expressive benefits are consistent with the observed importance of mass media coverage (especially stigmatizing coverage) and party campaigning in conditioning voters' reactions.

Table 4.7 may also be radically simplified for different types of voters. Some people may complete the first part of the expected utility line for each outcome $(T_A - T_B + Q_A - Q_B)$ in so clear-cut a fashion that they need no further information to be assured how they should vote. Some (cosmopolitan) voters may care only about national governmental outcomes, and ignore constituency results completely, unless there is a prospect of a local tie. Other (localist) voters may judge local outcomes to be more important than national outcomes, especially in calculating or in discounting exogenously set expressive benefits (X_A etc.).

Multi-level elections also fit closely with an approach to understanding voting behaviour which sees it as a form of experimental behaviour. Recent research into interest-group joining suggests that people often join endogenous groups (as defined by Dunleavy)[13] in which they are interested as a way of finding out more about them, information which is intrinsically more observable for members than non-members.[14] Members then evaluate whether to maintain (and later step up) their involvement from a much better information base about what the organization does and the kind of people involved. Table 4.7 suggests that voting in a parliamentary democracy is a somewhat analogous problem in decision-making terms. In order to gather information on the various benefits and probabilities involved, the simplest and probably most effective solution is for voters to participate, and then to evaluate their success before repeating the experience. Voting becomes part of a basically Bayesian approach in which initial assumptions are made, the experience of voting generates consistent or inconsistent information as feedback, and the individual maintains or adjusts her initial premises accordingly.

Multi-level elections provide a powerful reinforcement for continued voting participation by broadening the base of voters who receive some reinforcing feedback from participating. Far more voters receive success messages in terms of their alignment conforming with those of other groups of voters and hence being accorded institutional recognition in one form or another. To see this effect consider Britain, the limiting case of a unified and undivided government system amongst established Western democracies—a single elected chamber with unconstrained legislative sovereignty, where a majority commonly secures single-party government, and with the fewest and least constitutionally protected local governments of any liberal democracy. Plurality voting means that contemporary governments almost permanently govern on 42 per cent or less of the popular vote. Yet if we broaden our definition of political efficacy to encompass not just determining the national government but also electing a local MP and determining the control of the most immediate local government unit, then few British voters are complete losers. Table 4.8 shows the proportion of voters in the 1992 general election who were triple, double, or single winners at one or another level.

While fewer than 43 per cent of voters supported the Conservatives who secured a national majority, nearly 70 per cent of voters were partial winners in one sense or another. If we include in the winning category voters whose general election votes were ineffective either nationally or at constituency level but who at least lived in a council area with no overall control, the successful proportion rises to 81 per cent of the total, close to doubling the winning party's vote share. Thus only 19 per cent of voters were completely unsuccessful, and some proportion of this figure must live in areas where there was a realistic potential for an alternative result. Probably under one-sixth of British voters participated in the general election while living in areas where it was completely infeasible for their chosen vote to be institutionally effective.

This revisionist reading of the efficacy (and hence rationality) of participation should not blind us to the severely distorting impact of plurality voting in the British system. The proportion of winners and losers varies sharply across political parties. Scoring a complete loser as zero, NOC in council politics as a half point, and single, double, or triple winning at 1, 2, and 3, respectively, the average Conservative voter had an efficacy score of 2.1 (with 71 per

TABLE 4.8. *The percentage of all voters whose votes were successful at one of three levels, British general election 1992*

Constit.	Council	Win nationally	Lose nationally		
		Conservative	Labour	Liberal Democrat	Other
Win	Win	10.5	16.5	0.4	—
Win	NOC	10.8	2.7	0.3	0.1
Win	Lose	9.3	1.1	0.5	0.3
Lose	Win	0.3	3.8	1.2	—
Lose	NOC	1.8	5.2	5.2	0.8
Lose	Lose	10.3	5.9	10.2	2.6

Level of success	% of all voters	% of each party's voter			
		Con	Lab	LibDem	Other
Triple winners	10.5	24	0	0	0
Two-and-a-half wins	10.8	25	0	0	0
Double winners	26.5	22	47	2	0
One-and-a-half wins	4.9	4	8	2	3
Single winners	17.2	24	14	9	8
Half a win	11.2	0	15	29	21
Triple losers	19.1	0	16	58	68
Total	100	100	100	100	100
% of electorate	100	43	35.2	18.2	3.8

Notes:
NOC means no overall control.
Cell entries are percentage shares of the votes in Great Britain (N = 32,825,439), excluding Northern Ireland.

cent of their voters double winners or better); for Labour the figure was 1.2 (with 47 per cent double winners). The same scores were just 0.2 for the Liberal Democrats and other parties (mainly nationalist parties in Scotland and Wales and the Greens): three-fifths of voters opting for these third and fourth parties were complete losers.

These sharp party differences in efficacy rates look certain to have major implications for the long-term evolution of political alignments in Britain.[15] Table 4.7 strongly suggests that political support for locally dominant parties should consolidate over time, with people progressively accommodating to the majority view, unless the opposition parties can demonstrate efficacy in one way or another. Obviously, winning control of national government is the quickest way to reinforce the efficacy of all a party's voters. Where this effort fails, an opposition party must expand a local bridgehead by winning constituencies or control of local government to create an impression of efficacy. The importance of local authority efficacy is that many council elections occur on a fixed timetable in general election mid-terms, when governments are often unpopular, thereby boosting the opposition parties' chances. An opposition party which seems incapable of achieving even that (as Labour has been increasingly unable to do across much of south-east England outside London) may lose support, while an apparently worse-placed alternative opposition (the Liberal Democrats) attracts increased support. Mapping the dynamics of local efficacy and understanding the models of political change and salience held by voters should allow us to render comprehensible these otherwise irrational (because immediately less efficacious) shifts in voter allegiances.

A final way in which we should not lose sight of the outlier quality of the British system is to contrast the results in Table 4.7 with the likely equivalent results for a Western European country with a proportional representation system and a federal constitutional structure. At a guess the proportion of, say, German voters who would view their vote as completely inefficacious in affecting the party composition of their local *Gemeinder*, *Länder*, *Bundestag* constituency or the shape of the national government would be very much lower than in the UK—probably below 4 per cent at the last legislative elections. And although the distribution of these inefficacious votes in Germany may be markedly affected from one election to another by the national 5 per cent vote threshold for *Bundestag* representation, in most PR systems there will not be sharp inequalities in efficacy levels across different political parties' voters. Hence, contrary to Downs's thinly veiled suspicion that voting in PR systems is 'irrational', these countries' arrangements embody considerable sophisticated incentives for 'undeformed' participation.

6. CONCLUSIONS

The conventional public-choice focus on pivotality as somehow intrinsic to rational action is fundamentally misguided. Is it ever rational to expect to be decisive in settling social outcomes, in making a complex product market decision or a political choice in a mass behaviour context? It seems more pathological than rational to let individual decisions be swayed or negated by such consideration. Yet this does not mean that rational voters switch in one move from making a strategic choice dependent on other people's behaviour to making a parametric choice (like deciding whether to take an umbrella in case it rains, where the other actor is nature, presumably unaffected by my choices).

Instead, rational actors will operate with aspiration levels for their personal influence or efficacy which are fixed endogenously within the political process itself. James March elegantly summed up the very basic Bayesian process envisaged here in the discourse of organization theory:

Aspirations adapt to actual performance. Organizations [we can substitute 'actors'] learn what it is reasonable to expect by observing what they achieve . . . Behaviour that is associated with success tends to be repeated; behaviour that is associated with failure tends not to be repeated. Typically, however, such adaptation takes time (and, of course, performance also changes simultaneously).[16]

A second general conclusion is that the stark contrast between decision-making in markets and political processes envisaged by Brennan and Lomasky is misplaced. Disaggregating expressive and instrumental benefits, we have shown that the choice contexts in complex product markets and elections have many points of comparison. Especially important are the effects of default instrumental benefits, exogenously set expressive benefits, and the probabilities of majority choices in conditioning individual decisions. We have also argued that it is highly implausible to assume that elections deliver solely public-goods outcomes. By contrast a (rather conservative) public-choice construction of how voters can own some instrumental outcomes of their decisions yields a detailed model of voting participation which fits closely with empirical research. It also offers a detailed account of how multi-level (and multi-component) elections create incentives for greater participation, but also in plurality-rule voting systems strong systemic conditioning effects on the evolution of alignments.

Perhaps the most potent themes for future research on understanding rational participation explored here are those which have been increasingly stressed in modern philosophy, about the expressive and instrumental benefits which arise from taking a position, and about the importance of external sources in conditioning individuals' appreciation of exogenously set expressive benefits. About the first of these, Taylor remarks:

My identity is defined by the commitments and identifications which provide the frame or horizon within which I can try to determine from case to case what is good, or valuable, or what ought to be done, or what I endorse or oppose. In other words, it is the horizon within which I am capable of making a stand.[17]

About the second, Rorty remarks: '[T]he best way to cause people long-lasting pain is to humiliate them by making the things that seemed most important to them look futile, obsolete and powerless'.[18] Somewhere between the affirmation of identity and the pressures of others, rational individuals strike a balance in electoral choices as much as in other aspects of their social lives. A public-choice theory which seriously connects with this dialectic can enhance our empirical understanding of contemporary politics.

NOTES

1. G. Brennan and M. Lomasky, *Democracy and Decision* (Cambridge: Cambridge University Press, 1993).
2. For the sake of simplicity we do not discuss possible variations in k between situations where a product clearly loses out in competition to an overall winner, and those where there is no overall winner.
3. However, if the k discount rates were different across A and B, such that X_A was much more heavily discounted than X_B, then with sufficiently large X values relative to T, Q, and C benefits it is just conceivable that the voter might choose B in a tied situation.
4. E. Noelle-Neumann, *The Spiral of Silence* (Chicago: University of Chicago Press, 1984).
5. Brennan and Lomasky, *Democracy and Decision*, 32–53.
6. However, it is also possible to envisage settings of k and p_A and p_B

where a different outcome would follow, even though voters' choices are set solely by expressive benefits. For example, if we retain all the values assumed above but set $k = 0.1$, $p_A = 0.1$, and $p_B = 0.9$, then from Table 4.5 the pay-off matrix becomes:

	Public goods elections	
	Majority A	Majority B
Vote A	10	37
Vote B	−14	40
U_A	$(0.1*24) + (0.9* - 3) = - 0.3$	

Here, although $T_A > T_B$ and $X_A > X_B$, the voter should still choose B.

7. Brennan and Lomasky, *Democracy and Decision*, 54–73.
8. See K. Dowding, *Rational Choice and Political Power* (Aldershot: Edward Elgar, 1991), 56–63, for a discussion of pivotality as an algebraic device versus pivotality in actual life.
9. W. Berns (ed.), *After the People Vote* (Washington, DC: American Enterprise Institute Press, 1992).
10. A. Downs, *An Economic Theory of Democracy* (New York: Harper and Row, 1957), 150.
11. Downs, *Economic Theory*, 154.
12. S. Brams, D. Kilgour, and W. Zwicker, 'A New Paradox of Vote Aggregation', (paper presented to the 89th Annual Meeting of the American Political Science Association, Washington DC, 2–5 Sept. 1993).
13. P. Dunleavy, *Democracy, Bureaucracy and Public Choice* (Hemel Hempstead: Harvester-Wheatsheaf, 1991), 62–71.
14. L. S. Rothenberg, *Linking Citizens to Government* (New York: Cambridge University Press, 1992); G. Jordan, W. Maloney, and A. McLaughlin, 'Collective Action and the Public Interest Problem: Drawing a Line under Olson?' in P. Dunleavy and J. Stanyer (eds.), *Contemporary Political Studies 1994*, ii (Belfast: Political Studies Association, 1994), 519–43.
15. There may also be implications for turnout levels, but the implication of Table 4.7 is that declining efficacy primarily affects how voters cast their ballots, rather than whether they vote or not.
16. J. March, *Decisions and Organizations* (Oxford: Blackwell, 1988), 190.
17. C. Taylor, *Sources of the Self* (Cambridge: Cambridge University Press, 1992), 27.
18. R. Rorty, *Contingency, Irony and Solidarity* (Cambridge: Cambridge University Press, 1989), 178.

5

Working for Benefits: Rational Choice and Work-Welfare Programmes

DESMOND KING AND HUGH WARD

The last decade has witnessed a shift to 'work-welfare' programmes in a number of advanced industrial democracies, notably the United States and Britain, though they are not the only practitioners. Under these programmes the recipients of welfare or unemployment benefits are required to undertake a work or training activity. It is a condition of receipt of the benefit that this exchange be agreed and the activity discharged. These programmes are not identical across countries but their aims are similar. In specification such programmes can reflect a policy either of deterrence (the purpose being to extract an exchange from the recipient to deter his or her application for benefits) or assistance (the purpose being to assist the recipient to acquire skills or competences necessary to enter the labour-market). Examples of the former are found in several US states under the Community Work Experience Program; the latter is exemplified by Swedish policies.[1] Such programmes reflect the integration of employment and welfare policy during the last decade. Our interest is with the former sort.

In Section 1 we describe the adoption of these programmes in the US and Britain and in Section 2 we relate them to alternative conceptions of social citizenship. Section 3 is taken up by a discussion of the possible incentive structure underpinning this public policy development. We argue that governments design such policies to generate a partial separating equilibrium under which some claimants identified by the state as undeserving are discouraged

An earlier version of this chapter was originally published in *Political Studies*, 40/3 (Sept. 1992), 479–95, and is reproduced with the permission of Blackwells Publishers.

from seeking benefits. These programmes are intended to overcome problems of free-riding and false claiming viewed, by the New Right, as inherent in state-administered benefit systems. The appeal of such schemes is magnified during economic recession when tax-payers' concern about taxes is greatest.

1. THE GROWTH OF WORK-WELFARE PROGRAMMES IN THE US AND BRITAIN

United States

In the United States, Title II of the Family Support Act of 1988, the JOBS programme, amended Title IV of the Social Security Act of 1935 by making the receipt of welfare benefits conditional upon the discharge of a work or training requirement.[2] Each state was required to draft and enact (with the approval of the federal government) a law implementing Title II, the Jobs Opportunities and Basic Skills Training Program,[3] operative from October 1990. The 1988 Act includes details about 'participation rates', the percentage of welfare recipients who must participate in the work-welfare programmes, specified for the next five years at an ascending rate: 7 per cent in FY 1990 and FY 1991; 11 per cent in FY 1992; 15 per cent in FY 1994; and 20 per cent in FY 1995. Under federal regulations, to satisfy these participation requirements the states will be compelled to force participants to engage in unproductive work; to limit the states' ability to give volunteer participants first consideration; and to limit child-care provision.[4] This mandatory clause (and its specifications) was included in the Family Support Act against the protests of the National Governors' Association and many members of the Congress and at the insistence of the Reagan White House.

Each state's JOBS programme must offer the following services:[5]

(1) where necessary educational activities to provide high school graduation literacy equivalent and English as a second language (this clause can include post-secondary education);
(2) job skills training;
(3) job-readiness programmes;
(4) job development and placement services;
(5) child-care and transportation support services.

The programme's work-welfare component can vary but the states are compelled to provide two of the following four options:

(1) job search assistance;
(2) on the job training;
(3) work supplementation—under which option a welfare recipient's benefits are used to subsidize his/her employment rather than given directly to him/her;
(4) CWEP—the Community Work Experience Program, the scheme originally earning the term 'workfare'. Each state must evaluate the educational ability, work skills, support services needs, and work experience of all JOBS scheme participants in order to formulate an individual 'employment' plan.

Eligibility for participation in a state JOBS programme is widely drawn. Those AFDC parents with children aged 3 and above must participate for up to twenty hours a week, a specification which can be lowered to children aged 1. The following groups are exempted from participation: the ill and incapacitated elderly; individuals required at home to care for persons in the first category; parents looking after children under 3 years of age; recipients working thirty or more hours a week; children under 16 or in full-time education; and pregnant women.

There is an explicit linkage of the major federal welfare and training programmes. Included in the JOBS programme section of the Family Support Act is the injunction that state welfare administrators should co-ordinate their work with state administrators of the Job Training Partnership Act (JTPA) 1983, the principal federal-state training programme.[6] JTPA is based in the private sector. In many states JTPA was linked to the administration of welfare policies allowed under the Omnibus Budget Reconciliation Act 1981 (OBRA), which empowered the states to introduce 'demonstration' work-welfare programmes. This trend increased as employment grew after 1983 and the need for JTPA declined. It is exemplified in Massachusetts.[7] It is this linkage which will have to be adopted in all the states to cope with the implications of the Family Support Act of 1988.

Britain

The British Employment and Social Security Acts of 1988 and the Social Security Act of 1989 introduced significant changes to unemployed people's participation in training programmes and their eligibility for social security benefits;[8] these changes themselves built upon modifications to the law introduced after 1979. From July 1990 training courses became compulsory for those unemployed for two years or more and who reject offers of help at their Restart interview.[9] There is a significant overlap in the clauses of the 1988 Employment Act, the 1988 Social Security Act, and the 1989 Social Security Act. Thus the Social Security Act 1988 contained a clause mandating participation, for young people, in a YTS scheme; refusal to participate (or premature withdrawal from a scheme) can result in the loss of benefits. Part II of the Employment Act 1988 complemented this social security ruling by disqualifying unemployed persons from receiving unemployment benefit if they withdrew from a training scheme, or were dropped for misconduct, or declined a YTS place 'without good cause'. Finally, under section 10 of the Social Security Act 1989, unemployed persons must demonstrate that they are 'seeking employment actively' as a condition of receiving unemployment benefit.[10]

These changes represent a new emphasis by the government for unemployed persons to participate in a work-welfare scheme and a broadening of the government's training programme for the unemployed. Non-participation can result in lost benefits. These changes have provoked considerable opposition amongst interest-groups representing affected persons and, initially at least, from the Labour Party, though the latter has now modified its position.

The design and implementation of these initiatives in Britain borrows extensively from the United States.[11] This imitation is particularly true of the extensive training programmes—culminating in the 1988 ET (Employment Training) programme administered by eighty-two local TECs (Training and Enterprise Councils) in England and Wales and nine LECs (local enterprise councils) in Scotland—developed under the Training Agency (previously called the Manpower Services Commission and then the Training Commission). The White Paper, *Training for Employment*, which preceded the formulation and implementation of the ET programme, stressed three characteristics of the unemployed: skills inadequacy; low motivation; and the erosion of labour-market incentives by benefits.[12] On the latter issue the White Paper reported the Government's intention to 'ensure that unemployed people are aware that they will be financially better off in employment.'[13] The ET programme, launched in September 1988, was designed to overcome these problems: it combined the existing thirty-seven training programmes and, initially at least, planned the creation of 600,000 training places on schemes lasting up to twelve months.[14] The implementation of this programme has been placed with local TECs, directly modelled on US Private Industry Councils (PICs), whose membership is composed predominantly of business people. Representatives of trade unions participate on TECs only by invitation.

That these schemes amount to compulsory participation on the part of recipients of welfare or unemployment benefits has been vigorously refuted by government ministers.[15] Labour MP Michael Meacher asked why, 'if the schemes are so good and the quality of training offered is so high and valuable . . . not allow people to choose them?'[16] The then Secretary of State for Employment, Norman Fowler, rejected the claim of compulsory loss of benefits in discussion of the Employment Bill 1988: to lose benefits would require a 'range of evidence [that the claimant has] refused three or four jobs and three or four places on a training programme. That is where the training programme argument is applicable . . . The new programme is not compulsory in the way that it is argued that YTS is compulsory.'[17]

This assurance did not satisfy critics of the work-welfare programmes, and there is undoubtedly an important element of compulsion contained in these social security and training measures. Though it has been a gradual process, work and welfare have been effectively integrated in both the US and Britain.

1. A NEW SOCIAL CONTRACT?

Rights versus Obligations in Welfare

At the core of work-welfare programmes is an assumption about citizenship as mutual responsibility: welfare recipients or unemployed people, as citizens entitled to receive benefits, in turn hold obligations to the state and to their fellow citizens.[18] In the United States this conception of mutual responsibility and obligation drew political support from amongst liberal Democrats such as Senator Daniel Patrick Moynihan, conservative Republicans such as

Ronald Reagan, and intellectuals such as Charles Murray. On the political right and left work was conceived of as a natural and crucial step on a trajectory leading from welfare.[19] Whether the movement to that step should be compulsory or voluntary depended on political ideology.

This emphasis upon obligation differs from the values dominant in post-war British welfare policy and the Great Society initiative of the Johnson administration. Programmes enacted during these periods emphasized the social rights, over the obligations, of citizenship.[20] This essentially social democratic conception reflected the arguments of T. H. Marshall about citizenship and equality. In contrast New Right theorists stress recipients' obligations and the importance of maintaining a system of inequality. New Right theorists oppose collective solutions to welfare or unemployment problems, advocating in their place individual effort and the freedom to exercise individual choice.[21] For such theorists the market is the framework through which many rights can best be realized.

New Right arguments have many historical antecedents, not least in their conception of unemployed people and the fear of idleness likely to result from providing unemployment benefits. Such a concern about the labour-market disincentive effects of state assistance featured during the introduction of unemployment insurance in Britain in 1911. One reason why insurance was distributed through employment exchanges was because they could operate a 'work-test' to ensure that unemployment was genuine, a principle imitated from German practice. Labour exchanges provided a mechanism less crude than the Poor Law but effective in differentiating between workers, as Churchill explained to Parliament in 1909: 'it is not possible to make the distinction between the vagrant and the loafer on the one hand and the *bona fide* workman on the other, except in conjunction with some elaborate and effective system of testing unwillingness to work such as is afforded by the system of labour exchanges.'[22]

Churchill's concern about the 'loafer' or undeserving recipient persisted after 1920,[23] despite the difficulties of assessing whether unemployment was voluntary or involuntary. The legislation enacted in the 1920s requiring claimants to demonstrate that they were 'genuinely seeking work' (replaced in the 1930s by equally resented means-tests[24]) appeared increasingly absurd as unemployment mounted.[25]

Obligations and Work-Welfare Programmes

Claims about the contractual obligations of receiving welfare were articulated at the passage of work-welfare legislation in both the United States and Britain. In the US the National Governors' Association, a crucial advocate of reform, used this language in their proposals: 'the principal responsibility of government in the welfare contract is to provide education, job training and/or job placement services to all employable recipients . . . The major obligation of the individual in the public assistance contracts we propose is to prepare for and seek, accept, and retain a job'.[26] In saluting the 1988 legislation the New York Times also reverted to the language of contract. In an editorial titled 'Real Welfare Reform, at Last,' the newspaper proclaimed that the Family Support Act,

amounts to a revision of the social contract between the nation and the needy. Instead of maintaining poor children and their parents above the starvation level but in dependency, the Government will offer financial support plus education and training to help people move from welfare to work . . . Education and job training, leading toward employment, are the heart of welfare reform.[27]

Comparable statements were issued in Britain as the changes to social security and employment laws were enacted. In the House of Lords debate on the 1988 Social Security Bill, Lord Boyd-Carpenter emphasized the work-welfare linkage: 'nothing could be worse than to give them [young people] encouragement to remain without training, living on public benefits—a pointless existence without any of the ambitions or the incentives which they will obtain under the Youth Training Scheme.'[28] The fullest statement of the language of contract and obligation came from the Minister for Social Security, Nicholas Scott, addressing the Standing Committee dealing with the 1989 Social Security Bill. Scott stated that the 'state . . . has the task of advising and guiding people towards available job opportunities. But surely the unemployed person has a duty, as his part of the contract, not to sit passively waiting for a job to turn up but to take active steps to seek work.'[29] In the Commons, Scott argued thus:

the principle at the heart of the clause is that the State rightly accepts a duty to provide benefits for the unemployed under an insurance scheme;

if their unemployment is longer than the insurance period, to provide income support for those without other means; and to provide advice, guidance and encouragement for the unemployed. While it accepts the responsibility, as far as is compatible with broader economic aims, to create an environment of enterprise and job creation, the State is entitled in return to expect individuals to take the trouble actively to seek work. This is not . . . some monstrous imposition on the unemployed. It is a genuine effort to provide a path from the misery of unemployment towards self-respect and the ability of individuals to provide for themselves and their families.[30]

This statement provides a vivid illustration of the influence of the social obligation argument in recent British social policy, in particular those measures collectively constitutive of a work-welfare programme. The language of the debate is not dissimilar to that issued in the US during the passage of the Family Support Act.[31] As one observer notes, the promotion of such views in Britain fitted with the prevailing New Right ideology: 'the emphasis on claimants actively seeking work can . . . be seen as a response of economic neo-liberalism to a tightening labour market.'[32]

The obligations implied by work-welfare programmes are not confined to British and American practice. Some Swedes argue that their unemployment benefit system (an integral component of the Swedish active labour-market policy) constitutes a form of work-welfare policy. The national labour-market board (AMS) in Sweden is a mechanism through which recipients of unemployment or welfare benefits can be directed towards alternative employment or, failing that, a training programme designed to effect their return to employment. The head of the AMS has contrasted this system with that of the 'dole' in other countries, maintaining that the Swedish system rejects the 'hand-outs approach followed by other European countries who pay their unemployed to stay at home with nothing to keep them occupied.'[33] The Social Service Act of 1982 determined that 'eighteen- and nineteen-year-olds who were not in training or apprenticeship positions were required to work in municipal jobs in exchange for their allowances.'[34] Heclo and Madsen observe that 'because none of the opposition parties wanted to argue that it was better to pay young persons for not working, the new law commanded near unanimous consent.'[35] Thus the Swedish programme can be characterized as a work-welfare one, since the state enforces a work availability test to prevent people from living off the dole.

Thus there are deterrent and assistance versions of work-welfare programmes, the former most commonly associated with the term 'workfare'. It is the shift to adopting the deterrent programme by New-Right-influenced governments in the US and Britain since 1980 which we address with game theory.

3. RATIONAL CHOICE AND THE GROWTH OF WORKFARE

In this section we explain why some (New Right) governments have chosen punitive work-welfare systems, that is workfare, and others (social democratic) have not.

The arguments are clearer if we first examine why the state in advanced industrial democracies administers unemployment benefit schemes. Diverse answers have been provided to this question. From a rational-choice perspective perhaps the most obvious argument is to invoke market failure and inter-party competition. Under this argument unemployment insurance is only provided in sub-optimal amounts, if at all, by processes operating in civil society, whether in the community or in some form of market. Especially after the widening of the franchise, parties which sought to win elections could gain votes by introducing or expanding unemployment insurance schemes, and competitors for office had to match the new policies, even if this strategy was ideologically repugnant to them.

The long history of state-run schemes funded out of some compulsory or semi-compulsory form of taxation suggests that there had always been under-provision and political gains to be earned, such as legitimacy or social control, by addressing this problem. But unemployment insurance has also been provided historically in one form or another by families, communities, friendly societies, trade unions, employers, and profit-making insurance companies.

We review three possible forms of insurance provision: family or community-based schemes, market schemes provided by insurance companies, and public programmes. The first sort is applicable to small communities only, while the second fails to satisfy profit criteria. We argue that free-rider solutions and ideological considerations associated with the third solution generate workfare programmes.

The Benefit Game 1: Family and Community Insurance

Two ideal-type forms of provision within families and communities can be identified. The first ideal type was based around reciprocity practices between households which were of roughly equal power and economic capacity and lived within strong communities.[36] One game-theoretic model which might be appropriate here is the Prisoners' Dilemma (PD). In the two-person variant, each player stood to gain if a practice arose whereby help was provided, if feasible, in hard times. However, in a single-play game, each actor would most prefer to take the other's help if he or she were hard-pressed, but not to help the other when this assistance was needed. If the other chose not to assist, each would get his or her worst pay-off. A PD illustrating this outcome is shown in Fig. 5.1. In the one-shot game each participant has a dominant strategy of not helping.

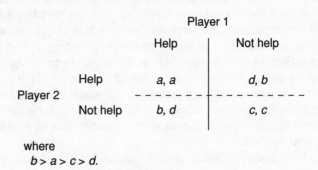

where
$b > a > c > d.$

Fig. 5.1 Family and community insurance modelled as the Prisoners' Dilemma

In practice, the insurance problem in strong, stable communities was not a one-shot game but a repeated one. This characteristic facilitated the development of stable conditional co-operation: by making their help in the current round conditional on what the other player did in previous rounds, the individuals might be able to set up a mutual threat system which cemented co-operation. The conditions for this outcome are that: the players either do not know for certain when the game will end or treat it as an infinite game; they are relatively far-sighted, in the sense that they do not discount future pay-offs too heavily; and the short-term increment in pay-off from breaking away from the reciprocity practice, thus taking the other player for a free-ride in one round, is low compared with losses in future rounds if reciprocity breaks down. In a more realistic *n*-person variant of the basic argument, reciprocal insurance would be plausible if the community was small enough, or inter-personal relationships were sufficiently dense, for free-riders to be identified.

Although reciprocal insurance practices of this sort may have led to the provision of benefits in strong communities, they broke down as communities grew larger, weaker, and less stable. Free-riders became less easy to identify; social practices such as the ostracism of malingerers were harder to maintain; and as community stability declined, time-discounting increased. For those leaving the community the game would become finite, and thus strategically equivalent to a one-shot game. Industrialization weakened the extended family, agricultural communities, and craft organizations such as guilds in which reciprocity had operated. Another form of free-riding might also have become more prevalent: as communities disintegrated it may have been easier to make an undetected false claim for help when, relative to the standards of the community, this claim was not warranted.

The second ideal type involves a preference asymmetry between the players, based on unequal endowments of resources. In the simplest, two-person variant, the poorer player has PD preferences, but the richer player, although he or she, too, gains from help in the (rare) event that he or she needs it, prefers to provide help to the poorer player, whether or not the poorer player is free-riding. The reasons for this preference may include: the declining marginal utility of money and subsistence commodities for the rich; the prestige accruing to the charitable; power over potential dependents deriving from providing for their needs; or the removal of a potential threat to law and order.[37] The second ideal-type game has the structure set out in Fig. 5.2.

The only equilibrium outcome in this game, whether it is repeated or single-play, is the asymmetric one in which 'rich' helps and 'poor' does not. In a realistic *n*-person context, the patterns are more complex. Collectively the rich might gain both in terms of legitimacy and public order from providing for the unemployed, but these public goods would go to the rich whether or not they

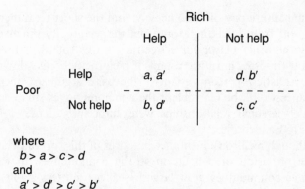

FIG. 5.2 Family and community insurance modelled in terms of
preference assymetry

helped. If public-good incentives predominated over individual
incentives such as prestige and personal power, and if an effective
system could be funded by a subset of the rich, the game among
the rich might resemble repeated Chicken,[38] with equilibria in
which some of the rich free-rode and others conditionally co-operated with the danger of the non-equilibrium 'collision' outcome in
which all the rich were committed to non-contribution.

Charitable prestige and power in the community are, then, central to this second ideal type. Again, however, as communities disintegrated, this form of provision became less successful, because
there would be less status and personal power to be gained in
unstable, eroding communities, while the costs of provision would
rise with the increased difficulty of identifying malingerers, and the
number asking for help might rise. If a collective-action game
among the rich emerged, erosion of community might make conditional co-operation among them less likely for precisely the same
reasons that it eroded collective action in the first ideal-type. In
cases where the two ideal-types were mixed, much the same would
be expected.

The Benefit Game 2: Market Provision

Now consider the provision of unemployment insurance for profit.
One problem for insurance companies is that those most likely to
buy cover are those holding the most risky jobs: the insurer's

customers would tend to be 'adversely selected' as bad risks. For the insurer there is an informational asymmetry problem since those purchasing the insurance know more about whether their jobs are high or low risk than does the insurance company. The possibility of making false claims creates a second form of adverse selection: if it is difficult or expensive to detect whether a claimant is malingering, in the sense that they had access to another job or deliberately left their first job, the insurer's customers may also be adversely selected for malingering.

Adverse-selection insurance problems are a sub-class of principal–agent problems.[39] In the insurance context, the problem has been whether the insurer can offer an equilibrium contract which tends only to be bought by good risks, so that there is a 'separating equilibrium' under which the strategies chosen by good and bad risks are different. With highly asymmetric information, there is often no separating equilibrium satisfying a non-zero profit constraint in this general type of game, suggesting that insurance would not be offered on the market. In the particular context of unemployment insurance, contracts demanding job disclosure would allow a lowering of asymmetries of information in relation to the riskiness of the policy-holder's job. It is less obvious that there exists a mechanism which would force those who intended to make false claims to reveal their status in advance of the signing of contracts. Neither is there any obvious penalty clause, to which all claimants would be subject, which would deter those intending to make false claims. For example, it would not be legally permissible for an insurance company to make those who claimed on its policies work for them for nothing—a mechanism which might deter some false claims.

Thus provision of unemployment insurance for profit looks problematic theoretically and, indeed, it has been unusual historically. Although trade unions have provided insurance cover, some would argue as a selective incentive to contribute towards the collective goods that unions can provide,[40] the adverse-selection problem might arise here, too: for a trade union wishing to cream off a surplus for collective good provision from insurance premiums, the infeasibility of discouraging bad risks would also be a concern. Neither provision for profit not trade-union provision would be a plausible substitute for disappearing forms of community-based provision.

The Benefit Game 3: State Benefits and Work-Welfare

Community-based benefit schemes are vulnerable to the problems of free-riding and false claiming as the community's size increases. Profit schemes developed by insurance companies confront two adverse selection problems: insufficient information about claimants' job security and about claimants' search for jobs. Through compulsory contribution the state can simultaneously solve the free-riding inherent in both forms of communal provision and by-pass the false-claims problem by pooling the risk with a large number of contributors not adversely selected to make false claims. The modern capitalist state's provision of benefits also concerns adverse selection. While office-seeking parties would not be concerned about profitability, historically speaking they have sought to make unemployment insurance schemes largely self-financing, with contributions set at some politically acceptable level. An important worry has been that false claims might put pressure on the system's financial viability, while ever-increasing contributions might also lose votes. Many voters react negatively if they believe that a large number of false claims are being made, a reaction exploited by New Right politicians.

We maintain that, depending on the particular preferences (New Right or social democratic) of the party in office, public policy may be used to generate a partial separating equilibrium, in which some claimants identified by the state as undeserving are discouraged from applying through workfare. Workfare was often employed in the past,[41] particularly by local government, as a means of separating out those seen as undeserving. Ideological changes both within parties of the right and the electorate have resulted in the re-emergence of a filtering mechanism repugnant to social democrats, because it also discourages legitimate claims.

Let us assume that governments seek to differentiate between the deserving and undeserving unemployed. The deserving are those who are seen as genuinely unable to find appropriate work given the current state of the labour-market, whereas the undeserving have jobs open to them, even in the absence of job-related training associated with workfare, which they choose not to take. Let us assume that the government places a probability of p on an unemployed individual being deserving and $(1-p)$ on the unemployed individual being undeserving, where $1 > p > 0$. If we further assume that the government's cardinal pay-offs are:

assist deserving claimant x
assist undeserving claimant y
no assistance given 0

then governments are motivated both by the desire for re-election and by policy aims.

Now we assume two sorts of government with the alternative views of social rights outlined in Section 2. First, social democratic governments with preference ordering $x > y > 0$, and second, New Right governments with preference ordering $x > 0 > y$.[42] Both sorts of government are assumed to receive a greater pay-off from helping the deserving claimant than from providing no help when a claim has not been made: because of the widespread support among the electorate for such help, in the light of the failure of other forms of provision, there are electoral pay-offs, at least in the sense that the issue is electorally defused, assuming that the other party is proposing such a policy. For a social democratic government this policy is compatible with its policy aims; even if a New Right government were ideologically opposed to such help, electoral considerations would plausibly offset this preference.

For a New Right government, helping an undeserving claimant is assumed to be worse than not providing any assistance: to provide help is, or is likely to be perceived by a New Right government as, a vote-loser; and to help the undeserving conflicts with New Right principles. In contrast, for a social democratic government some positive utility flows from assisting an undeserving claimant: even if there are, or there are perceived to be, electoral costs, providing such help is consonant with social democratic policy beliefs which emphasize the equal treatment of all citizens and assume that unemployment is not a consequence of personal failing. One possible objection to our argument here is that under a median-voter model, social democrats will be just as reluctant to assist undeserving claimants as are politicians of any other political party: that is, the electoral costs of transferring resources from the representative voter to the representative undeserving claimant will outweigh the benefits, a position which would account for the lack of support for universal schemes, often amongst unionists, when unemployment insurance was first developed.[43] This criticism is inapplicable here for two reasons. First, if there is any possibility of the representative voter moving towards the representative undeserving claimant position—that is, if risk is perceived as potentially generalizable[44]—then electoral preferences will shift accordingly. The perceived effects of recession can easily expand the percentage of the population who believe themselves vulnerable to hardship. Second, the preferences that lie behind the social democratic or median voter model need not necessarily be egoistical. Rational-choice arguments assume a set of well-defined preferences and these could be either for narrowing or for enlarging unemployment insurance schemes. Social democrats may feel disinclined to blame undeserving claimants, perhaps on the grounds that, even if they do not take appropriate available work, this decision partially reflects social facts (such as inflated wage expectations generated by irresponsible unions) or facts about the individual for which he or she cannot be held responsible (such as failure to be socialized to accept work disciplines).[45]

Two implicit assumptions deserve mention. First, governments are indifferent between claimants who enter the programme as undeserving individuals but are converted in some way into deserving individuals, and claimants who enter the programme as undeserving and remain so. Second, governments are also indifferent between those who enter the programme as deserving and become undeserving and those who enter the programme as deserving and remain so. Thus, what happens to individuals within programmes might count. To model this aspect of the problem would involve additional and unnecessary complexity at this stage. Since politicians are largely responsive to electoral concerns about false claims made on unemployment programmes, it is the initial status of people making claims, rather than considerations relating to the efficiency of labour-markets, that matters.

Potential claimants face a number of choices when deciding whether or not to search the job-market, whether or not to accept any current vacancy they are aware of, and whether or not to claim including: the costs of search in the labour-market; the availability of different sorts of job (defined by pay, other conditions of employment, and transport costs); time costs associated with making a claim, such as signing on and other forms of attendance necessary to obtain benefit; the level of unemployment benefit; benefits associated with workfare-related training, including job prospects, and personal esteem; and the social stigma associated with making a claim. From the individual's point of view some of these costs and benefits are dependent on the particular form of unemployment programme that is in place, while others are dependent on the job market.

To simplify the analysis we will assume that all unemployed people claim under traditional, non-workfare programmes. Furthermore we assume that the deserving do not claim under workfare with a probability

$$r, 1 > r > 0$$

(and claim with a probability of $(1-r)$); and the undeserving do not claim under workfare with a probability

$$q, 1 > q > 0$$

(and claim with a probability $(1-q)$). Some do not claim under traditional programmes, partly, no doubt, because they see the time costs and stigma attached to making a claim as too great when compared with the monetary benefits. Our assumption simplifies the analysis and the results are qualitatively similar to those under the more defensible assumption that, for a given state of the job-market, and a given type of unemployed person, the probability of a claim under workfare is lower than the probability of a claim under a traditional scheme, where all probabilities are strictly less than one.[46]

In principal–agent problems the relationship is treated as if it is a game. The extensive form of the game is examined for equilibria, even if no strategic interaction occurs. Because governments cannot make their choice of unemployment scheme contingent upon the particular individual making a claim, there is no strategic interaction here. We follow the convention of modelling the extensive form as if 'nature' makes moves with various probabilities which determine to which class a particular claimant belongs (Fig. 5.3). The state's pay-offs are placed at the tips of the game tree: for instance, if the unemployed person is seen as undeserving and the state chooses a traditional unemployment scheme, the assumption is that a claim is made and the state's pay-off is y, which we enter under the traditional branch which starts from the undeserving branch.[47]

The expected pay-off of the state if it chooses workfare is:

$$p (r\,0 + (1 - r)\,x) + (1 - p)\,(q\,0 + (1 - q)\,y)$$
$$= p\,(1 - r)\,x + (1 - p)\,(1 - q)\,y$$

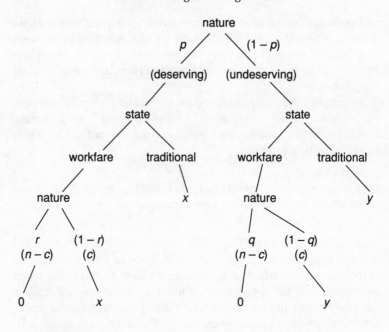

$n - c$ = non-claimant
c = claimant

Fig. 5.3 The extensive form of the unemployment game

The first term on the left corresponds to the state's expected pay-off if the unemployed person is deserving, since the state gets zero with probability r if no claim is made, and x with probability $(1-r)$ if a claim is made. The second term on the left corresponds to the state's expected pay-off if the unemployed person is undeserving, since the state gets zero with a probability of q if no claim is made and y with a probability of $(1-q)$ if a claim is made.

The expected pay-off of the state if it chooses a traditional scheme is:

$$px + (1-p)\,y$$

Because the simplifying assumption is that all unemployed people claim under traditional schemes, the state gets x with probability p if the unemployed person is deserving and y with probability $(1-p)$ if the unemployed person is not deserving.

The government chooses workfare if:

$$p (1 - r) x + (1 - p) y > px + (1 - p) y$$

Collecting terms, this is equivalent to

$$0 > prx + (1 - p) qy \tag{1}$$

For a social democratic government both x and y are greater than zero. Since the probability terms are also strictly positive, condition 1 can never hold. A social democratic government would choose a traditional unemployment scheme. Because all unemployed people claim under such a scheme, the equilibrium is pooling: the benefits of discouraging undeserving claimants are always too low relative to the opportunity costs of discouraging some deserving claimants for a social democratic government to choose workfare, even though it derives less pay-off from false claims.

In contrast, for a New Right government y is negative. Rearranging condition 1 we get:

$$-y/x > p/(1 - p) \ r/q \tag{2}$$

Depending on the values of parameters, condition 2 may be satisfied. If it is satisfied, the New Right government chooses workfare. Some of those seen as deserving and some of those seen as undeserving do not claim. *The equilibrium is partial, separating between those who do, and do not, claim.* If condition 2 is satisfied, even though a New Right government suffers opportunity costs because of the existence of deserving claimants who are deterred by workfare, these costs are compensated for by the ability of workfare to prevent some proportion of claims by the undeserving being made.

Condition 2 is more likely to be satisfied as $-y/x$ increases, that is, the losses associated with helping an undeserving claimant increase relative to the gains from helping a deserving claimant. Recalling our earlier discussion of government pay-offs, three factors might increase $-y/x$: the erosion of electoral support for helping deserving claimants; an increase in electoral reaction against undeserving claims; and increased policy priority being placed upon solving the problem of undeserving claims. Arguably all three of these factors operated in Britain and the US in the 1980s. (The electorate's changing position may, of course, have been linked with changes in party ideology.)

Condition 2 is also more likely to be satisfied as $p/(1 - p)$—the

relative frequency of deserving and undeserving unemployed—
falls. The notion of the erosion of moral order has been an important theme in certain strands of New Right thinking.[48] It seems
quite plausible to us that there has been a belief among the New
Right that, as part of the erosion of the moral order, the proportion of undeserving unemployed has increased.

Finally, condition 2 is more likely to be satisfied as r/q—the relative frequency with which deserving unemployed are deterred
from claiming compared to the frequency with which undeserving
unemployed are deterred from claiming—falls. This result makes
intuitive sense, since failing to help the deserving has costs for the
New Right, while deterring the undeserving has benefits.

4. CONCLUSION

In this chapter we have identified the growth of work-welfare programmes in the 1980s in the US and Britain and explained their
development by reference to competing conceptions of the social
rights of citizenship and rational-choice assumptions. Using the
latter we have explained why neither community nor market unemployment insurance schemes will provide sufficient coverage as
society industrializes. Consequently, it is state-organized systems
which have evolved to address unemployment and welfare needs.

Benefit programmes are periodically the object of criticism, most
recently by the New Right, whose ideology restores a historical
distinction between deserving and undeserving claimants. They are
regularly criticized for being too costly. New Right advocates har-
ness a public fear that malingerers will free-ride on other citizens
who contribute compulsorily to the provision of benefit schemes.
This logic results in the adoption of work-welfare programmes
alleged to be capable of distinguishing between these two sorts of
claimants.

Ideologically and substantively work-welfare programmes mark
an important break in the post-1945 approach to welfare and
unemployment assistance. Despite their association with politically
conservative ends they expose a general concern about the purpose
of benefit programmes and demonstrate the prominence of work
in debates about citizenship. Deterrent programmes represent one
method of integrating work and welfare priorities but there is likely

to be considerable debate about the desirability of these schemes and the formulation of alternatives in coming years.

Although it is useful to analyse work-welfare programmes by reference to preference and incentive structures, a complete account would also require attention to be paid to political struggles and economic pressures. Even where work-welfare programmes have the potential to be of an assistance rather than a deterrence character financial constraints and political pressures often force them towards the latter category. Thus, the US federal deficit and the multiple fiscal problems of individual states, including Massachusetts and California, compel state policy administrators to devise programmes under the Family Support Act which minimize expenditure. In both Britain and the US financial constraints produce a common pressure to cream off the best participants and to fail the least well advantaged for labour-market participation. Many of these problems reflect the dominance of the deterrence imperative in work-welfare programmes associated with New Right principles which we have explained in this chapter.

NOTES

1. A caveat is the difference in the institutional structure of the welfare state in these countries, which will influence any work-welfare programmes adopted.
2. For details see D. S. King, 'Citizenship as Obligation in the United States: Title II of the Family Support Act of 1988', in M. Moran and U. Vogel (eds.), *The Frontiers of Citizenship* (London: Macmillan, 1991). There were a number of measures introduced before 1988 empowering the states to impose such conditions upon welfare recipients, but their implementation was optional.
3. Almost half of the states had implemented their own work-welfare programmes after 1981, when the Omnibus Budget Reconciliation Act empowered such programmes. These state programmes range on a continuum from liberal (in which participation is voluntary, such as Massachusetts) to punitive (in which participation is mandatory and the range of activities available is limited, such as West Virginia and California).
4. See 54 Federal Register 156, 38–95.
5. See Family Support Act 1988 (Public Law 100–485), Title II, sect. 482.
6. For an account of JTPA's legislative passage see R. Fenno, *The Making of a Senator: J. Dan Quayle* (Washington: Congressional

Quarterly Press, 1989). The Job Training Partnership Act is an altogether different approach to training and employment needs from that of its major predecessor—the Comprehensive Employment and Training Act of 1973 (CETA)—which was based in the public sector.

7. See Department of Employment Training, *Annual Report 1988* (Boston, Mass.: 1988).

8. For a comprehensive overview see D. Finn and L. Ball, *Unemployment and Training Rights Handbook* (London: Unemployment Unit, 1991).

9. See *Working Brief* (London: Unemployment Unit, 1990).

10. For a recent introductory survey of these reforms see M. Hill, *Social Security Policy in Britain* (Aldershot: Edward Elgar, 1990).

11. D. S. King, 'The Establishment of Work-Welfare Programmes in the USA and Britain: Politics, Ideas and Institutions', in S. Steinmo, K. Thelen, and F. Longstreth (eds.), *The New Institutionalism* (Cambridge and New York: Cambridge University Press, 1992).

12. White Paper, *Training for Employment*, Cmnd. 316 (London: HMSO 1988).

13. Ibid. 38.

14. In fact, the implementation of ET has involved significant revision of this target as the TECs have been slow to be established. See *ET in London* and *ET: There are Alternatives* (London: Centre for Alternative Industrial and Technological Systems, 1989). The revival of unemployment in 1991 has again made ET central to the government's strategy, with the restoration of previous cuts in its budget and the introduction of another programme, Employment Action, for the long-term unemployed.

15. During the Committee stage of the 1987 Social Security Bill the then Under-Secretary of State for Health and Social Security, Minister Michael Portillo argued: 'I entirely rebut the . . . repeated allegation about compulsion. It is true that we are withdrawing income support from 16 and 17 year-olds who have left school, are not in work and have not taken up a YTS place, but the choices for young people are still there. They can stay at school. They can go to college. They can, if they are lucky, take a job. Or they can take the YTS place that is on offer to them. I persist in saying, therefore, that there is no compulsion. We are talking about the guaranteed option of a place on a YTS and the response of the Government and the taxpayer to that new situation.' Parliamentary Debates (Hansard), Official Report House of Commons Standing Committee E (1 Dec. 1987), col. 313. Whether these choices amounted to compulsion is obviously a matter of interpretation.

16. Parliamentary Debates (Hansard), Official Report House of Commons Standing Committee F (21 Jan. 1988), col. 632.

17. Ibid., col. 639. It has been argued by some critics of the government proposals that loss of benefits is based upon far fewer criteria.

18. For the obligation argument see L. Mead, *Beyond Entitlement: The Social Obligations of Citizenship* (New York: Free Press, 1986).

19. See D. Ellwood, *Poor Support* (New York: Basic Books, 1988); J. D. Moon, 'The Moral Basis of the Democratic Welfare State', in A. Gutmann (ed.), *Democracy and the Welfare State* (Princeton, NJ: Princeton University Press, 1988); and C. Murray, *Losing Ground* (New York: Basic Books, 1984).

20. For the rights-based argument see T. H. Marshall, 'Citizenship and Social Class', in id., *Citizenship and Social Development* (New York: Doubleday, 1964); D. S. King and J. Waldron, 'Citizenship, Social Citizenship and the Defence of Welfare Provision', *British Journal of Political Science*, 18 (1988), 415–43; and A. L. Schorr, *Common Decency* (London: Yale University Press, 1986). For a discussion of social democratic principles see D. Miller, *Market, State and Community* (Oxford: Clarendon Press, 1989).

21. See the discussion in N. Barry, *Welfare* (Buckingham: Open University Press, 1990), and also D. Anderson, D. Marsland, and J. Lait, *Breaking the Spell of the Welfare State* (London: Social Affairs Unit, 1981).

22. Parliamentary Debates (Hansard), House of Commons, vol. 5 (19 May 1909), col. 503.

23. Similar language and claims can be found amongst contemporary socialists as illustrated by I. McLean in *The Legend of Red Clydeside* (Edinburgh: John Donald Publishers, 1983), 177.

24. See discussion in A. Deacon, *In Search of the Scrounger* (Occasional Papers on Social Administration No. 60; London: G. H. Bell & Sons, 1976).

25. See discussion in R. McKibbin, 'The "Social Psychology" of Unemployment in Inter-war Britain', in id., *The Ideologies of Class* (Oxford: Clarendon Press, 1990).

26. National Governors' Association, *Job-Oriented Welfare Reform* (Washington, DC: NGA, 1987), 1–2.

27. *The New York Times*, 1 Oct. 1988, 1, 26:1.

28. Parliamentary Debates (Hansard), Official Report House of Lords, vol. 492 (25 Jan. 1988), col. 438.

29. Parliamentary Debates (Hansard), Official Report House of Commons, vol. 493 (26 Jan. 1989), col. 134.

30. Ibid. (31 Jan. 1989), col. 164.

31. One difference between Britain and the United States is the object of obligation: in the US it is society whereas in Britain it is more legalistically directed towards the state.

32. N. Wikeley, 'Unemployment Benefit, the State and the Labour Market', *Journal of Law and Society* 16 (1989), 304.
33. Quoted in R. Taylor, 'Mediator in an Economic Arena', *The Financial Times*, 2 Oct. 1989, 37.
34. H. Heclo and H. Madsen, *Policy and Politics in Sweden* (Philadelphia: Temple University Press, 1987), 171.
35. Heclo and Madsen, *Policy and Politics in Sweden*, 171.
36. See J. C. Scott, *The Moral Economy of the Peasant* (New Haven, Conn.: Yale University Press, 1976), and S. Popkin, 'The Political Economy of Peasant Society', in J. Elster (ed.), *Rational Choice* (Oxford: Basil Blackwell, 1986).
37. See A. de Swaan, *In Care of the State* (Oxford: Polity Press, 1988), ch. 2 and D. S. King, 'Voluntary and State Provision of Welfare as Part of the Public–Private Continuum: Modelling the Shifting Involvements in Britain and the US', in A. Ware (ed.), *Charities and Government* (Manchester: Manchester University Press, 1989).
38. M. Taylor, *The Possibility of Cooperation* (Cambridge: Cambridge University Press, 1987). In a Chicken game there is more than one equilibrium: the equilibria are such that one person gains and the other loses. In a two-person game both players want a good provided and each can individually do the work completely but each has a preference that the other player do all the work. Taylor gives the example of two neighbouring farmers whose crops depend upon flood control: 'there is a minimum amount of work which must be done; either individual alone can do it all, but each prefers the other to do all the work. The consequences of nobody doing the work are so disastrous that either of them would do the work if the other did not', 35. This preference structure is that of a Chicken game.
39. For an introduction see J. E. Stiglitz, 'Principal and Agent', in J. Eatwell, M. Milgate, and P. Newton (eds.), *The New Palgrave: A Dictionary of Economics* (London: Macmillan, 1987), iii, 966–71.
40. M. Olson, *The Logic of Collective Action* (Cambridge, Mass.: Harvard University Press, 1965).
41. J. Lewis, 'Back to the Future: A Comment on American New Right Ideas about Welfare and Citizenship in the 1980s', *Gender and History*, 3:159–73 1991 and M. B. Katz, *In the Shadow of the Workhouse* (New York: Basic Books, 1986).
42. The assignment of a zero pay-off to not helping a claimant is arbitrary, making no difference to the analysis, while simplifying the algebra.
43. See the discussion in W. J. Braithwaite, *Lloyd George's Ambulance Wagon* (ed.) H. N. Bunbury and R. Titmuss (Bath: Cedric Chivers Ltd., 1957).

44. For such a case see J. Dryzek and R. E. Goodin, 'Risk-Sharing and Social Justice: The Motivational Foundations of the Post-War Welfare State', *British Journal of Political Science*, 16 (1986), 1–34.

45. An implicit assumption is that governments are indifferent between not assisting deserving unemployed people who do not claim and undeserving unemployed people who do not claim. This assumption is reasonable because governments cannot test individual non-claimants' worthiness and are likely to have only imperfect information about the relative probabilities that a non-claimant is or is not deserving.

46. Training benefits only open to claimants might encourage some to claim under workfare who would not do so under traditional schemes. Where substantial resources are put into training, as in Sweden, workfare might even increase the probability of a claim (as has reputedly occurred in Israel). However, while some individuals might be encouraged to claim in less well-resourced systems, any perceived training benefits will tend to be more than offset by the increased stigmatization of the unemployed which has been associated with, if not caused by, workfare, together with the higher costs to the individual of claiming.

47. We do not need to put precise values on the pay-offs of the unemployed to determine what the equilibria are.

48. See, for example, H. Parker, *The Moral Hazards of Social Benefits* (London: Institute of Economic Affairs, 1982) and G. Gilder, *Wealth and Poverty* (New York: Basic Books, 1981).

6

Party Competition in Interlinked Political Markets: The European Union and its Member States

MOSHE MAOR

The institutional development of the European Union (EU) will affect the interplay of government and opposition in each of the Member States. The interplay—par excellence one of interaction—is a feature of party systems. Surprisingly, it is entirely absent from the literature on systemic properties used to characterize and differentiate party systems. Party systems are characterized by the number of parties and their relative size, the extent of polarization, movement in party support, and societal cleavages as they are reflected by the parties. These characteristics do not necessarily reveal the nature of government–opposition interaction, although the extent of polarization in the party system may be an approximate guide.

1. THE PROBLEM

This chapter presents a general model of élite decision-making during party competition in interlinked political markets. 'Interlinked political markets' are multi-party systems where the structure of party competition in one system affects the structure of party com-

An earlier version of this paper was presented to the workshop 'The Convergence of West European Party Systems', at the London School of Economics in October 1992, as well as to the ECPR joint sessions of workshops in April 1993. I would like to acknowledge the useful comments from Peter Mair, Mogens Pedersen, Hans Daalder, Peter Pulzer, Knud Heidar, Vincent Wright, Giofranco Pasquino, Gunar Sjöblom, Gordon Smith, Howard Machin, and Alan Ware. They bear no responsibility for the opinions expressed in the paper.

petition in another. Five determining factors create the structure of party competition: the number and relative size of parties; their ideological distance and the extent of polarization; movement in party support or party-system volatility; societal cleavages as transmitted by the parties; and government–opposition relationships.[1] Issues are then discussed according to the particular combination of these factors together with the influence of the constitutional setting. When a change in one of the above dimensions arises from processes which occur in another system, one can conclude that a linkage between the two systems exists. A classic example is the relationships between regional/local and national political competition in federal systems.

This chapter focuses on the linkages between party competition in EU Member States and at the Union level. It constructs a common framework to address two questions. First, what are the linkages between European and national party competition? Secondly, what are the inter-party consequences of those linkages? The chapter then explores a variable—namely, the institutional context within which party competition takes place—which intervenes in the relationship between market *A* and market *B*.

A complete description of party competition in interlinked political markets must take into account both the intra-system channels of influence (e.g. amongst different party élites in a given market) and the inter-system channels of influence (e.g. amongst party élites which operate in different markets). This chapter incorporates both channels, presenting a general model of élite decision-making in contexts in which party competition in one market imposes significant constraints on party competition in another.[2] These constraints shape the motivation of party élites in both parliamentary and electoral arenas. The assumption underlying this argument is that party élites participate in games in two different arenas: the parliamentary and the electoral. Each move they make has consequences in both arenas, as well as in the electoral arena of the interlinked market.

The concerns of this chapter are therefore patterns of inter-party conflict and co-operation, and inter-systemic influences amongst interlinked political markets. The arguments are theoretical, that is, conditional statements independent of temporal or spatial specifications. Section 2 describes the concept of 'interlinked political markets' and the effects of such markets on the evolution of inter-party co-operation. To account for such behaviour, Section 3 introduces a game-theoretic framework in which the divergent interests and evaluations of the political situation by élites generate a co-operative game in the parliamentary and electoral arenas. Section 4 presents the intervening variable, the institutional and constitutional context within which political actors operate, and Section 5 provides a tentative list of indicators of government–opposition co-operation. The conclusion discusses the advantages of this framework in generating hypotheses for research.

2. PARTY COMPETITION IN INTERLINKED POLITICAL MARKETS

Interlinked political markets are multi-party systems where the structure of party competition in one market affects the structure of party competition in another. The markets are competitive, with parties competing over both penetration into a parliamentary system at time t, and the maintenance of political power at time $t + 1$.[3] In the electoral system power distribution is determined by votes: the more votes a party obtains in the elections, the more powerful it is. The power-seeking parties are thus, by definition, maximizers of votes through the electoral system.[4]

To understand the process through which political processes in one market trigger processes in the interlinked one, it is important to appreciate two conditions at the electoral level which establish a linkage: (1) both markets share, partly or fully, each other's electorate (for instance, the German local and national markets), or (2) both markets share similar historical and cultural experiences (for instance, the Danish, Swedish, and Norwegian markets). Political competition at the level of the member states and at the Union level falls under the former condition. Electors in each EU Member State are part of the electorate eligible to vote in the European elections. In addition, part of the electorate which participates in European elections is eligible to vote in any given Member State.

Under either one of these conditions, parties operating in the electoral and the parliamentary arenas in one market may be exposed to influences derived from party competition in another. For the former condition, the emergence of a coalition at the national level may have an impact on party competition at the regional level. In Germany, for instance, parties tend to follow a well-known convention by declaring their potential coalition partners before the election. This enables German voters to establish a balance between the national and *Land* levels by voting for a specific coalition in the national parliament—the *Bundestag*—and a different one in the regional parliament—the *Bundesrat*. During 1972–82, the Social Democratic Party and the Free Democrats controlled a majority in the *Bundestag*, whereas the Christian Democrats obtained a majority in the *Bundesrat*. In contrast, after the 1990 elections, the Christian Democrats together with the Free Democrats controlled a majority in the *Bundestag*, whereas the SPD obtained a majority in the *Bundesrat*.

Regarding the second condition, when a new cleavage (or division) emerges in a system, it will be diffused to systems which share a similar societal context. The formation of the Progress Party in Denmark during the 1970s, for instance, triggered the creation of the Norwegian Progress Party, and, later on, the Swedish New Democracy Party.

The above examples demonstrate how party competition in one market may impose significant constraints on party competition in another. One reason for this is that party competition over the dominant dimension is often geared to take into account issues which emerge within society without disrupting the party system. Issues which are generated by an interlinked market may threaten to disrupt the existing institutional system, destabilize the electorate, or threaten the internal unity of the major parties. These issues, when emerging from an interlinked market, are less susceptible to accommodation by the recipient parties. This constraint shapes the motivation of party élites in the parliamentary and electoral arenas towards growing co-operation or collusion over impending issues of importance.

Understanding of the consequences of this constraint on party behaviour is enhanced by an economic analogy. The competitive relationships in the electoral and parliamentary party systems have several characteristics in common with oligopoly. The term 'oligopoly' refers typically to an industrial structure in which a few sellers control the market and supply a significant percentage of its output—much like the system of few parties formulating public policy. It is in the interests of all the firms in such markets to block potential rivals from benefits at the consumer level (electoral support). This can be done by tacit co-operation (collusion) between the firms, which may affect consumer-level variants such as the price and product differential. Beyond the object of activity, an important difference between economic and political markets is that in the former regulations against collusion usually exist to protect consumer interests. In political markets, on the other hand, the collusion of parties (i.e. political coalitions) is one of the characteristics of political life.[5]

Adoption of the logic of oligopolistic interactions enables us to identify the nature of party competition in interlinked markets. In economic markets, where formal co-ordination of activities is illegal, tacit price co-ordination is often possible. Under certain conditions, firms may find it easier to agree on a mutually acceptable co-operative outcome, to achieve that outcome smoothly, and to maintain it over time in the face of exogenous shocks and private incentives to deviate. In political markets, formal co-operation between government and opposition is not one of the characteristics of political life, as it subverts the basic objective of rational politicians: the maximization of votes through the electoral system.[6] Such co-operation might blur the differences between the parties at the electoral level, thus undermining their attempts to maximize their votes. Tacit co-ordination, however, may bring about an outcome which is compatible with the interests of the parties involved whilst avoiding any negative by-product in the electoral arena.

Studies of the effects of tacit price co-ordination in economic markets conclude that incumbent firms can maintain the stability of monopoly price whilst deterring the entry of new rivals or even after entry occurs.[7] In the former case, Bain and Sylos-Labini's models demonstrate that threats to limit prices can act as a rational deterrent to entry.[8] Those models suggest that it is irrational for an incumbent and dominant firm to deter entry by setting a low limit price before entry occurs. Instead, the incumbent could increase his profits by setting the higher monopoly price before entry and threatening to reduce his price in the event that entry actually occurred. Given the threat, it is argued, no actual entry would occur, because the prospective entrant would anticipate earning insufficient profit at the lower post-entry price. This argument is usually countered by the observation that the incumbent's threat to lower the price after entry lacks credibility. Once entry occurs, it is generally in the incumbent's interest to accommodate the entrant by behaving co-operatively. (This explanation, of course, implicitly assumes that tacit co-ordination will be successful.)

Similarly, in political markets, governmental and opposition parties could decide to collaborate either in parliament or in elections, or in both.[9] For most of the wartime years the major parties in Britain, for example, agreed to collaborate: coalition cabinets were formed, and elections were delayed until after the war ended. In Austria from 1947 onwards, the People's Party and the Socialist Party formed a coalition government that denuded the Parliament of opposition; yet at each election the two parties vigorously fought one another for votes. Coalescent strategies have also been pursued by government and opposition parties after the wartime period. Austria is the most interesting example, and the German model follows close behind.[10]

The outcome of coalescent strategies is often the formation of oversized coalitions. Such alliances are the rule in the proportional representation system as practised in Switzerland and the Netherlands. They can also be a feature of a system with one dominant party.[11] There have been cases of such a party including a smaller partner in the government, although this was not necessary to secure a majority in parliament. Grand coalition can also be found in systems where majorities tend to crumble due to the lack of party discipline. Lastly, in semi-parliamentary semi-presidential systems (Finland, the Weimar Republic in Germany), where the President has considerable influence on the formation of the government, oversized coalitions can also be a characteristic of the system.[12] An essential conclusion to be drawn from these examples is that coalescent strategies during peaceful periods may be encouraged by 'a system in which constitutional rules and practice prevent any site [i.e. political arenas for encounters between government and opposition] from being decisive and where opportunities for preventing or inhibiting government action are numerous'.[13]

My analysis focuses on co-ordination of activities between government and opposition in interlinked political markets. This pattern is elaborated in the following section. Focusing on party competition at the national level during a process of regional integration, the first question considered is: what is the rationale of government–opposition co-operation?

3. THE RATIONALE OF GOVERNMENT–OPPOSITION CO-OPERATION DURING A PROCESS OF REGIONAL INTEGRATION

It is now well established in political science that traditions of consultation between all major parties about electoral arrangements enable their leaders to discriminate against new entrants by colluding to create entry barriers.[14] Parties engage in a competitive struggle for monopoly privileges.[15] The introduction of party competition in an interlinked market into the above process, however, creates some obstacles for those actors seeking monopoly privileges. Instead of protecting the existing privileges, party competition in one market may affect the content of electoral competition in the other, in ways which are incompatible with the interests of the parties.

Parties operating in a supranational system may increase the incentives of parties operating at the national level to compete. This can be done by airing an issue that threatens to disrupt the existing institutional system—a process which may lead to electoral reform. In the electoral arena, parties operating in a supranational system may force items onto the agenda to which the established parties are unprepared to react, or alternatively, issues that destabilize the electorate or threaten the internal unity of the major parties.[16]

One element which accounts for successful oligopolistic co-ordination is agreement about the co-operative outcome. Agreement is easiest whenever parties' interests correspond, but the difficulties in reaching an agreement are compounded when one takes into account each actor's preference ordering. To capture these differences, I employ the following model. Each actor considers a legislative strategy in the light of sources of instability at three levels: the institutional environment within which it operates; the intra-party environment; and the electoral environment. There are three types of issues to be considered: those which may disrupt the existing institutional system; those which may threaten the internal unity of a party; and those which may destabilize the electorate. Each party must choose between two different strategies: to co-operate with other parties (C) or to be intransigent (I). The choices available to government and opposition are the same, but their respective preference ordering for outcomes differ. Table 6.1 presents the generic pay-off matrix of two-person games.

TABLE 6.1. *Pay-offs of possible games between government and opposition*

	C(ompromise)	I(ntransigence)
C(ompromise)	$R1, R2$	$S1, T2$
I(ntransigence)	$T1, S2$	$P1, P2$

$Ti > Pi > Ri > Si$:	Deadlock
$Ti > Ri > Pi > Si$:	Prisoners' Dilemma
$Ti > Ri > Si > Pi$:	Chicken

In parliamentary competition, the preferred outcome for the government is to be intransigent when the opposition is willing to co-operate (pay-off T). In this case, governmental parties can use their state power to alter the rules of the game which structure electoral competition. By so doing, they articulate pressures exerted by parties operating in the interlinked market consistent with their interests (i.e. those of the governing party). The scope for the activity of the governmental parties, in this sense, depends on constitutional factors.[17] Similarly, in electoral competition, the most preferred outcome for the government is to be intransigent when the opposition is willing to co-operate. Acting in the long term, such parties can counter-play expectation-boosting by opposition parties. The governmental parties consider the converse situation (they are willing to co-operate while the opposition parties remain intransigent) the worst possible outcome. Let us call this pay-off S. This case may emerge when governmental parties recognize negative influences which are exerted by parties operating in the interlinked market. In the parliamentary arena, improving competitiveness by forcing an issue of electoral reform onto the agenda will favour newcomers and small-to-medium opposition parties. In the electoral arena, improving competitiveness by airing an issue which divides the governmental party (or the coalition government) will undermine its electoral fortunes. The unwillingness of the potential beneficiaries to compromise (e.g. to co-operate) stems from the nature of these strategies.

A third alternative is mutual co-operation. Call it R. Joint institutional manipulation allows government and opposition parties to discriminate against new entrants by colluding to create electoral system thresholds.[18] Parties would therefore focus on a competitive struggle for monopoly privileges to preserve oligopolistic rather than open competition. They will be able to acquire a degree of control over campaign financing and access to mass media. These provisions enhance the ability of established parties to neutralize negative influences from the interlinked market. Furthermore, both the government and the opposition could alter constitutional factors which limit their scope for joint institutional manipulation. Thus, they can increase leverage for future manipulation and at the same time restrict the leverage of the parties operating in the interlinked market to structure electoral competition in the given market.

In electoral competition, mutual co-operation implies joint agenda-setting. Since voters' decisions necessarily echo the choices they are offered,[19] parties can reshape the voters' preferences by avoiding inter-party competition over issues on which they are internally divided. They can also avoid or delay a competition over potentially volatile issues which may undermine their traditional support at the level of the electorate. Once a divisive issue is aired by parties operating in the interlinked market, both government and opposition parties may neutralize the negative effects of the issue by offering a similar policy stance. As a result, voters are offered no choice.

Finally, mutual intransigence (P) is the worst outcome, as it implies possible tit-for-tat behaviour if a viable opposition gains office in the future.

For the opposition, the most preferred outcome is to be intransigent when the government is willing to co-operate. In the face of pressures derived from the interlinked market which are consistent with the opposition interests, and, given that they are confident that future alternation in power is likely, such parties will prefer to avoid co-operation with the government. The opposition parties consider the converse situation (they are willing to co-operate while the governmental parties remain intransigent) the worst possible outcome. The fact that they would like to co-operate often implies that they would have to share responsibility for governmental policies. Once the opposition decides to co-operate it is immediately restricted in its ability to criticize the government and present itself as a viable alternative.

A third alternative is mutual co-operation. Opposition parties could use their party power and engage in joint institutional manipulation. Furthermore, both the government and the opposition could alter constitutional factors which limit their scope for joint institutional manipulation.[20] Finally, mutual intransigence is worse than mutual co-operation as it implies further institutional manipulation by the government when it is confident that future alternations of power are unlikely.

If mutual co-operation is preferred we face a classic Prisoners' Dilemma in parliamentary and electoral competition in interlinked political markets. For both government and opposition parties, a dominant strategy of intransigence holds. Regardless of the strategy pursued by the opponent, each actor's dominant strategy is to avoid co-operation. Party élites, furthermore, are afraid of the consequences of compromise whilst everybody else is intransigent. By choosing not to engage in co-operative activity, both players find themselves in a sub-optimal outcome, that is, they find themselves worse off than if they had chosen the co-operative strategy. We therefore face the following ordering of preferences in the parliamentary and electoral arenas of interlinked political markets:

$$T_{pi} > R_{pi} > P_{pi} > S_{pi}$$
$$T_{ei} > R_{ei} > P_{ei} > S_{ei}$$

The subscripts p and e refer to the parliamentary and electoral arenas respectively, and the subscript i refers to the parties participating in the game.

Given that mutual co-operation is preferred, its relative success is not inevitable—even in highly concentrated party systems protected by insurmountable barriers to entry. The key to this insight is the recognition that even though parties' fates are interdependent, the individual self-interests of MPs and MEPs are not perfectly consonant.[21] As a result, parties may find it difficult to agree on a mutually acceptable co-operative outcome, achieve that outcome smoothly, and maintain it over time in the face of exogenous shocks and private incentives to deviate. In the language of game theory, the joint vote-maximizing point may not be a Nash equilibrium.

However mutual the success of the co-operation may be, an important question is, what happens to the status of the competing party as vote-maximizer? Co-ordination of activities between government and opposition is most likely to be executed at the invisible level of politics (for instance, informal contacts in committees or private meetings). This process may be achieved by an understanding minimizing the impact of any dimension which may destabilize their internal cohesion, or their electoral or institutional environment. Certain issues need to be subsumed to protect the position of the established parties. Alternatively, parties may opt for the strategy of competing over specific aspects of the destablizing issues. Instead of competing over European integration, for example, they may focus on the social chapter.

So far it has been argued that parties competing in the interlinked markets are likely to face mounting incentives for government–opposition co-operation. An essential factor which may affect those incentives, however, is the institutional context within which party competition in a given market takes place. The interplay between institutions and the opportunities they afford for co-operation, and the way institutions evolve, are all part of the complex set of intervening variables that we would like to understand when looking at party behaviour in interlinked markets. The discussion now turns to a brief examination of this topic.

4. CONSTITUTIONS AND INSTITUTIONAL INFLUENCES[22]

The observable dimensions of institutions are the contracts (implicit or explicit) made between parties at all levels of political exchange: constitutions, statute law, and common law.[23] The response of parties to rules will result in a more or less elaborate structure of informal procedures and norms of behaviour determined by the institutional context within which party élites operate and by their preferences. The more defined the lines of political accountability connecting government and opposition parties, the greater the incentives for incumbents to co-ordinate their activities with their rivals. And the more fractured, confused, and weak the linkage between public policy, incumbents, and opposition parties, the more probable that governmental parties will act independently. Table 6.2 shows that there are four features of constitutional and institutional arrangements which magnify or reduce the possibility of tacit government–opposition co-ordination.

TABLE 6.2. *Constitutional and institutional influences on the choice of tacit government–opposition co-ordination*

	Relatively high-level of co-ordination	Intermediate situation	Relatively low level of co-ordination
Structure of government	Federal states	Unitary states with strong or entrenched sub-national governments	Centralized unitary states with weak-sub-national governments
Constitutional arrangements	Codified constitution/ strong judicial review		Uncodified constitution/ no judicial review
Separation of powers	Strong separation/ independent election of legislature and president		Weak separation/ one election decides legislature and government
Electoral system	Proportional representation system		Plurality rule or non-PR system

Source: Adopted from P. Dunleavy, *Democracy, Bureaucracy and Public Choice* (Hemel Hempstead: Harvester Wheatsheaf, 1991), 137.

The Centralization of State Power

The degree of control over public policy exercised by the incumbent party at the national level is the background against which party élites consider some kind of tacit co-operation with rival parties. Federal systems, such as Germany or Switzerland, restrict national government by requiring consultation with actors operating in sub-national arenas. These constraints are expressed in opposition parties' control of state or regional governments or local authorities; they can use their control in these arenas to oppose and undermine government policies. Attempts by the governing party to influence public policy without prior consultation might provoke strong sub-central reaction. A high degree of tacit co-ordination between government and opposition parties is almost inevitable.

Unitary states which lack alternative centres of state power provide the most scope for national governments solely to shape public policy, secure in the knowledge that no alternative centres of state power exist from which opposition parties could organize countervailing efforts. The British polity springs to mind.[24] An intermediate degree of tacit co-ordination occurs in cases of greater restrictions on the ability of national governments to act independently. This applies in most unitary states where local government plays an important part in structuring party politics and political recruitment, as in France, or implements almost all welfare state policies, as in Denmark or Sweden. Here the national government cannot easily implement divisive changes in local government structures or financing, either because special procedures are needed for institutional restructuring, or because the centre is dependent on local governments for effective public service delivery.

A Codified Constitution

More general constitutional constraints—such as judicial review and restrictions on the politicized use of power—increase the likelihood of tacit co-ordination between government parties and opposition parties. The UK, for example, has an uncodified constitution so that a government with a parliamentary majority may use its unconstrained powers to engage in institutional manipulation without any possibility of judicial review. Other liberal democracies have codified constitutions, but in some cases the constitution is relatively easy to change and contains little effective opportunity for judicial review of the constitutionality of government actions. In all these systems, a governing party with a clear majority will not be unduly constrained in using state power for partisan ends. By contrast, where the constitution is very codified, difficult to amend, and embodies extensive judicial review, as in Germany, the use of institutional manipulation by the incumbent parties is harder. Incentives for tacit co-ordination are therefore most likely to be found in the German polity, and to a lesser degree in the French one rather than in the British system.

The Separation of Powers

The likelihood of tacit co-operation is also enhanced where there is an effective separation of legislative and executive powers. A high level of tacit co-operation occurs when the two branches of government can be controlled by different parties. In France and in the US, a directly elected president may lack a majority in the lower house of the legislature. By contrast, where a majority government can be confident of passing almost all its legislation unamended through parliament, the scope for government–opposition co-operation declines sharply. The Westminster system exemplifies this case. To summarize, where policy measures initiated by the incumbent party can be amended by the opposition in the legislature before implementation, the scope for tacit government–opposition co-ordination is enhanced.

The Electoral System

The electoral system has an important influence on the possibility of tacit co-ordination between government and opposition parties. Countries in which electoral rules assign a high priority to achieving proportionality between votes tend to have multi-party systems and coalition governments where tacit co-operation strategies prevail. By contrast, in countries with plurality-rule elections, the voting system is oriented instead to delivering legislative majorities to the largest party. This type of system makes tacit co-ordination less feasible or attractive to incumbent governments.

The overall impact of these considerations is complex in any political system, since they pull in different directions. The Westminster-model constitution and the derived two-party system and adversarial political competition embody multiple pressures which make tacit government–opposition co-ordination unattractive for party élites and difficult to implement.[25] On the other hand, the German constitution and government structure generate multiple factors which impel party élites towards tacit co-ordination. To sum up, tacit government–opposition co-ordination takes place within a given institutional arena and this arena influences the character and extent of co-operation subsequently observed. This is a problem of constitutional political economy. The extent of tacit government–opposition co-ordination is not the only important variable in evaluating a political market, but the issue clearly deserves to be on the agenda of relevant considerations.

5. FROM DEDUCTIVE REASONING TO INDUCTIVE RESEARCH: A TENTATIVE LIST OF INDICATORS

Moving from rational-choice logic to empirical research requires first and foremost the identification of the relevant variables. Tacit (and express) co-operation often results in extraordinary majorities. Extraordinary majorities have the effect of restricting the set of winning coalitions while simultaneously admitting a new kind of coalition, a blocking coalition.[26] Such coalitions can (only) ensure the status quo, as they make it more difficult to move away from existing policies towards new ones. It is therefore easier to form blocking coalitions because it is easier to maintain the status quo than to produce a new set of policies with majority support. Based on this insight, empirical research must study voting patterns in parliamentary arenas by addressing such questions as; 'How often is opposition split in division lobbies?', 'How often are amendments proposed by the opposition accepted?', 'To what extent does voting in the European Parliament follow national lines?' and 'How often are extraordinary majorities recorded?'.

A complementary strategy examines the policy variant in the relationships between government and opposition. It addresses such questions as: 'What are the policies which separate government and opposition?', 'Does a shift in government composition lead to a policy change?', 'To what extent does a change of government bring about a change in policy?', and finally, 'Do parties try to present a common view on issues which may destabilize their institutional, electoral, or internal environments?'

Understanding the conditions which facilitate government–opposition co-operation also requires an appreciation of the institutional environment within which parties operate. I refer here to the creation of facilitating practices as an indicator of inter-party co-operation. There are two types of facilitating practices: information exchange and incentive management.[27] The former facilitates both explicit and tacit co-operation by eliminating uncertainty about a rival's actions. Classic examples of information exchanges are government–opposition negotiations within committees, and advance notice by government of policy initiatives. In each case, the exchange of information shortens or eliminates misunderstandings and, therefore, the time intervals spent in states of asymmetric willingness to co-operate. By decreasing the transitional gains from each actor implementing its dominant strategy, incentives are altered to facilitate a co-operative outcome. Such facilitating practices function by directly altering the structure of the pay-off matrix, rather than by working through the medium of information exchange. By restructuring pay-offs, the incentives for government–opposition co-operation may be directly affected. Similarly, a government may change its incentives to match strategy change initiated by the opposition, thereby affecting its rival's incentives to initiate such strategic alterations. In this way, the adoption of facilitating practices can convert competitive oligopoly outcomes into simple Nash equilibria at the co-operative point. Perhaps a classic example of the use of an incentive management device is the allocation of top ministerial jobs and other perks to members of opposition parties.

Finally, an effort ought to be made to assess the relevance of the structure of parliament as a factor which significantly affects the policy costs of being in opposition.[28] An index of the potential influence of oppositions, constructed by Strom, aggregates the following indicators: the number of standing committees, whether or not these standing committees have fixed areas of specialization, whether such jurisdiction corresponds to ministerial departments, the number of committee assignments per legislator, and whether committee chairs are proportionately distributed among the parties. These dichotomized indicators may provide a clue to the ability of the opposition to prevent or inhibit government action.[29]

Attention now turns to the advantages of the theoretical framework in generating hypotheses for empirical research. I hope to show that studies concerning the impact of European integration on parties and party systems ought to focus on the similarities in the way political actors react to the pressures of integration, and the derived consequences in terms of party system change.

6. CONCLUSION

This chapter has examined the relationship between interlinked political markets at the national and European Union levels. The theoretical framework generates two hypotheses:

(1) Political parties, that is, government and opposition, operating in interlinked markets, will tend to implement coalescence strategies to minimize the impact of any issue which may destabilize their internal cohesion, or their electoral or institutional environments.

(2) As a result of the institutional development of the European Union, West European party systems are undergoing restricted change in the nature of the interplay between government and opposition. This hypothesis implies that there are growing similarities between systems in terms of increasing government–opposition co-operation or convergence.

Empirically, there is considerable evidence to suggest that strategies of tacit co-ordination exist and are adopted by party leaders competing in interlinked political markets. Classic examples are the co-ordination of activities between government and opposition in Germany over European integration, immigration policy (1992), German Unification (1990–1), and economic policy (1992–early 1993). In Britain, tacit collusion is often recorded over issues related to Northern Ireland, electoral reform, capital punishment, and many others. The results of the European elections in 1994 suggest that such trends are unlikely to diminish in any West European polity.

NOTES

1. For the first four factors, see J.-E. Lane and S. Ersson, *Politics and Society in Western Europe* (London: Sage, 1991). For the fifth, see M. Maor and G. Smith, 'Government–Opposition Relationships as a Systemic Property', paper delivered at the ECPR joint sessions of workshops, April 1993.

2. G. Tsebelis, *Nested Games: Rational Choice in Comparative Politics* (Berkeley, Calif.: University of California Press, 1990).

3. D. R. Mayhew, *Congress: The Electoral Connection* (New Haven, Conn.: Yale University Press, 1974).

4. A. Downs, *An Economic Theory of Democracy* (New York: Harper and Row, 1957).
5. W. H. Riker, *The Theory of Political Coalitions* (New Haven: Yale University Press, 1962). The reader may also note that, although this chapter's interest lies in the competitive relationships in economic and political markets, it is important to mention the differences between the two. First, businesses are primarily producers of private goods (newspapers, appliances, health care) that are either purchased and enjoyed by individuals or else left alone; parties are primarily producers of public goods (governments and their policies) that are imposed on everyone. Second, where businesses are expected to pursue the private interest of the firm and its owners, parties and their leaders are expected more or less altruistically to pursue the public interest.
6. Downs, *Economic Theory*.
7. See, for example, R. A. Posner, 'Oligopoly and Antitrust Laws: A Suggested Approach', *Stanford Law Review*, 21 (1969), 1562–1606; R. Porter, 'Optimal Cartel Trigger Price Strategies', *Journal of Economic Theory*, 29 (1983), 313–38; S. C. Salop, 'Practices that (Credibly) Facilitate Oligopoly Co-ordination', in J. F. Stiglitz and G. F. Mathewson (eds.), *New Development in the Analysis of Market Structure* (Cambridge, Mass.: MIT Press, 1986), 265–90; G. J. Stigler, 'A Theory of Oligopoly', repr. in id., *The Organization of Industry* (Homewood, Ill., 1968), 39–66; C. d'Aspremont, A. Jacquemin, J. Gabszewics, and J. Weymark, 'On the Stability of Dominant Cartels', *Canadian Journal of Economics*, 14 (1982), 17–25.
8. Independently of one another, J. S. Bain, *Barriers to New Competition* (Cambridge, Mass.: Harvard University Press, 1956) and P. Sylos-Labini, *Oligopoly and Technical Progress* (Cambridge, Mass.: Harvard University Press, 1962) proposed the idea that scale economies in the firm can cause entry barriers, resulting in positive profits for the firms in the industry. Overall, they identified four types of barriers which characterize oligopoly. First, a firm in an industry may own essential raw materials or essential technology that is unavailable to potential competitors. Secondly, the firms may be protected from competition by government regulation. For instance, a licence may be needed to fly a particular route or import certain goods. Thirdly, economies of scale are often a significant barrier to entry where large firms may be able to produce more cheaply than small firms. Fourthly, the firm may be protected by a limit price which deters the entry of new rivals.
9. R. A. Dahl, 'Patterns of Opposition', in R. A. Dahl (ed.), *Political Oppositions in Western Democracies* (New Haven, Conn.: Yale University Press, 1966), 332–47.

10. See, for example, P. Gerlich, E. Grande, and W. C. Muller, 'Corporatism in Crisis: Stability and Change of Social Partnership in Austria', *Political Studies*, 36 (1988), 209–23; G. Smith, *Democracy in Western Germany* (Aldershot: Gower, 3rd edn., 1986).

11. K. von Beyme, *Political Parties in Western Europe* (Aldershot: Gower, 1985).

12. Ibid. 325–6.

13. Dahl, 'Patterns of Opposition', 345.

14. See, for example, G. Doron and M. Maor, 'Barriers to Entry into a Political System: A Theoretical Framework and Empirical Application from the Israeli Experience', *Journal of Theoretical Politics*, 3 (1991), 175–88; M. Maor, 'Barriers to Entry into a Political System', M.A. thesis (Tel Aviv, 1988); R. Taagepera and M. S. Shugart, *Seats and Votes: The Effects and Determinants of Electoral Systems* (New Haven, Conn.: Yale University Press, 1989).

15. G. Tullock, *Towards a Mathematics of Politics* (Ann Arbor, Mich.: University of Michigan Press, 1967).

16. M. Maor and G. Smith, 'Government-Opposition Relationships as a Systemic Property: A Theoretical Framework', paper presented to the ECPR joint sessions of workshops, Leiden, April 1993; M. Maor and G. Smith, 'On the Structure of Issues', in: T. Bryder (ed.), *Party Systems, Party Behaviour and Democracy* (Copenhagen: Copenhagen Political Studies Press, 1993).

17. P. Dunleavy, *Democracy, Bureaucracy and Public Choice* (Hemel Hempstead: Harvester Wheatsheaf, 1991); P. Dunleavy and H. Ward, 'Exogenous Voter Preferences and Parties with State Power: Some Internal Problems of Economic Models of Party Competition', *British Journal of Political Research*, 4 (1981), 351–80.

18. Taagepera and Shugart, *Seats and Votes*.

19. B. Page, *Choices and Echoes in American Elections: Rational Man and Electoral Democracy* (Chicago: University of Chicago Press, 1978).

20. Dunleavy, *Democracy and Public Choice*.

21. M. Maor, 'The Dynamics of Minority Rule: Intra-Party Politics and Coalitional Behaviour in Western Europe', Ph.D. thesis (London, 1992); M. Maor, 'Intraparty Conflicts and Coalitional Behaviour in Denmark and Norway: The Case of "Highly Institutionalized" Parties', *Scandinavian Political Studies*, 15 (1992), 99–116; M. Maor, *Political Parties: Comparative Approaches and the British Experience* (London: Routledge, 1995).

22. This section relies on Dunleavy's analysis of preference-shaping strategies, see Dunleavy, *Democracy and Public Choice*, 112–46.

23. The section's interest lies within legally enforceable contracts. Verbally stated agreements are thus excluded.

24. D. S. King, 'Political Centralization and State Interests in Britain', *Comparative Political Studies* 21 (1989), 467–94.
25. M. Duverger, *Political Parties* (London: Methuen, 1964), 414.
26. P. Ordeshook, *Game Theory and Political Theory* (Cambridge: Cambridge University Press, 1986), 378.
27. S. C. Salop, 'Practices that (Credibly) Facilitate Oligopoly Co-ordination', in Stiglitz and Mathewson, *New Development*, 271–3.
28. K. Strom, *Minority Government and Majority Rule* (Cambridge: Cambridge University Press, 1990).
29. Ibid. 71.
30. Lane and Ersson, *Politics and Society*.

7

Railway Regulation as a Test-bed of Rational Choice

IAIN MCLEAN

1. INTRODUCTION: HYPOTHESES TO BE TESTED

It is commonplace for theorists to explore some historical event from a rational-choice perspective, and (typically) to claim that it explains more than do rival perspectives.[1] The procedure of this chapter is the other way round. We take a historical event (the passage of the Regulation of Railways Act 1844), try to explain why it is substantively significant and unexpected, and then judge which of a number of rival schools, including two versions of rational choice, performs best at explaining what happened.

Government regulation of the railways in the United Kingdom dates back to the 1840s. Inspectors of Railways were first appointed under an Act of 1840. Because the Act stipulated that the inspectors must not have a connection with any railway company, they were recruited from the Royal Engineers and their reports always stated their military rank. Although the ban on connections with railway companies was repealed in 1844, these features have remained unaltered. The Railway Inspectorate's first report in 1841 demanded that their powers of regulation be

An earlier version of this chapter appeared as a joint paper with Sir Christopher Foster: 'The Political Economy of Regulation: Interests, Ideology, Voters and the UK Regulation of Railways Act 1844', *Public Administration*, 70 (1992), 313–31. Many thanks to my co-author, and also to colleagues at Stanford University and the 1991 meetings of the Public Choice Society, for comments on earlier versions; to computer support staff at Stanford and Warwick Universities for help with running a large and old data-set on SPSS and SAS; and to the editor and publishers of *Public Administration* for permission to republish material which has appeared there.

strengthened, a demand partly met in 1842. The companies had set up a Railway Society in 1839. It did not last, but an *ad hoc* trade association met in 1841 under the leadership of George Hudson, a leading entrepreneur and promoter of company mergers, known in his own time as the 'Railway King'. To head off government-imposed safety regulation, it drafted common safety rules for its member companies. No permanent organization was set up. In 1842 the Railway Clearing House was created to deal with inter-company allocation of revenues. It survived until 1923, and in an attenuated form until 1963. It had to process a remarkable volume of information about the movement of goods and passengers between companies, and patrolled the companies to try to ensure that they co-operated.[2] Perhaps because of these considerable burdens, it did not become a lobbying organization. In 1844 the directors of the Liverpool & Manchester Railway deplored the lack of 'a *professional advocate* in the House of Commons, as was the practice with the West India Interest, the Canadian Interests, &C'.[3] A stable Railway Companies' Association, run through the Railway Clearing House, emerged in 1867. Thus by then both the regulators and the regulated had evolved interest groups which interacted in a corporatist way.

The radical Regulation of Railways Act 1844 (7 & 8 Vict. c85) was enacted by W. E. Gladstone, President of the Board of Trade, despite fierce opposition from the railway companies led by Hudson. Section 1 of the Act gave Parliament the power, from 21 years after its passage, to cap the rates of any new line which was earning more than 10 per cent a year on the value of its paid-up stock. Section 2 empowered Parliament, after the same period of time, to nationalize any new railway company which was making over 10 per cent annual profits. Section 6, which was to apply to any company, old or new, whenever it sought new parliamentary powers, required every company to run at least one train each way every weekday which stopped at every station and carried third-class passengers in covered accommodation with seats at an average speed (including stops) of not less than 12 m.p.h. and a fare of not more than 1d. a mile. Children under 3 must travel free; those between 3 and 12 at half price; and each passenger must be given a free baggage allowance of ½ cwt. The Act introduced a change in Private Bill procedure to enable the Board of Trade to scrutinize all railway bills affecting the same part of the country together, and to decide which route it was most in the public interest to permit.[4] Other sections imposed obligations on the companies to carry the mail (at any safe speed not over 27 m.p.h.); to carry troops or police; to allow public telegraph lines to be erected along their rights-of-way; and to open their own telegraph systems to public use.

As might be expected, the 'Parliamentary trains' mandated by section 6 tended to leave their starting-points around 6 a.m. and companies complied with the section as minimally as possible. ('The idiot who, in railway carriages, | Scribbles on window-panes, | We only suffer | to ride on a buffer | of *Parliamentary trains!*')[5] This pattern of service was still visible in the timetable of British Railways in 1962, immediately before the Beeching cuts.[6]

The origins of railway regulation are of interest for several reasons.

1. Gladstone's Bill was the grandfather of Anglo-American regulation of natural monopolies. It was the model for the US 1887 Interstate Commerce Act, which itself became the model for subsequent regulation in the USA.[7] There has been far more interest in the political economy of regulation in the USA than in the UK, among practitioners and academics alike. The hypotheses to be described shortly have mostly been developed by Americans on American data; here they can be tested on an event of founding importance for regulation on both sides of the Atlantic. The politics of regulation has only recently been rediscovered in the UK. Since large-scale privatization of public services began in 1979, it has become painfully clear that privatization of a public monopoly entails creating either an unregulated private monopoly or a regulatory framework. The political economy of regulation has been reimported from the USA, with little recognition that it was a British invention in the first place. Yet the Victorian pattern of railway regulation had lain there almost undisturbed for a century and a half. The 1844 Act was supplemented but not abandoned; its basic pattern of price and quantity regulation was not abolished until the Transport Act 1960. The safety regulation survives to this day, and investigations into railway accidents are still conducted by retired officers of the Royal Engineers. Not until 1992 was the Railway Inspectorate fully incorporated into the Health and Safety Executive.[8] Between 1844 and 1923 there were further highly publicized attempts to tighten the regulation of railway safety and/or

of rates. *Bradshaw's Railway Almanack* published a list of the 'railway interest'—MPs and peers who were railway directors and who could be relied upon to oppose regulation—every year from 1847 until 1923. But few scholars have studied them.[9]

2. Almost every railway historian assumes that the 1844 Act was important and beneficial; almost every economic historian has argued that it was misconceived but, fortunately, unimportant because it was emasculated in Parliament.[10] Railway historians are usually amateurs; economic historians usually professionals, and the second can be witheringly sarcastic about the quality of evidence and argument used by the first.[11] I shall argue that in this case the railway historians are right and the economic historians wrong.

3. Regulation is a test-bed for theories derived from political economy. We shall consider four schools and seven hypotheses. (*a*) Marxism, or more broadly structuralism, argues that politicians' actions are determined by their economic role. Note that this assumption is common to Marxists and to their ideological opponents, (*b*) the followers of Sir Lewis Namier. Marxists and Namierites agree that political actors are driven by their economic roles, but differ at the level of analysis (macro for Marxists and micro for Namierites). (*c*) Modern normative political economy ('public choice') has several strands. Buchanan and others insist that politicians should be viewed as maximizing their probability of re-election, not the public (dis)interestedness of their policies. Olson predicts that over time politics in a democracy will become dominated by 'distributional coalitions' of producer-group interests; Olson's theory implies that coalitions of capital make more formidable special interests than coalitions of labour. Tullock and others add that interests can be expected to engage in continuous rent-seeking: that is, use resources to lobby for protected monopolies or other means of securing economic rent.[12] (*d*) The recent manifesto edited by Alt and Shepsle on behalf of 'positive political economy' (hereafter PPE) seeks to distance PPE both from 'atheoretical . . . thick historical description' and from the normative orientation of public choice. PPE 'seeks out principles and propositions against which actual experience can be compared in order to understand and explain, not judge, that performance'.[13] For our case-study, the crucial distinction is that public-choice analysts assume that legislators are driven wholly or largely by the re-election imperative,

whereas PPE is agnostic on their motives. Our hypothesis testing is intended to distinguish among the different schools of political economy.

There clearly is something odd about the Parliament of 1841–7. The Tories, the party of agriculture and protection, held a comfortable majority; and yet a third of them voted with Peel in 1846 to repeal the corn laws. This action damaged the economic interest of many Tory MPs and their constituents, and it destroyed the Tory Party as a serious contender for power for a generation. Why should MPs act so apparently self-destructively? Analogously, the 3rd Reading of the railways Act was unopposed even by the railway interest. And it has an extra twist which repeal of the Corn Laws does not. The ideology of classical economics, in which the bureaucrats of the Board of Trade were soaked and to which Peel and Gladstone were both converted,[14] strongly favoured free trade, but not regulation. Thus our case poses stiff challenges to orthodox political economy.

We will test seven hypotheses about the motives for regulation.

(1) The *hegemonic ideology* thesis endorses Marx's dictum that in every era the ruling ideas are the ideas of the ruling class. So regulation, like the repeal of the Corn Laws, could be an ideological move associated with the triumph of classical economics. Not only Marxists are associated with this sort of idea[15] but we will call it Marxist for short.

(2) The *party interest* thesis argues that the parties represented bundles of socio-economic interests, and that the actions of Ministers and MPs were designed to forward their party's (and hence, by proxy, their socio-economic group's) interest. Again, 'Marxist' will be used as shorthand for a more comprehensive label.

(3) *Individual wealth-maximization* is consistent with the public choice or PPE approaches, but is most associated with Namierism. It hypothesizes that politicians act so as to make themselves rich, outside and inside Parliament.

(4) *Bureaucratic advancement* is most associated with public choice, but is consistent with PPE: it suggests that regulation is introduced by and for bureaucrats in order, among other things, to boost their pay and prestige.

(5) The *vote-motive* hypothesis suggests that politicians introduce regulation in order to win or gain votes at the next general

election. A variant of it insists that politicians vote for what
they perceive to be the interest of their district. The vote motive
hypothesis emanates from public choice and is consistent with
PPE.

(6) The *regulatory capture* hypothesis suggests that regulation is
introduced with the connivance of the industry to be regulated
to its own (at least ultimate) advantage. This also emanates
from public choice and is consistent with PPE.

(7) The *public interest* hypothesis is that politicians introduce regulation because they perceive it to be in the public interest.
Although assumed true by Whig historians, this idea is supported by none of the schools of political economy except PPE.

In summary:

Hypothesis	Consistent with
Hegemonic ideology	Marxism
Party interest	Marxism
Individual wealth-maximization	Namierism, public choice, PPE
Bureaucratic advancement	public choice, PPE
Vote motive (district interest)	public choice, PPE
Regulatory capture	public choice, PPE
Public interest	PPE

2. GLADSTONE'S REASONING

Every railway that wished to open to the public had first to obtain
a private Act. Parliament gave the company the right to purchase
land and operate across public highways; in return it laid down
maximum toll rates. Railway Acts were modelled on earlier acts
authorizing entrepreneurs to build turnpike roads. At first, MPs
assumed that the railways would, like turnpike roads, provide the
track, and others would run goods and passenger vehicles on them.
Therefore, railways' tolls for track use were regulated, but the
charges for carriage were not. The Stockton & Darlington Railway
(1825) did indeed operate as a turnpike on rails for passenger traffic, but it carried freight itself. Soon after the first trunk line, the
Liverpool & Manchester Railway, opened in 1830, it became clear
that the turnpike model was impracticable: technically, because

increasing speeds and long braking distances meant that some single body had to be responsible for deciding when a train could enter a section of track; and economically, because anybody who tried to put a private locomotive on the track would be at the mercy of the railway company as soon as he ran out of water. In 1841 the Officers of the Railway Department argued bluntly.

That Railway Companies using locomotive power possess a practical monopoly for the conveyance of passengers . . . the result of circumstances contemplated neither by the Legislature nor by the Companies themselves. . . . under these circumstances, the Legislature is bound to provide that the public interests shall not suffer from the mistaken view taken in the infancy of the science of locomotion, and that for this purpose the powerful monopolies, in whose hands a large and increasing portion of the internal communication of the country is placed, should be subjected to the supervision and control of the Board of Trade.[16]

The Railway Department, unlike the Board of Trade proper, was not a nursery of classical economics. But Gladstone, the minister responsible *de facto* during 1841–3, and *de jure* during 1843–5, sympathized with his officials.

Gladstone's classical education did not expose him to economics or Liberalism. He entered politics as a Tory determined to protect the Church of England as a state church. Church and state dominated his life from his entry into Parliament in 1832 until he resigned from Peel's cabinet over a grant to the Catholic seminary in Maynooth in 1845. Peel gave him a junior government job in 1834–5, and in 1841 offered him the Vice-Presidency of the Board of Trade. This disappointed Gladstone, who wanted to govern Ireland: 'the science of politics deals with the government of men, but I am set to govern packages'.[17] Gladstone's education in free trade, regulation, and lobbying continued intensively through his four years in office. His colleague Sir James Graham, the Home Secretary, said 'Gladstone could do in four hours what it took any other man sixteen to do, and he worked sixteen hours a day.'[18] In what follows it is important to remember that trade policy dominated neither his time nor his emotions.

Gladstone's conversion to free trade gave him no reason to oppose regulation. During the tariff reductions of 1842 he was confronted by aggrieved producer-groups who stood to lose their monopoly rents: 'B of Trade and House 12 3/4—6 3/4 and 9 1/4–1 1/2 [i.e. 12.45 pm to 6.45 pm and 9.15 pm to 1.30 am]. Dined at

Abp of Yorks. Copper, Tin, Zinc, Salmon, Timber, Oil, Saltmeat, all are to be ruined, and all in arms.'[19] Perhaps out of embarrassment at his father's role as a lobbyist on behalf of West Indian sugar (and thus by proxy of slave-holding), Gladstone detested lobbyists. In 1844, when the railway companies lobbied Peel against Gladstone's bill, Gladstone published a sharp exchange of letters with them, which forced them to admit that the delegation had not been authorized by the Boards of the railways represented.[20]

Gladstone's bill of 1844 was 'a personal rather than a departmental measure' disliked by the rest of the Cabinet: only Peel spoke in Parliament in Gladstone's support.[21] The Railway Department had a reform agenda, mostly concerning safety. Their annual reports noted that, although railways were the safest means of travel, yet many accidents were due to avoidable human error or inadequate equipment. They drew attention to an accident on the Great Western Railway at Sonning, near Reading, on Christmas Eve 1941. A train was derailed after hitting a landslip. The passengers in the open third-class carriages were thrown out, and eight killed. This gave rise to pressure from the department on railways to enclose their third-class carriages and provide buffers.[22] However, the immediate impetus for the Bill, and the strategy for getting it carried, were due to Gladstone alone. He ascribed the need for regulation to 'the great and almost unparalleled extent of capital unemployed' in Britain. Early railways had seemed to be dubious investments. By 1844 they had proved themselves technically and economically and they were earning large dividends. Therefore there was a sudden rush to promote new schemes, and the private Bill Office had more railway bills in hand than ever before. Gladstone did not think that the entry of new railway companies would bring the railway business into competitive equilibrium. Rather, if Parliament were to allow competing routes between the same towns, 'it would afford facilities to exaction . . . an increase of the evil . . . a mere multiplication of monopoly'.[23] Gladstone proposed the rate-capping and nationalization powers that appeared in the final Act, although in a more draconian form.

Gladstone's economic reasoning was sophisticated, especially for a self-taught politician writing before Cournot's work on oligopoly was known in the English-speaking world. Most companies were discriminating monopolists.[24] They charged fares which guaranteed a substantial operating profit, but which just undercut stage-coach fares. They were reluctant to put third-class coaches on first- and second-class trains for fear that passengers would leak on to the cheaper coaches. They negotiated exclusive deals with some road carriers to take passengers and goods to places not on the railway, and excluded others from station yards or refused to carry their goods.[25] Gladstone perceived that it was difficult or impossible to enforce competitive behaviour by direct regulation. It was also unrealistic to expect competition between companies to do the job. A promise by a new company to provide effective competition should be treated with suspicion because such companies' Acts might be 'improperly used as efficient instruments of extortion against the subsisting Companies, to whom might be offered only the alternative of losing their traffic or of buying off opposition.' Even if a rival company were to construct its line rather than let itself be bought off, Gladstone 'cannot conceive that two bodies, or even three, acting by compact executive Boards, and secure against the entrance of any other party into the field, will fail to combine together.' George Hudson, the Railway King, cheerfully admitted to Gladstone's Select Committee that he had offered the rival Leeds & Selby Railway a sum of money to 'shut up their line', which they had accepted.[26]

Using what would now be called game-theoretic reasoning, Gladstone concluded that the railway market was bound to fail. There were two games to consider: the game between an existing (natural monopolist) company and the government, and the game between an existing company and a new entrant. In the first game, the company was likely to be able to fend off attempts to regulate its rates directly because of information asymmetry. The company knew its full schedule of rates and the government did not; therefore attempts to regulate rates simply led to the company reformulating them in a slightly different form, so that regulators or plaintiffs had to start all over again. As to the second game, Gladstone saw further than Cournot. Companies would not simply adjust their production in response to each other's activities. Rather, they could be expected to collude and share monopoly rent: as they were 'acting by compact executive Boards' they could be expected to arrive at the co-operative (collusive) equilibrium in their Prisoners' Dilemma.[27] Gladstone therefore asserted 'the undoubted right and power of the State to promote the construc-

tion of new and competing Lines of Railway, as a means of protection to the Public against the consequences of the virtual
monopoly which former Acts have called into existence'.[28]

3. GLADSTONE'S TACTICS

Gladstone began by appointing a Select Committee on Railways,
on to which he co-opted his Whig predecessor, Henry Labouchere,
who sided with Gladstone throughout, and two railway directors,
who did not.[29] Between March and June 1844, the Select
Committee produced six reports and took minutes of evidence
which occupy 682 pages of the large-format *Parliamentary Papers*.
All evidence suggests that the enquiry was dominated by Gladstone
from start to finish. According to one of the two railway-interest
members of the Committee, Gladstone came to it with a ' "hypothetical outline", which he fully intended to cram down their
throats'. This was a draft agreement between the government and
the railway companies, which, according to Gladstone, offered
some advantage for both sides. He then 'dressed his fly very skil-
fully', and persuaded some of the company chairmen who
appeared before the Committee to agree to it. But when two of
them refused to accept the draft agreement, 'it was then found to
be no more than an Indian-rubber body with gauze wings'. When
Hudson refused to rise, 'the hypothetical outline was quite
blown'.[30]

Gladstone's hypothetical outline asked the railways to guarantee
'a means of communication for the poorer classes, in carriages protected from the weather, at a moderate charge'. These rules need
only apply to one train a day, and railways could carry other third-
class traffic (if any) by whatever arrangements they liked. He
offered in return '[t]he principle that competing lines, as such, and
without a legitimate traffic of their own, ought not to be encouraged when better arrangements can be made'.[31] The company
chairmen who appeared before the Committee failed to understand
this early corporatist bargain. Hudson was delighted at the offer of
protection from competition—'it will be a great boon to railway
property'—but appeared unprepared to accept that any interests
other than those of existing lines required protection. He was
obsessed with blocking the future East Coast Main Line from

King's Cross to York, which would eventually take the traffic away
from the roundabout route to York via Rugby, Derby, and
Normanton which he controlled. He did not appear to understand
Gladstone's proposal.[32]

After the companies had rejected the hypothetical outline,
Gladstone forced the Third Report of the Select Committee over
the objections of the railway-director members. This stated that the
railways' monopoly 'is . . . regarded, even at the present day, with
considerable jealousy by the Public at large', jealousy which could
be expected to grow 'if the profits of Railways generally should be
augmented in any very great degree'. Gladstone held two trump
cards. One was that the railways needed an Act to reverse a recent
rating (property tax) decision hostile to them. The other was that
many railways had been issuing illegal and unsecured 'loan notes'
over and above the debt they were allowed by their Acts to issue.
The companies needed, and Gladstone proposed, clauses in the
regulatory bill to legalize the notes that had been already issued.
Gladstone played these cards in order to get the parliamentary
train clause applied to all companies, old and new, without incur-
ring the accusation of retrospective legislation. Such an extension,
Gladstone silkily argued, was not confiscatory

as it rests upon the principle that the Companies affected by it are voluntary Suitors for the aid of the Legislature, to enable them, in some
instances, to legalise transactions which they have conducted without the
sanction of the law; in others to extend and enlarge, for their own benefit, the concerns in which they are engaged; and that it is open to those
Companies to accept the aid, with the conditions attached to it, or to
decline both the one and the other.[33]

The Bill which he introduced was much more hostile to the railway interest than the hypothetical outline. It contained detailed
terms for nationalization and rate-capping which gave wide executive powers to the Board of Trade. For instance, it was to have the
power to deduct money otherwise due to rate-capped or purchased
railways if it considered that their assets had been badly managed,
and the power to make 'such regulations . . . as shall appear to [it]
to be required for the public convenience, and necessary for securing to the public the full benefit of such revised scale of tolls, fares
and charges'.[34] After an unsuccessful attempt by the railway interest to have the Bill rejected without discussion, Gladstone introduced it with an aggressive speech. He complained that, in

discriminating against some road carriers, 'the Railroad had gone among individual traders very much like a triton among the minnows'. He evoked the spectacle of a sinister interest combining railway directors and the 'deeper power in the opposition, and he might as well use plain language . . . Parliamentary agents and solicitors'. He ridiculed the claims of the railway interest that the Bill was 'a shock' to property, and pointed out that railway shares had continued to rise since the Third Report announced Gladstone's intention to legislate, and even since the companies petition to Peel to withdraw the bill had been rejected. He concluded:

I shrunk from a contest with Railway Companies . . . but being persuaded that justice is not with them, but against them . . . I do not shrink from the contest. I say that although Railway Companies are powerful, I do not think they have mounted so high, or that Parliament has yet sunk so low, that at their bidding you shall refuse your sanction to this bill. . . . (Loud cheering).[35]

The Second Reading was carried by 186 to 98—'a satisfactory division'.[36] However, Gladstone was forced to enter further discussions with Hudson, in order to preserve the bill's chances of passing in the 1844 session before Parliament rose in August to shoot grouse.[37] In Committee, Gladstone withdrew the clauses giving the Board of Trade executive power over nationalized and rate-capped companies, and the Bill passed without a division. The rate regulation and state purchase powers remained, but with a declaratory statement that they could not be triggered except by Act of Parliament and that it was not the Act's intention that nationalized companies should compete against existing private ones.[38] By comparison with his Bill, Gladstone had certainly suffered a defeat, and it is this defeat which has led economic historians to conclude that the Act was a dead letter. The sophisticated proposals of the Bill might have enabled the government to enforce regulation in spite of the information advantages the companies had; the version enacted did not. Even so, the knowledge that the state control plans remained must have influenced rational railway investors and managers. One sure way of avoiding nationalization would be to ensure that your rate of return remained below 10 per cent; a way to ensure that in turn was to build unprofitable branch-lines, as occurred conspicuously in late Victorian times, and avoid regulation by over-capitalization. The history of British railways from

1844 to 1923 may therefore be evidence for the Averch–Johnson hypothesis that regulated industries evade the effects of regulation by over-capitalization. Furthermore, by comparison with his start-ing position, the hypothetical outline, Gladstone had gained more regulation. The rate revision power was in the hypothetical outline, but the state purchase power was not. The powers relating to the telegraph, also absent from the hypothetical outline, passed unchallenged, perhaps because there was no distributional coali-tion of telegraph manufacturers and operators. The removal of local MPs from the pork-barrel of Private Bills affecting their con-stituencies also passed unchallenged.

In 1864, when the opportunity to purchase or rate-cap railways under the 1844 Act was imminent, Gladstone was Chancellor of the Exchequer in a Liberal government. He still had no ideological objection to state purchase, and he drew up a scheme for imple-menting his own legislation. But the government did not pursue it.[39]

We now turn to evaluating the hypotheses. Hegemonic ideology may explain the repeal of the Corn Laws (though even here it faces problems[40]), but not railway regulation. The classical economists had no clear prescription for regulation of natural monopoly. For some, Gladstone's Bill was a relic of an earlier age:

It has seldom been our lot to see . . . such a mass of antiquated, exploded, and objectionable principle as we find in Mr Gladstone's Railway Bill now before us—involving such a total disregard to all the great principles preached by himself and, we may say, by every other public man of emi-nence for the last half century. Mr Gladstone here asks his followers to accompany [him] back at least a century.[41]

Others saw that, even within the framework of classical econom-ics, there was a case for the regulation of natural monopoly. The most prescient was James Morrison MP, who made a cogent speech in favour of railway regulation in 1836, in which he developed classical economic thinking in application to natural monopoly.[42] However, Gladstone did not acknowledge Morrison in 1844, and there is no reference to Morrison in his diaries during the Peel Administration. Even if he was influenced by Morrison, Morrison's views were not hegemonic ideology. Party interest is not supported: the Bill was not a party measure and the Cabinet did not support Gladstone strongly. (The party profile of votes on the Bill is examined in the next section.) Individual wealth maximization is not supported either. Theoretically, those with interests in every industry other than railways stood to gain from railway regulation; but the gain to any individual is much too small to account for his or her behaviour. It would be ludicrous to apply it to Gladstone. By 2 March 1844 ('An awful day') he had already threatened to resign from Peel's government over Maynooth. On 8 July, the same day as his aggressive speech introducing the Railways Bill, Gladstone discussed the timing of his future resignation with Peel; he duly resigned in February 1845.[43] A long conversation between Gladstone and Peel, recorded by Gladstone immediately after Peel's resignation, shows that Peel had no wish to be re-elected either.[44] These facts also falsify the vote-motive hypothesis. Most discussion in the Second Reading debate revolved around the parliamentary train clause, and MPs regaled the Commons with stories of the horrible things that had happened to their constituents. But most third-class travellers did not have the vote. The vote-motive hypothesis cannot be rescued, for either Gladstone or Peel, by asserting that they were maximizing their long-run probability of re-election. It could be said that Gladstone was nurturing a long-run reputation for probity, but this cannot be fitted into public-choice assumptions about politicians' motives without making them vacuous. The bureaucratic hypothesis gets some support from the evidence. Gladstone's bureau, the Railway Department, had led the pressure for safety regulation and had made, in its report of 1841, the second coherent economic case for regulation. However, in 1844 Gladstone led them rather than *vice versa*. Bureaucratic self-advancement may plausibly explain tariff and sanitary policy,[45] but not railway policy. The regulatory capture hypothesis is not supported. Gladstone actually offered the companies a 'capture', that is to say a corporatist bargain, in the hypothetical outline. But the companies rejected the deal. So Gladstone drew up a fiercely interventionist Bill, which became a moderately interventionist Act. The companies admittedly saw off the clauses they most disliked; but if regulatory capture were true, they would have been able to see off the rest as well. The public-interest hypothesis stands as the most correct of those examined. The case of Gladstone directly contradicts the public-choice assumption that politicians are maximizers of their re-election chances, rather than of the public interest as they see it.

4. AN ANALYSIS OF THE VOTES ON THE
SECOND READING

In this section five of our seven hypotheses will be tested against
MPs' votes (the votes cannot help evaluate the bureaucratic or regulatory capture hypotheses). MPs are assumed to be motivated by
some mixture of ideology, party interest, personal interest, constituency interest, and (their perception of the) public interest.
These are often concurrent and intercorrelated, but the data help
us to distinguish among them. Personal interest may be measured
both by MPs' personal status (their wealth, connection with the
land, and relationship to the aristocracy) and by their known economic interests. Constituency interest may be measured by constituencies' location, how rural they were, and the number of
voters. The data do not directly measure MPs' dependence on constituency patrons—as Namierites insist, this was still a marked feature of politics at the time, Gladstone's own constituency of
Newark being a case in point.[46] However constituency size is a
rough surrogate: not all small boroughs were rotten, but all rotten
boroughs were small.

Of the 188 votes (including tellers) in favour of the second reading of Gladstone's Bill, 141 came from Conservatives and 47 from
Liberals; of the 101 votes against, 29 were from Conservatives and
72 from Liberals.[47] Thus both parties were divided, but the proportion of Liberals who voted in favour was higher than the proportion of Conservatives who voted against. Table 7.1 shows a
cross-tabulation of vote by party, and also of vote by a more
detailed party breakdown. 'Peelites' are those who voted with Peel
to repeal the Corn Laws in 1846, the act that splintered the
Conservative Party. A number of them including Gladstone later
joined the Liberal Party. The labelling of Liberals is mostly derived
from their self-description in *Dod's Parliamentary Companion*. It is
possible to regard this five-way party breakdown as a unidimen-
sional measure of radicalism, with the non-Peelite Conservatives
on the right and the Radical Reformers and Repealers on the left.
These terms must of course be handled with great care. However,
W. O. Aydelotte has collected data on 186 Commons divisions in
the 1841–7 Parliament: 120 of them can be shown by Guttman
scaling to lie on one dimension such that propositions and MPs

TABLE 7.1. *Votes on the Second Reading of the Railway Bill, 11 July 1884, by party* (column percentages in brackets)

A. Two-party breakdown

	Party		
	Conservative	Liberal	Total
Positive vote	141	47	188
	(82.9)	(39.5)	(65.1)
Negative vote	29	72	101
	(17.1)	(60.5)	(34.9)
TOTAL	170	119	289
	(58.8)	(41.2)	(100.0)

B. Five-party breakdown

	Party					
	Non-Peelite Cons.	Peelite	Whig-Liberal	Reformer	Repealer	Total
Positive vote	91	50	28	18	1	188
	(77.8)	(94.3)	(37.3)	(42.9)	(50.0)	(65.1)
Negative vote	26	3	47	24	1	101
	(22.2)	(5.7)	(62.7)	(57.1)	(50.0)	(34.9)
TOTAL	117	53	75	42	2	289
	(40.5)	(18.3)	(26.0)	(14.5)	(.7)	(100.0)

can be ranged from the most left-wing to the most right-wing. The technique involves showing that almost nobody who voted left on a more left-wing proposition voted right on a more right-wing one and *vice versa*.[48] This produced the ordinal variable BIGSCALE in Aydelotte's analysis. He finally produced no fewer than twenty-four Guttman scales, or ideological dimensions, out of the 186 divisions. MPs' votes on the Railways Bill are strongly associated with their positions on many of the scales. However, the Railways Bill vote is not itself one of the components of any of the scales.[49]

This is because, as Table 7.1 shows, the strongest partisans of the Bill were those who later became Peelites. On the BIGSCALE, the

Peelites appear as the more moderate or left-wing Tories and their protectionist rivals as the more extreme or right-wing. On issues which appear in the BIGSCALE and which divided the Tories, the Peelites were more likely to vote with the centrist Liberals than with the protectionists on their own side, as they did on the Repeal of the Corn Laws itself. There are other issues, especially related to factory reform, which displayed something of an alliance of right and left (Protectionists and Radical Reformers) against the centre. The Railways Bill does not fit this pattern: Table 7.1 shows that the opposition to it cannot be described as a coalition of right and left against the centre. As it is a component of none of Aydelotte's twenty-four Guttman scales, it did not fit well into any clear ideological dimension understood (even subconsciously) by MPs.

Table 7.2 lists the variables which were found to be related to MPs' votes.[50] The following groups were found to be significantly more likely to vote for the Bill than their respective opposites: those who did not have a connection with business or finance, and specifically with the railway, shipping, or dock industries; those who held or had held government office (in either party); the landed upper class; those whose election had been uncontested; those whose constituency was either in southern England or in Ireland;[51] those who sat for county seats (with small borough Members intermediate and large borough Members least favourable); and Peelites. Noteworthy variables found not to be significant at this stage included the number of voters per constituency (a measure of electoral and patronal pressure on Members), whether or not an MP was a lawyer (despite Gladstone's attack on them while introducing the Bill), and MPs' personal wealth.

Many of the significant variables simply repeat the same information derived in different ways. In particular, Tories were more prone to support the Bill than Liberals, and Tories were more likely to sit for southern seats, for county seats, and to be members of the upper classes. So are all the associations reported in Table 7.2 simply spurious? No, because when one variable affects another through a third, intervening one, it is not obvious which association is truly spurious. Different types of constituency elected MPs of different parties, who then took different lines on the Bill. Is party merely an intervening variable which should be disregarded? On this matter British and American intellectual traditions

TABLE 7.2. *Variables significantly associated with the vote on the Second Reading of the Railways Bill, 11 July 1844*

Variable name	Description	Degree of association (Spearman's rho)
ENCANWHT	Guttman scale on divisions ideologically related to Canada Wheat Bill, June 1843. Low value = 'left'	−.491
BIGSCALE	Guttman scale on 120 divisions between 1841 and 1947. Low value = 'left'	−.396
RAILWAY[a]	Had connection with railways	−.310
PEELITE	Whether a Conservative who voted with Peel to repeal the Corn Laws, May 1846	.291
BUSINT	Whether an active businessman	−.267
CONSTLOC	Location of seat: Ulster, rest of Ireland, southern England & Wales, Scotland, northern E & W	.225
CONTEST	Whether MP's election to the 1841 Parliament was contested	−.221
SOCINDEX	Whether landed and university–educated	.213
CONSUMM[b]	Type of seat: county, small borough, large borough	.185
SHIPPING[a]	Had connection with shipping and navigation	−.161
FINANCE[a]	Had interests in finance	−.125
DOCKS[a]	Had interests in docks	−.119
GOVTOFF	Had held government office by 1847	.117

[a] Variables shown are those found to have $p < .05$ on both Pearson chi-square and Spearman's rho.

[b] Interpreting the sign of the coefficients: on all dichotomous variables, 'Yes' was coded as 1 and 'No' as 2. For multi-valued variables the lowest code is for (the fullest) agreement with the description above or with the first of the descriptions given. Therefore, for example, a 'left' position on the Canada Wheat scale is significantly associated with a 'No' vote on the Railways Bill; voting with Peel on the Corn Laws is significantly associated with a 'Yes' vote on the Railways Bill.

diverge. The British tradition, despite Namier, is to regard party as fundamental and variables of the sort listed in Table 7.2 as showing nothing that is not already conveyed by knowing an MP's party. The American tradition, influenced by the extreme weakness of Congressional parties, is to regard party as not just an intervening variable but a transparent one. This model assumes that politicians respond to their districts' demands, not to party cues.

Table 7.3 therefore controls all the *prima facie* significant variables by party. This shows that the railway interest was indeed distinctive, and after controlling for party, is the most marked predictor for a Conservative to fail to support the Government. This is an association in the expected direction. The same is true of Conservative businessmen in general.[52] The other variables which remain significant fall into four groups. CONSTLOC, and probably SOCINDEX, reflect the fact that Conservative MPs from certain parts of the country were more likely to support the Bill than others. Support for the Bill was strongest in Ireland and in southern England, and weakest in northern England. PEELITE and GOVTOFF reflect the fact that the Bill appealed more to government-minded than to backbench MPs. The reasons are probably partly ideological and partly administrative. The scales show that attitudes to

TABLE 7.3. *Variables significantly associated with Railways Bill vote for MPs of at least one party after controlling for party*

Variable name	Degree of association (rho) for Conservatives	Degree of association (rho) for Liberals
RAILWAY[a]	−.450	n.s.
CONSTLOC	.351	n.s.
BIGSCALE	n.s.	−.245
ENCANWHT	−.208	−.238
BUSINT	−.236	n.s.
GOVTOFF	.218	n.s.
PEELITE	.204	n.a.
CONTEST	−.164	n.s.
SOCINDEX	.157	n.s.

Notes: For descriptions of variables, significance tests and interpretation of sign of coefficients, see key to Table 7.2.
n.s. = not significant; n.a. = not applicable.

railway regulation remained associated with attitudes to other issues in ways which are not simply captured by party labels, and are the only variables that remain significant for Liberals alone. Finally, CONTEST shows that Conservatives who had not faced an election were significantly more likely to support the Bill than those who had.

Tables 7.2 and 7.3 ensure continuity with previous discussions, which have used similar bivariate methods. However, the correct way to evaluate the relative weights of a large number of interconnected independent variables on a single variable is by multiple regression analysis. Conventional multiple regression cannot be used in this case, because the dependent variable—vote on the Railway Bill—is dichotomous. All the variables in Table 7.2 were therefore entered as independent variables in a logit model with DIV059 as the dependent variable. Only five were significant, in the following order: ENCANWHT, RAILWAY, CONTEST, PEELITE, and CONST-LOC.[53] The logit analysis thus tends to support the American rather than the British approach, since party disappears as a significant predictor of vote. What is left is, in descending order of significance:

(1) a tendency for those who favoured reduction in trade barriers to oppose railway regulation;
(2) interest in the railway industry—those with the interest opposed regulation;
(3) whether or not the MP faced a contest in 1841—those who had not were more favourable to regulation;
(4) those Conservatives who joined Peel in 1846 were more pro-regulation than other MPs;
(5) MPs for rural areas were more pro-regulation than those from industrial areas.

Findings (2) and (5) are consistent with findings on the politics of railway regulation reported elsewhere.[54] People who dwell in the country are more likely than those who live in cities to be confronted with railways' monopolistic behaviour. A passenger or goods forwarder in a city is more likely than one in the countryside to have more than one railway to choose from. So discriminating monopolist railways will offer more attractive fares and charges to people in towns. This was already happening in 1844, according to witnesses at Gladstone's Select Committee.

Of our hypotheses, hegemonic ideology gets some support from the significance of ENCANWHT in the logit. But note that the railway vote did not align sufficiently with other votes to get on to any of Aydelotte's Guttman scales. Party interest disappears as a significant explanatory variable in the logit analysis. Wealth maximization is confirmed by the behaviour of the railway interest. Constituency interest is confirmed by the significance of location and the rurality of seats. It is harder to assess how far MPs were motivated by public-interest considerations. However, we interpret the strong showing of the variable PEELITE in these terms: Peelites, by definition, are those who supported an action which they knew would destroy their own party and in many cases damage their chances of re-election. That action is hard to interpret except in perceived public-interest terms. (Recall that 'Peelite' is defined as 'Conservative who voted with Peel to repeal the Corn Laws in 1846': thus they are defined in relation to an event which had not yet taken place.)

5. CONCLUSION

In 1886, when another controversial railway regulation bill was before Parliament, the *Aberdeen Daily Free Press* perceived that 'Powerful as the railway interest is it has to deal, in the House of Commons, with a tribunal elected by constituencies in every one of which the predominating interest, with regard to railways, is that rates and fares should be as low as possible'.[55] This was just as true in 1844. Peel and Gladstone launched fierce attacks on the railway interest, with Gladstone making a powerful appeal to MPs' self-esteem. In the weeks between the Bill and the Act, the companies clawed back some of the ground they had lost. This reflects a common pattern of regulatory politics: regulated industries are typically more successful in negotiating with the executive than in securing favourable legislation. But they did worse than if they had accepted Gladstone's hypothetical outline. Olson's *Rise and Decline of Nations* argues that normal politics is the politics of distributional coalitions, in which producer groups secure monopoly privileges from governments at the expense of consumers. If so, the politics of railway regulation is not normal politics, and the Administration of 1841–6 was not a normal administration.

Our test of seven hypotheses about the origins of regulation has shown that the only one which is strongly supported is that both Gladstone and the MPs who voted on his bill were moved by their perceptions of the public interest. This is both a very old-fashioned and a very novel conclusion. Of the schools of political economy we have reviewed, the only one which can encompass such an idea is the positive political economy thesis (PPE) associated with Alt and Shepsle and some of their fellow-contributors and co-authors (notably R. Bates, P. Ordeshook, and B. Weingast). The contrast between PPE and public choice is instructive. PPE is both broader and weaker than public choice: broader, because it encompasses the public-choice hypotheses about political motivations and others besides; weaker, because it cannot predict which set of motives are dominant in any particular case. Ours is the sort of case in which standard public choice has been in trouble before. Faced with the apparently un-selfinterested behaviour of a constitution-maker like James Madison, it can only suppose that Madison's utility maxim and incorporated 'posthumous deference'.[56] Posterity is deferential to Gladstone and to Peel, but to write posthumous deference into their utility functions is to remove all predictability from them. It is more illuminating to return to an older rational-choice perspective and to conclude that Gladstone rationally did what he thought best advanced the public interest.

NOTES

1. See e.g. S. Popkin, *The Rational Peasant: The Political Economy of Rural Society in Vietnam* (Berkeley, Calif.: University of California Press, 1979); G. W. Cox, *The Efficient Secret: The Cabinet and the Development of Political Parties in Victorian England* (Cambridge: Cambridge University Press, 1987). The latter, together with other work by similarly minded writers, is discussed in I. McLean, 'Rational Choice and the Victorian Voter', *Political Studies*, 40 (1992), 496–515.
2. See P. S. Bagwell, *The Railway Clearing House in the British Economy 1842–1922* (London: Allen & Unwin, 1968).
3. Quoted by G. Alderman, *The Railway Interest* (Leicester: Leicester University Press, 1973), 273; emphasis in original.
4. This procedure was extended to all Private Bills in 1855. By removing local MPs from considering private bills affecting their constituencies, it considerably reduced the power of the pork-barrel: see McLean, 'Rational choice', 502.

5. W. S. Gilbert, from *The Mikado* (1885). The stanza comes from the song in which the Mikado explains that his 'object all-sublime' is to 'let the punishment fit the crime, the punishment fit the crime'.

6. Until the Beeching cuts in 1963 there was a pattern of daily trains starting from railway centres early in the morning and calling at all wayside stations—sometimes being the only train of the day to call. For examples see the 06.50 Edinburgh to Oban, 06.44 Edinburgh to Carlisle via Hawick, and 06.53 Edinburgh to Berwick-upon-Tweed, in *British Railways—Scottish Region Timetable September 1961–June 1962*, Tables 20, 23, and 28. This pattern of service cannot possibly have reflected contemporary demand. Any traffic from Tynehead or Grantshouse would have been to Edinburgh in the morning and from Edinburgh in the evening. Therefore, I interpret these services as the fossilized remains of Parliamentary trains.

7. C. Foster, *Privatisation, Public Enterprise and the Regulation of Natural Monopoly* (Oxford: Blackwell, 1992), ch. 1.

8. Other aspects of railway regulation due to the Railway Clauses Consolidation Act 1845 have been equally long-lived. The penalty imposed by the 1845 Act of forty shillings for leaving a gate across a railway unlocked, still to be seen on thousands of cast-iron signs on gates and bathroom doors, was repealed only by the Transport and Works Act 1992.

9. But see Alderman, *Railway Interest*; H. Parris, *Government and the Railways in the 19th century* (London: Routledge, 1965); W. C. Lubenow, *The Politics of Government Growth: Early Victorian Attitudes towards State Intervention 1833–1848* (Newton Abbot: David & Charles, 1971); G. R. Hawke, *Railways and Economic Growth in England and Wales 1840–1870* (Oxford: Clarendon Press, 1970); P. M. Williams, 'Public Opinion and the Railway Rates Question in 1886', *English Historical Review*, 67 (1952), 37–73. The first study of railway regulation by a modern economist is Foster, *Privatisation*, chs. 1 and 2. Studies of early railway management include T. R. Gourvish, *Mark Huish and the London & North Western Railway* (Leicester: Leicester University Press, 1972) and R. Kostal, 'Common Law, Common Lawyers and the English Railway Industry 1830–80: A Study in the History of Law and Industrial Capitalism' (D.Phil. thesis, Oxford, 1989). Though neither explicitly considers the 1844 Act, they illustrate the divergence of interest both within the railway industry (between trunk companies charging high fares in an inelastic portion of the demand curve and local companies in working-class districts charging low fares in an elastic portion, for instance) and between railway operators and those they depended on, such as their lawyers and the courts, with whom they clearly suffered a principal–agent problem.

10. For a representative of the first view see C. H. Ellis, *British Railway History 1830–1876* (London: Allen & Unwin, 1954), 128–31. Representatives of the second include Alderman, *Railway Interest*, 17 and Lubenow, *Government Growth*, 114–16, 182. Lubenow's argument depends crucially on his assumption that the Railway Inspectorate could not interfere in the operations of the companies; but Parris, *Government and the Railways*, 93–9, shows that this assumption is false, though not until the 1890s did the Inspectorate have formal powers of enforcement. Foster, *Privatisation* is the first economist to see any merit in Gladstone's Bill.

11. See 'The Reputation of Dr. Lardner', in Hawke, *Railways and Economic Growth*, 93–9.

12. J. M. Buchanan, *Liberty, Market and State: Political Economy in the 1980s* (Brighton: Wheatsheaf, 1986); M. Olson, *The Rise and Decline of Nations* (New Haven, Conn.: Yale University Press, 1982), chs. 1–3; C. K. Rowley, R. D. Tollison, and G. Tullock, *The Political Economy of Rent-Seeking* (Dordrecht: Kluwer, 1987).

13. J. E. Alt and K. A. Shepsle (eds.), *Perspectives on Positive Political Economy* (Cambridge: Cambridge University Press, 1990), 1–2.

14. See L. Brown, *The Board of Trade and the Free Trade Movement 1830–1842* (Oxford: Clarendon Press, 1958), 20–33, 214–31; E. J. Feuchtwanger, *Gladstone* (London: Macmillan, 2nd edn., 1989), 43; R. Shannon, *Gladstone*, i. *1809–1865* (London: Hamish Hamilton, 1982), 117–20.

15. A non-Marxist exponent of hegemonic ideology is S. Krasner, 'State Power and the Structure of International Trade', *World Politics*, 28 (1976), 317–47.

16. *Report of the Officers of the Railway Department to the Rt. Hon. the President of the Board of Trade, Parliamentary Papers, House of Commons, 1841 First Session, vol. xxv.*

17. Quoted by Feuchtwanger, *Gladstone*, 41.

18. Quoted by Shannon, *Gladstone*, 115–16.

19. Gladstone, diary for 15 Mar. 1842. In M. R. D. Foot and H. G. C. Matthew (eds.), *The Gladstone Diaries*, iii. *1840–1847* (Oxford: Clarendon Press, 1974), 187.

20. *Copies of any Memorial to Sir Robert Peel, by certain Directors and others connected with Railway Companies, against the Railways Bill now before this House; and of any Correspondence thereupon between the Board of Trade and the aforesaid Memorialists*, P.P. 1844, xli, Gladstone wrote of the deputation: 'My temper was moved by the proceedings of the Railway people today: & a kind of sediment of anger remained long after, though the opportunity was really a good one for discipline': *Gladstone Diaries*, 3 July 1844.

21. Parris, *Government and the Railways*, 55–6; Hansard, 3rd ser. vol. 76, col. 478.
22. Parris, *Government and the Railways*, 45–6; Ellis, *British Railway History*, 95, 130.
23. Hansard, 3rd ser., vol. 72, cols. 232–6.
24. Hawke, *Railways and Economic Growth*, 360; Gourvish, *Mark Huish*, 34–44, 71. Parliament and the courts both tried to curb railways' price discrimination—the former in the Railway Clauses Consolidation Act 1845 and the latter in the *Pickford* v. *Grand Junction Railway* case (on which see also Kostal, 'Common Law', ch. 5). Both failed.
25. For ample evidence on these practices, see *Fifth Report of the Select Committee on Railways, Minutes of Evidence*, P.P. 1844), xi.
26. *Fifth Report*, Report, p. xii; Minutes of Evidence, p. 333, q. 4395: P.P. 1844, xi.
27. For the railways' strategies in the first game see the sources cited in the previous notes in this paragraph. The characterization of the second as a Prisoners' Dilemma assumes that each railway's ordering of the outcomes is (1) You keep prices high, I cut them; (2) Both of us keep them high; (3) Both of us cut them; (4) You cut prices, I keep them high.
28. *Fifth Report*, p. xii.
29. Hansard, 3rd ser., vol. 72, cols. 232–55, 286–95. 471.
30. Thomas Gisborne, MP, 11 July 1844: Hansard, 3rd ser., vol. 76, col. 663.
31. 'Hypothetical Outline of Considerations which may be give to, and asked from, Railway Companies, as equivalents in an amicable Agreement', Appendix to *Fifth Report*, P.P. 1844, XI. See Parris, *Government and the Railways*, 77–80. Parris sees the importance of 'the doctrine of "equivalents" ' as an early piece of corporatism, but is too tentative in his attribution of it to Gladstone.
32. *Fifth Report*, Minutes of Evidence, 320–33, qq. 4203–4395. Quotation from q. 4203: P.P. 1844, XI.
33. *Third Report* and *Fifth Report* P.P. 1844, XI.
34. A Bill to attach certain conditions to the construction of future Railways . . . and for other purposes in relation to Railways: quoted at cl. 6; see also cl. 2, 9, 10, 11. P.P. 1844, IV, 415–35.
35. Hansard, 3rd ser., vol. 76, cols. 465–509, quoted at 489, 502, 508–9.
36. *Gladstone Diaries*, 11 July 1844.
37. R. S. Lambert, *The Railway King* (London: Allen & Unwin, 2nd edn., 1964), 106–7; F. Hyde, *Mr Gladstone at the Board of Trade* (London: Cobden-Sanderson, 1934), 159–77. On 5 July Gladstone wrote of the railway interest: 'More blind and unreasonable conduct I have never yet known. . . . But from me, those who are leading this movement

... will not obtain one jot or tittle of concession'. (Hyde, *Gladstone*, 177). By the end of the month he had had to give several jots and many tittles, probably because Peel was not prepared to back a fight.

38. 7 & 8 Vict. cap. 85 s. 4.
39. H. C. G. Matthew, *Gladstone 1809–1874* (Oxford: Clarendon Press, 1986), 119.
40. T. McKeown, 'The Politics of Corn Law Repeal', *British Journal of Political Science*, 19 (1989), 353–80; I. McLean, ' "The Politics of Corn Law Repeal": A Comment', *British Journal of Political Science*, 20 (1990), 279–81.
41. *Economist*, 1 (1843–4), 962. See also John Bright's speech in the Second Reading debate on the Railways Bill: Hansard, 3rd ser., vol. 76, cols. 626–34, which however was not sophisticated in its economic argument.
42. Hansard, 3rd ser., vol. 33, cols. 977–88. For a discussion, see Foster, *Privatisation*, ch. 1.
43. *Gladstone Diaries* for dates stated.
44. *Gladstone Diaries*, 13 July 1846. 'He said he had been twice prime minister & nothing should induce him again to take part in the formation of a Government: the labour and anxiety were too great: & he repeated more than once emphatically with regard to the work of his post, "no one in the least degree knows what it is. I have told the Queen that I part from her with the deepest sentiments of gratitude & attachment—but that there is one thing she must not ask of me & it is to place myself again in the same position" '. Peel had no reason not to tell the truth to Gladstone, whose diary was not intended for publication.
45. See respectively Brown, *Board of Trade*, and Lubenow, *Government Growth*, ch. 3.
46. On the general position, see G. Kitson Clark, 'The Electorate and the Repeal of the Corn Laws', *Transactions of the Royal Historical Society*, 5th ser. 1 (1951), 109–26; N. Gash, *Politics in the Age of Peel* (Hassocks: Harvester, 2nd edn., 1977), pp. ix–xxv. On Newark, see Feuchtwanger, *Gladstone*, 17–18.
47. Unless otherwise stated, the source for all data is the data-set 'Members of the House of Commons 1841–47' compiled by W. O. Aydelotte and made available through the ESRC Data Archive, University of Essex. The total of 'No' votes exceeds the number reported in Hansard by one, because the Speaker disallowed one railway chairman's vote against the Bill.
48. See the following papers by W. O. Aydelotte: 'Voting Patterns in the British House of Commons', *Comparative Studies in History and Society* 5 (1963), 134–63; 'Parties and Issues in Early Victorian

England', *Journal of British Studies*, 5 (1966), 95–114; 'The Country Gentlemen and the Repeal of the Corn Laws', *English Historical Review*, 82 (1967), 47–60; 'The Disintegration of the Conservative Party in the 1840s: A Study of Political Attitudes', in W. O. Aydelotte, A. G. Bogue, and R. W. Fogel (eds.), *The Dimensions of Quantitative Research in History* (Princeton, NJ: Princeton University Press, 1972), 319–46; and 'Constituency Influence on the British House of Commons, 1841–1847', in W. O. Aydelotte (ed.), *The History of Parliamentary Behaviour* (Princeton, NJ: Princeton University Press, 1977). Where not otherwise explained, information on the data is derived from the codebook: W. O. Aydelotte, *Study 521 (Codebook) 'British House of Commons 1841–1847'*, Regional Social Science Data Archive of Iowa (Iowa City, 1970).

49. Significance was measured as follows. The Railways Bill votes were cross-tabulated against each of the scales, and against a wide range of variables describing MPs' interests, constituencies, and personal characteristics. Those which showed $p < .05$ on a Pearson chi-Square test were retained for further analysis. Each of these was either a dichotomous or an ordinal variable, and so rank-order correlations (Spearman's rho) were calculated. The value of rho for the Railways Bill against BIGSCALE was −.396. Six of the scales scored a higher absolute value against it. The variables left in the analysis were then tested to see whether they remained significant after controlling for party (see below).

50. On Aydelotte's own admission ('Disintegration', 336–7), the Guttman scales are more difficult to interpret than to detect. To avoid overburdening the tables with hard-to-interpret data I have therefore deleted all the scales from Tables 7.2 and 7.3 except BIGSCALE and ENCANWHT—the latter being the scale with which votes on the Railways Bill were most closely associated.

51. The only region to produce a unanimous vote in favour of railway regulation was Ulster, where only 36 miles of railway were either open or under construction (see F. Whishaw, *Whishaw's Railways of Great Britain and Ireland* (London: John Weale, 1842), 430–71).

52. Interests in shipping and in docks also remain good predictors after controlling for party; however, the number of MPs with these interests was small (17 for shipping, 21 for docks) and more than half of them had railway interests as well, so I have dropped them from Table 7.3.

53. In forward or stepwise models, these variables correctly predicted 85.0 per cent of pairs (gamma = 0.725). A backward regression model produced similar results but with a slightly poorer prediction (CONSTLOC failed to pass the 5 per cent significance threshold). The independent

variables were tested for intercollinearity with negative results (combined r^2 = 0.07).

54. R. Noll, 'The Illinois Constitutional Convention of 1870', paper presented to Political Economy Seminar, Hoover Institution (Stanford University, November 1990).
55. 7 May 1886, quoted by Williams, 'Public Opinion and Railway Rates', 46. 'Every one of which' may be too sweeping, but Williams found that the MPs for four of the biggest railway centres—Crewe, Derby, Rugby, and North Bucks—supported the 1886 Bill.
56. J. M. Buchanan and V. Vanberg, 'A Theory of Leadership and Deference in Constitutional Construction', *Public Choice*, 61 (1989), 15–27.

8

Rational Decision in International Crises: A Rationalization

MICHAEL NICHOLSON

1. THE PROBLEM

Decision-making in international crises has been widely discussed for thirty years and is a perennial topic of interest for students of foreign policy decision-making. This is not surprising. Wars are often preceded by crises and why some crises result in wars and others do not is not clearly understood despite much study. Furthermore, crises can be looked at as a reasonably self-contained phenomenon as compared with most issues in international relations and hence one for which one might hope to formulate a reasonably simple theory.

It is generally conceded that crisis decision-making behaviour is different from that in non-crisis situations.[1] There is also broad agreement that there is a dichotomy between crisis and non-crisis behaviour such that a situation switches from non-crisis to crisis mode and does not proceed down a continuum becoming more and more crisis-like. While this is not beyond controversy, I shall nevertheless accept this conventional wisdom for the purposes of this paper. Decision-making in crisis is compared with normal decision-making to the former's detriment, often being interpreted as 'irrational' according to the normal precepts of rational behaviour as this term is used in decision theory. At least it frequently, though

Some of the central arguments of this chapter appeared in M. Nicholson, *Rationality and the Analysis of International Conflict* (Cambridge: Cambridge University Press, 1992). The analysis has been significantly revised here. I am grateful to Maurice Yolles and John Vogler of Liverpool Sir John Moore's University, the members of the PSA Rational Choice Group, and in particular the editors of this volume for their helpful comments.

not invariably, appears to be inefficient given the ostensible goals of the group. While sometimes people's behaviour in crises is well adjusted towards sensible and comprehensible goals, often it is not. Rationality seems to be abandoned when it should be paramount. The crisis of 1914, the Suez crisis, and the Bay of Pigs crisis are merely some of the most frequently cited cases of apparently irrational decision-making procedures.

In this chapter I shall show that some of the apparently irrational behaviour of the decision-making group as a whole is nevertheless a perfectly rational, or at least comprehensible, response to extreme situations as far as the individual members of the group are concerned, given the basic structure within which they are operating. Furthermore, it follows very directly from a slight modification of a perfectly standard approach to decision-making in groups. Once we consider that intense work and pressure, closely associated with stress, is something that decision-makers can reasonably be expected to avoid or at least reduce, a number of issues fall quite naturally into place.

The purpose of this chapter is to interpret some of the generally accepted results of the empirical investigations into crisis behaviour in terms of a theoretical decision-making model such that the crisis mode falls quite naturally out of the more general considerations.

I do not wish to defend a particular definition of 'crisis' in international relations other than to assert how I shall use the term and why. The following definition is conventional. It involves two definitional characteristics: first issues of central importance to the state decision-makers are in question, such as perhaps the very existence of the society. That is, the probability of disastrous consequences resulting from the crisis situation are perceived to be high: there may always be some probability of a war but in a time of crisis there is a high one. Secondly, a crisis is a short-period phenomenon where 'short period' means a matter of a few days, or a few weeks at most. These defining characteristics almost always lead to two contingent characteristics of crises. First, there is a lot of information to be handled by decision-makers, which leads to the second contingent characteristic: in a crisis the rate at which decisions have to be made and information circulated, both within and between the various foreign decision-making organizations, is much greater than is normal. In other words, there is a lot of work, not much time, and the work concerns important decisions; so decision-takers are under pressure. This speed of operation has a number of consequences. The full decision-making and consultative process cannot always be gone through properly, meaning a more superficial and rapid selection and inspection of the documentation takes place, while the individuals involved in the decision-making process are put under severe mental and physical pressures which may distort their judgements. This picture, or something like it, is widely accepted.

This is a narrower definition of crisis than that in a major recent study of crises by Brecher, Wilkenfeld, and Moser (*Crises in the Twentieth Century*).[2] They regard a finite time as being a central distinguishing characteristic of a crisis rather than a short time as I have stressed. However, in this chapter I am concerned with decisions under pressure where the brief time available for decision is a major relevant feature and where this is not the norm. By definition, a crisis is an abnormal situation in the life of an organization. This definition would exclude some cases that Brecher, Wilkenfeld, and Moser include.

Some features recur in crises, though by no means invariably. First, the number of decision-makers involved is small as compared with normal situations, and its members comparatively easy to identify as compared with the loose boundaries in most noncrisis situations. Secondly, the members of the smaller group either start off by being or become more homogeneous in their attitudes towards the salient issues which have become more salient than in a normal decision-making situation. Thirdly, as a rather extreme form of this, 'Group-Think' and other forms of apparently irrational behaviour develop. Finally, though again not invariably as Brecher[3] has shown, the search for new information or novel alternatives is reduced, despite the greater apparent need for such a search. These forms of behaviour can be interpreted in terms of goal-directed behaviour on the part of the actors, once we explicitly bring into the picture the time available to make a decision.

In this chapter I shall stay as closely as possible to the standard definitions of rational choice. Hence, actors are assumed to be rational in the sense that their choices can be described by a utility function and that the other normal requirements of rationality, such as searching for information in situations under uncertainty (however difficult this may be to pin down precisely[4]) are also adhered to. This definition of rationality is often known as 'instrumental rationality'. It does not preclude the possibility of broader definitions of rationality being given.[5]

2. INDIVIDUAL DECISION-MAKING, WORK, AND PSYCHIC ENERGY

Decision-taking, whether done by an individual or a group, involves making choices from a continuously renewed set of novel situations in a changing environment. Initially I shall assume that the decision is taken by an individual and bring in the problem of groups later. Decisions are often strategic in the sense of involving an interaction with other actors who are normally rivals. Decision-takers have some underlying principles of preference, but these general preferences have to be constantly reinterpreted in terms of the contexts which arise. There are background principles of choice, but the situation develops with time and in the light of new information about the situation and the likely consequences of acts. Decisions involve the analysis of these in terms of the underlying preferences and form a utility function which, for the sake of simplicity, I shall assume to be of the Von Neumann–Morgenstern type. Static treatments of rational decision-making concentrate on the end product and not on the actual process. I shall highlight some of the problems of process.

For the present analysis we have to consider the process whereby the actors formulate their choices. The work of the decision-makers is the effort of the decision-makers in formulating their choices. 'Work' on my definition is an activity which involves energy and application on the part of the individuals involved which could have been applied elsewhere. The energy used in work, in this case the process of making a decision by an individual, I shall call 'psychic energy'. This is a not too distant relative of Freud's similarly named concept. In itself there is no direct measurement of psychic energy, though an ordinal measure would be possible. Nor is it directly observable. This does not deprive it of significance in a social scientific structure if we interpret it as a 'theoretical concept'.[6]

The work of a decision-maker consists of forming choices in a changing environment. The task is to determine what alternative actions are available and the sets of possible consequences of those actions with their probabilities. Thus information is sought and analysed. In the case of an individual's decisions, I hypothesize that the overall work involved increases according to the novelty of the situation and its complexity. However, if the preference of one over the other is clear-cut these do not matter very much. It is only when the alternatives are close to being equally preferred that the complexity or the novelty of the situation in which the decision-making problems are embedded become issues which generate work. Another dimension is added when we bring in the time constraints, common enough in decision-making problems and central in the case of crises. As the overall time in which the decision-maker has to solve the problem decreases, so the work per period, such as a day, increases. The time constraint may be an inherent feature of the decision-making situation or some subjectively perceived pressure. A short period of intense work, creating stress, can be involved when a problem has to be solved quickly, even if it is not an inherently complex one.

As long as the flow of new information and the degree of novelty are in some sense 'normal', then the group is accepting normal costs which we can regard as a base point. As the flow goes up so does the work. Either there is a reduction in efficiency or, at some point, the basic procedures have to be altered. Selecting a course of action in a complex world is not something which appears in a blinding flash of intuition. It is an activity which involves the intellectual and emotional resources of those involved. It gets harder and harder as there is more work to be done. If there is 'overload', a person feels stress and the work is done less efficiently in the sense of there being more mistakes. There is some finite limit to the amount of work which can be accomplished.

Work is not the only consumer of the finite resources of psychic energy. Other factors require the expenditure of psychic energy and are therefore potential sources of stress. I shall identify two, though I do not pretend these are exclusive or the only way of categorizing the factors. Still concentrating on the individual, there is the importance of the problem and the level of uncertainty, which are significant in their interactions with each other and work rather than in isolation. I shall analyse these in greater detail.

'Uncertainty' is frequently defined as a situation where the probabilities cannot be determined in any objective manner and 'risk' as one where they can be. On this definition, virtually all the issues we deal with in crisis decision-making involve uncertainty not risk.[7] However, uncertainty does not preclude characterizing the possible outcomes of some act by subjective probabilities and it can be argued that, to make any coherent sense of decision-taking under uncertainty, this must be done.[8] This is my view. Intuitively, at least, one feels one can order degrees of uncertainty and it is hard to see how one could have much of a theory of decision-taking under uncertainty without at least this. With full subjective probabilities, two individuals with the same information can still rationally disagree. Normally one would expect ordering relationships to be preserved, though this is not logically required.

Maximum uncertainty (or risk) comes when the probabilities, whether subjective or objective, of the relevant outcomes are around 0.5. Probabilities near 0 and 1 denote low uncertainty. One would expect agreement about whether an outcome was very uncertain or not, though again it is not a logical necessity. My empirical claim is that uncertainty produces stress, though only when inter-linked with importance.

'Importance' means the utilities are large compared with other possible alternatives. Thus there is some intuitive sense in which the choice of a career between being a lawyer and being a doctor is more important than learning the flute or learning the piano for an amateur musician. More of one's life is more different in the first case than in the second. In the case of choices facing foreign policy decision-makers, the choice between fighting a war or giving in is again a more important choice than fixing a tax on foreign-aircraft landing rights by the argument that more people are more affected in the first case than in the second.

However, if there is complete certainty about outcomes and the relevant attributes are few, important decisions can be simple to make and relatively stress-free. It is when there is uncertainty about the consequences that the problems arise. Consider the following example which I pose in terms of objective probabilities.

Suppose an individual is facing two gambles. One involves a stake of £10, a prize of £10, and a probability of winning of 0.5. The individual has difficulty in deciding whether to take the gamble or not—in other words is indifferent between the two alternatives. The second gamble consists of a stake of £10,000 and a prize of £12,000 and again the individual is indifferent between accepting the gamble or not. In the second case the outcomes are more important than in the first and the stress involved in reaching the decision is much greater. Stress involves excitement as well as costs. Serious gamblers in fact want to gamble significant sums. It is precisely the excitement they are looking for. Nevertheless there is a limit to this. This factor is strengthened if we assume that the result of the gamble is not announced until a week after the gambler has chosen which option to take. The gambler is in a state of uncertainty and this state can lead to stress, which is obviously greater if larger sums of money are involved than small ones. In the case of foreign policy decisions the uncertainty is presumably not sought after for its own sake in the way that gamblers seek for it. It is a necessary gamble. At best the reaction to uncertainty will probably be regarded as a cost. If so, then it would appear in a formal analysis as risk aversion.

The importance of the outcomes in this instance only produces stress because risk is involved as well. A choice between an outright gift of £10,000 and £12,000 involves no work or stress at all. It is the combination of factors, not each in isolation, which produces stress.

We can summarize the issues as follows. When an issue is unimportant it does not produce stress. If it is important it produces stress when linked with other factors as indicated below. I represent variables as dichotomous, High (*H*) and Low (*L*), or in the case of time as Constrained (*C*) or Unconstrained (*U*). All of course are continuous, but the points are more clearly seen in this

TABLE 8.1. *The interlinking of stress-creating factors*

Complexity and/or novelty	Time	Uncertainty	Consequences
H	C	H	Most stressful situation
H	C	L	Stress due to intense work
H	U	L	Low stress
H	U	H	Stress
L	C	L	Low stress
L	C	H	Stress
L	U	H	Stress
L	U	L	Low stress

simple framework. Notice that I am suggesting that when there is uncertainty in an important situation there is always stress, though uncertainty is not a necessary condition for the existence of stress. Like the others, this is an empirical assertion which may or may not survive more rigorous examination.

Stress

In decision-making contexts there is a normal level of expenditure of such psychic energy which is appropriate for the task in hand. If the expenditure of energy is high compared with some normal level (which would include some normal deviations) then this results in stress for the individual. Stress, unlike psychic energy, though itself not directly observable, has manifestations which are. We can identify the onset of stress. At least in principle we can obtain some measures of it. I do not propose to measure stress here, though the implication of my argument is that it is a measurable concept.

Though stress has a bad name in popular literature and is linked with all sorts of gruesome consequences, it is not necessarily harmful. I make two assumptions about stress. First, beyond some level, different for different individuals, the performance and efficiency of those individuals deteriorates. There seems a mass of psychological evidence to support this contention.[9] Secondly, even though some degree of stress might be welcomed, there exists some level of stress beyond which people try to reduce it. They may do this by either conscious or unconscious stratagems. Among the conscious stratagems may be the trading off of optimality against stress.[10]

3. A MODEL OF THE GROUP'S DECISION-MAKING PROCESS

I shall assume there is a defined group of people who take foreign-policy decisions which consists of career officials and political actors. I shall call this the bureaucracy. In normal times the boundaries of the decision-making group are vague and can go as far as including public opinion. To highlight the central problems of this paper I shall introduce a simplified model in which the bureaucracy is a group of individuals, possibly quite large, but nevertheless clearly defined. The bureaucracy takes decisions on behalf of the state, which might be conceived of as some abstraction or as members of the broader society who have no direct hand in the decision-making process as such. The central point is that, at least in principle, the members of the decision-making group are not taking the decisions for their own personal benefit but on behalf of some larger entity. I assume that the bureaucratic decision-making group has a utility function over those factors which are relevant to the state. The members of the decision-making group must have some amalgamation rules for combining their own individual perceptions of the interests of the state into some aggregate view within the decision-making group. While there is no unique specification of a rational procedure for such amalgamations (a majority vote, for example, is only one such procedure), we can specify some characteristics of the group decision which would be regarded as irrational given the function of the group.

The decisions of such a group can be described by a utility function in the standard Von Neumann–Morgenstern sense. I shall hypothesize that in normal times this is in fact the case. There are some caveats. Of the many categorizations of groups, a pertinent one for our current purposes is the distinction between groups which are taking decisions for the benefit of the group members (such as a tennis club operating on the principles of Athenian democracy) and those which are deciding on behalf of others (such as the committee of a tennis club). In either case, each individual member of the group also has a utility function from which the group utility function is formed. There are some well-known problems about group decisions such as the Condorcet/Black/Arrow[11] problem but, despite its prominence in the literature, it is arguable that its practical significance is exaggerated at least as far as small group decisions are concerned. I shall assume that the decision-making process for a group which is deciding about matters which concern its members alone is unproblematic (it is not particularly relevant here even if it is not so).

First let us consider a group decision under normal conditions. Our group is well defined in terms of membership and it is clear who is a member and who is not a member of the group. The group must select a group preference from the set of individual preferences. This also involves work on the part of the individual group members in the general sense considered above. Different options have to be considered and argued about; alliances are formed; log-rolling is undertaken, and so on. This, of course, is in addition to factors requiring energy in the case of individual decision. The broader the range of disagreements in the group, and the more fundamental their nature, the more effort (work) is required.

My first hypothesis is that the further apart people's views are on the matters about which a decision has to be made, then the more energy is needed to reach an agreed course of action. Even when voting is used, which in principle can be operated irrespective of the degree of divergence of views, it is normal to try to get as much agreement as possible before the vote is taken. Secondly, bureaucracies regard work, at least above a certain level, as a cost and try to reduce it. These are not particularly startling hypotheses but they have interesting implications. A group faced with great internal disagreements, and hence a lot of work, tries to contain them. They will look for ways of doing so, such as avoiding particularly contentious items or getting rid of members whose views differ markedly from the norm. These pressures are increased when there is a shortage of time and a tight deadline. The time constraint can produce stress and further stimulates the temptation to use quick procedures. This means, of course, that decision-makers in effect are not acting solely for the state but also for themselves, in that the reduction of stress and work is not of interest to anyone else.

This can be represented formally. Suppose there are n actors called $a(1)$, $a(2)$ . . . $a(n)$. Let us suppose there is a variable x where each of the actors chooses his or her most preferred value and that the initial most favoured value for each of the actors are respectively $X(1)$ $X(2)$ . . . $X(n)$. Let us suppose that $X(1)$ is chosen. Denoting the utility of point j to actor i as $u(j,i)$, the energy involved in making this point the group decision is

$$E(1) = e \sum_{1}^{n} [u(i, i) - u(1, i)], \tag{1}$$

where $e > 0$ is some scaling parameter. This expression can be regarded as the cost of disagreement. Normally we would suppose that there will be a collection of issues over which the actors must choose. For simplicity, assume there are just two variables p and q so that, for example $X(1)$, is now a point in two dimensions namely

($p(1)$, $q(1)$). This does not affect the above expression which can be interpreted in any number of dimensions. The higher this is, the greater the degree of psychic energy on the part of the group members required to solve it. Notice that I am regarding psychic energy as only a characteristic of individuals. I am not endeavouring to formulate some aggregative concept which relates to the group as a whole. I have doubts about the meaning of such a concept.

I assume that, in general, the bureaucracy tries to minimize the expenditure of energy. Clearly there are n such expressions $E(1)$, $E(2)$ . . . $E(n)$. In an optimizing framework we would expect that the $x(i)$ would be chosen for which $E(i)$ would be at a minimum, that is $E(i) \leq E(j)$ for all $j \neq$ i. Search involves energy too. In a problem of any complexity we would expect that a satisfying process would occur and the $x(i)$ is chosen which first comes up for which $E(i) < E(0)$ where $E(0)$ is some conventionally acceptable level. This can be regarded as part of the internal utility of the group. Now this happens for all items requiring choice. If lots of items come up for decision, then the cost in terms of psychic energy is large.

Individuals in the group run into stress in the same way as individuals on their own feel stress, though there are some modifications. First, obviously the range of work factors is larger in that there is the cost involved in attaining group agreement. There are other features relating to group decision which do not have clear analogues in individual decision, such as group dissension as a stress-making factor. The resolution of group dissension was one of the factors which appeared in work. It reappears as an independent factor here in that when group dissension involves personal animosities and arguments, it can be an independent source of stress. On the other hand, some features of group decision might reduce stress. Thus, fear of making an error might be reduced (the so-called 'risky shift factor'). This might reduce the significance of the importance of the issues as a creator of stress.

When groups are taking decisions on behalf of other people or some broader entity than themselves, as is obviously the case in any foreign policy decision or indeed any political decision outside an Athenian democracy, the situation becomes more problematic. Each member's utility function involves two different sorts of variable. First, there is that part which relates to the social utility function. In the cases relevant here these are preferences over the

foreign-policy alternatives. I shall call these the primary preferences and the criteria by which we judge them the external rationality of the group. Secondly, there are arguments in the function
which relate to the individual members but which do not concern
the society as a whole but the interests of the group alone. I shall
call these the secondary preferences and the relevant criteria the
internal rationality of the group. This can also be split into two
parts. Those factors which concern relations within the group, such
as group harmony, and those which concern the individual members of the group, such as reduction of stress or personal ambition.

The primary preferences are considered in terms of what each
individual actor believes is for the good of the group. Whatever
alternative is chosen has no direct effect on the actors' lives when
they are outside the group in the sense that they get more money,
or something of the sort. Thus a British decision-maker does not
(normally) get richer if his or her preferred policy towards, say,
India is approved.[12]

The secondary preferences concern factors within the group
itself. Goals relevant to these do not interest the society outside the
group on whose behalf the group is taking the decisions. They
involve the internal procedures by which the group formulates its
decisions. An individual has preferences over such things as relationships in the group. He or she might seek dominance in the
group (a common desire, I suspect, in groups of this importance),
win the favour of a leader, or something of the sort. Such features
of group behaviour are well known. I shall not dwell on their characteristics in this paper, though their existence is, of course, important to the argument.[13] From a set of disparate sets of preferences
a composite preference ordering somehow has to evolve and be the
basis of a decision.

There are two important factors to be considered. First, both
primary and secondary factors require the expenditure of energy
and effort. The expenditure of energy takes place over a particular
period of time. Within a certain period (e.g. a day) there is a certain amount of energy available for coping with decision-making
tasks. If the tasks requiring attention need energy greatly in excess
of that which is available then we run into difficulties, but this is a
matter for discussion below. Secondly, the existence of secondary
preferences means that the most preferred position over the primary preferences alone will normally be at a different point than

it would have been if no secondary preferences had existed. Suppose the set of primary alternatives is in two dimensions and is given by $X(i) = [p(i), q(i)]$. $a(1)$'s most preferred point on these alone is $[p(1), q(1)]$. Suppose now there is a secondary preference where $r(1)$ denotes $a(1)$'s most preferred point. If we denote the most preferred triple as $[p'(1), q'(1), r'(1)]$ there is no reason for $p'(1) = p(1)$, or likewise for the other variables. No rule of preference consistency requires it. Hence the actor's preferences over the primary alternatives might be (and normally will be) distorted by the existence of the secondary alternatives.[14] An example would be voting for the primary motion which was one's second preference in order not to upset a friend for whom it was a first preference. My argument is thus that the decisions made concerning the wider group are influenced by factors which have no concern for them whatever. It will normally be the case that these decisions will be different than if only those matters—the primary matters—which concerned them were taken into account.

4. DECISIONS IN CRISIS

It is now easy to show how behaviour which is often observed in crises fits easily into the framework we have discussed. In a crisis, the environment becomes increasingly novel. The work-load increases because of the increased flow of information and consequent complexity of the tasks involved. The general factors associated with crisis decision-making, as discussed above and by innumerable scholars, come into play. All these require an increase in psychic energy, which, as I have argued, is a limited resource, so stress rises, perhaps to a very high level.

The question then is how to reduce the expenditure of psychic energy. First let us look at it from the point of view of the group as a whole. Within any time period (say a day) the amount of information and the number of problems to be addressed increase. Hence, the quantity $e\Sigma(u(1) - u(i))$ increases, because of the increase in n, the number of issues which is raised before the group. This is likely to increase the stress of the actors and, beyond a point, we shall assume that a major factor in their secondary preferences is the containment of stress at or below some level. I suggest beyond some point that its containment becomes a major issue for the group. Formally, this increase in work can be constrained by cutting down i, the number of actors, or by cutting down $u(1) - u(i)$, which is the degree of difference of opinion between the actors. There are clear interpretations for both these formal operations. Cutting down i is simply cutting down the number of people involved, while cutting down $u(1) - u(i)$ can be done by eliminating those people who most disagree with the general lines of policy proposed. This is, of course, precisely what happens in crisis situations. The number of people in the decision-making group is small and, in general, there is a greater homogeneity of view, which is what this model predicts. Note that this comes about not through people altering their views, but due to a selection of people who are like-minded.

Selection accounts for part of the increasing homogeneity of the group's opinions, but other factors work in the same direction. Group-Think, which is sometimes observed in crises, involves people agreeing with each other and apparently adjusting their views and preferences in order to do so. Consider the problem from the point of view of the individual. Even though the group has been selected, or selects itself, to produce a high degree of agreement, there is still a highly stressful situation. Procedures are developed to reduce both work and stress. Suppose an individual in a group prefers A to B but finds that every other member prefers B to A. There is a strong temptation to argue to oneself that as all these colleagues have this preference, perhaps they have analysed it more carefully, and fuller and more mature consideration would mean that this would result in this being the deviant's preference too. Whether this is quite what happens is hard to establish, but something like this is not uncommon, though the process might well be nothing like so explicit. By imitating the preferences of others there is a great deal of stress saved as compared with doing the analysis oneself. If agreement as such is valued then this comes in as a secondary preference and the combination of primary and secondary preferences might switch the apparent ordering over the primary preference. This is a slightly different point, though it has the same result. This could be a conscious weighing up of alternatives. Group-Think is normally regarded as a process of changing preferences, though it could be regarded as the unconscious analogue of the conscious division of primary and secondary preferences. When there is plenty of time for making the decision this approach may not be adopted, but time is at a premium and this is a simpler way out, even if there may be residual qualms. The same thing applies, perhaps with more force, when more uncertainties are involved.

In such situations a culture of agreement is also likely to arise, also for the same reason—agreement is less psychically costly. The group is likely to value agreement as such as the psychic cost of disagreement goes up. This may or may not be the mechanism behind Group-Think. However, what can be affirmed confidently is that the Group-Think phenomenon is one which does away with the high costs of disagreement in contexts where the degree of disagreement is potentially high.

The reluctance to search for novel alternatives is also a common characteristic of crises, though there are exceptions.[15] This can be incorporated into this model, though it is fairly obvious even without it. Search increases the quantity of work and energy expended both at the individual and the group level. Resources, in terms of time and energy which are devoted to search in normal times, are now involved in finding out appropriate reactions to new stimuli in these abnormal periods.

5. CONCLUSION

The point of this chapter is to demonstrate that responses to crises which appear rather odd when looked at from the point of view of group decision-making are sometimes comprehensible forms of behaviour on the part of people who are under severe pressure. A decision procedure which may be appropriate when there is no time constraint may not be so when time is at a premium. This is not to argue that the apparent oddities which attend so much crisis decision-making can always now be seen as a disguised form of rationality; far from it. There are clear cases of decision-makers being overwhelmed by stress, such as Eden at the time of the Suez crisis and the Kaiser in 1914. Short of these extremes there seems much in the literature to suggest that decisions are taken anything but rationally, even allowing for the constraints. To improve the decision-making, however, the constraints need to be taken into account and built in to the analysis, as Janis attempts to do in his analysis.

NOTES

1. The literature on crisis decision-making is enormous, but bibliographies are likewise common and easily accessible (for example, in J. M. Roberts, *Decision Making during International Crises* (London: Macmillan, 1988) and M. Brecher and J. Wilkenfeld, *Crisis, Conflict and Instability* (Oxford: Pergamon Press, 1989). Some earlier classics in the discussion of crises are R. North, O. R. Holsti, M. G. Zanninovich, and D. A. Zinnes, *Content Analysis* (Evanston, Ill: Northwestern University Press, 1963), which is a study of the 1914 crisis in particular, and F. Hermann Charles (ed.), *International Crises: Insights from Behavioral Research* (New York: Free Press, 1972). These are still worth reading as subsequent work has added to rather than superseded them. More recently, the Brecher and Wilkenfeld book provides a useful discussion of their work in the general context of work on crises. O. Holsti, 'Theories of Crisis Decision Making', in P. C. Lamer (ed.), *Diplomacy: New Approaches in History, Theory and Policy* (London: Free Press, 1979) and Roberts, *Decision Making* also give useful accounts. In M. Nicholson, 'Stress and the Rational Decision Maker', *Journal of Conflict Processes*, 1 (1992), 17–25, I also discuss the issues in the general context of decision theory. See also G. T. Allison, *Essence of Decision: Explaining the Cuban Missile Crisis* (Boston: Little Brown, 1971); I. L. Janis, *Group Think*, 2nd edn. (Boston: Houghton Mifflin, 1982).
2. See M. Brecher, J. Wilkenfeld, and S. Moser, *Crises in the Twentieth Century* (Oxford: Pergamon Press, 1988).
3. M. Brecher, *Decisions in Crisis: Israel, 1967 and 1973* (Berkeley and London: University of California Press, 1980).
4. L. J. Savage, *Foundations of Statistics* (New York: Dover, 1972).
5. See S. Hargreaves-Heap, *Rationality in Economics* (Oxford: Blackwell, 1989).
6. I discuss the notion of 'theoretical concepts' in M. Nicholson, *The Scientific Analysis of Social Behaviour: A Defence of Empiricism in Social Science* (London: Frances Pinter, 1983), as applied to the social sciences. The issue is discussed in greater detail in R. B. Braithwaite, *Scientific Explanation* (Cambridge: Cambridge University Press, 1955). Essentially, they are concepts like, for example, gravity or centre of gravity, which, though not directly observable even in principle, play a central role in a deductive system whose implications are observable.
7. M. Nicholson, *The Scientific Analysis of Social Behaviour: A Defence of Empiricism in Social Science* (London: Frances Pinter, 1983).
8. L. J. Savage, *Foundations of Statistics* (New York: Dover, 1972).
9. For example, again from a large literature, C. R. Anderson, 'Coping

Behaviours as Intervening Mechanisms in the Inverted-U, Stress Performance Relationship', *Journal of Applied Psychology*, 61 (1976), 30–4; C. L. Cooper, 'Executive Stress', *Human Resource Management*, 23 (1984), 395–407, and V. H. Vroom, *Work and Motivation* (New York: Wiley, 1964).

10. The analysis can be worked out in terms of psychic energy alone and leaving out stress. However, as stress is widely used in the psychological literature, and draws attention to a feature I wish to highlight, it is convenient to use it for a situation where abnormal amounts of psychic energy are being used.

11. The Condorcet Paradox is that, for certain configurations of consistent and transitive individual preferences, the group preferences determined by voting is intransitive. Suppose we have three committee members, I, II, III, whose preferences respectively over three alternatives are $a > b > c$, $b > c > a$ and $c > a > b$. In a straight majority vote, a will defeat b, and c will defeat a, which one might assume means that c would defeat b. Contrary to intuition, a quick inspection of the orderings shows that in a direct vote, b will defeat c.

12. Bribery is a way of giving secondary incentives to alter primary preferences. Conversely, roles requiring the declaration of private conflicts of interest with public interests, for example in a legislature, try to mitigate the interactions.

13. Another goal of individual actors is to win in committee, in the sense that all actors wish to get their own most preferred alternative accepted. Casual observation suggests this is an important factor. This they want to do because they believe in it, but also because they get prestige through being successful in promoting their own policies.

14. Notice that this does not violate the widespread if not universally accepted assumption of the irrelevance of independent alternatives. The alternatives are not independent. That is, the independence of irrelevant alternatives concerns the 'or' connective, that is, the addition of 'or C' to the choice set of 'A or B' should (according to the principle) make no difference in the choice between 'A or B'. However, in the text we are considering 'A or B' in the context of ' "A and C" ' or "B and C" '. Clearly one might choose A in the first case but not in the second.

15. M. Brecher, *Decisions in Crisis*.

9

The Buck in Your Bank is not a Vote for Free Trade: Financial Intermediation and Trade Preferences in the United States and Germany

CHERYL SCHONHARDT-BAILEY
AND ANDREW BAILEY

This chapter examines the relationship between asset holdings and trade-policy preferences. We examine the interests and the incentives of share owners, who are the residual owners of firms that are directly affected by trade policies, to act collectively. Specifically, we examine characteristics of share ownership that affect the propensity of investors to form interests, around which they may mobilize, and in particular the institutional framework of national financial markets and the incentives embedded (accidentally or deliberately) in government policy. In doing so, we argue that the form and distribution of shareholding, both of which have been the subject of lively debate in the economics and finance literatures, have complicated the mobilization and exercise of interests. To illustrate our argument, we analyse financial intermediation in the United States and Germany, focusing on the growth of institutional share ownership in the former and changes in the role of banks in German industry, both of which we believe are neglected areas in the study of interest-group activity.

The authors are grateful for comments from Jeffry Frieden, Arye Hillman, Stephanie Hoopes, David Lake, Louis Pauly, Herbert Sawyer, and Chenggang Xu. An earlier version of the paper was presented at the 1993 American Political Science Association Annual Meeting. Gita Subrahmanyam and Lanier Saperstein provided us with valuable research assistance. The views expressed in this article are those of the authors and do not represent the views of the Bank of England.

1. THE PREFERENCES OF ASSET-HOLDERS

Public-choice theories of protection ideally fuse explanations of the demand for protection with the supply of such legislation by governments.[1] A fully specified demand side involves identifying economic interests, aggregating those interests into politically active groups, and specifying the institutional constraints under which such groups act while seeking to maximize the welfare of their members. Specifying the supply side may introduce the concept of an autonomous state,[2] social welfare, political support-maximizing politicians,[3] or the nature of the political structure.[4] We focus solely on the demand for protection.

Factor Specificity

Two familiar models in the trade literature—the Heckscher–Ohlin and the Ricardo–Viner specific factors—offer different predictions for the policy preferences of capital owners. Whereas the Heckscher–Ohlin model assumes perfect inter-industry factor mobility, the Ricardo–Viner model defines some factor inputs as industry-specific (immobile) and others as perfectly mobile between industries. These two are often depicted as long-run and short-run models respectively (even in a Ricardo–Viner world factors trapped in the short run will, given sufficient time, migrate to other industries where returns are higher),[5] and they differ in their predictions of coalition formation. Equalization of factor returns in the Heckscher–Ohlin model means that owners of a particular factor will incur similar costs or benefits from a given trade policy; thus coalitions are expected to form along factor lines. In the Ricardo–Viner model, where factors are specific to industries at least in the short run, coalitions will divide along export- versus import-competing industry lines.

The first step is therefore to consider the degree of (im)mobility of capital. In doing so, we draw an important distinction between capital as the ownership of assets (investment capital) and capital as part of the production process (production capital). Specialization of production is advantageous, while specialization of asset ownership involves concentrated exposure to risk, and hence can be disadvantageous.[6] Inter-sectoral mobility of investment capital suggests that owners may easily adjust to adverse shocks to the firms or industries in which their capital is employed. In contrast, when investment capital is concentrated and immobile, owners will expect to suffer losses and are likely to be in the vanguard of calls for policy changes that redistribute income. In the case of trade policy, such industry-specific factors will give rise to industry-specific interests that may either favour or oppose protection, depending upon the form of trade competition facing the industry. Owners of factors specific to the domestic import-competing industry gain from protection (via the relatively higher price), while owners of factors specific to the export sector lose (via the relatively lower price). The preference of a mobile factor (for example, labour) is ambiguous: although workers can move into the protected sector, their welfare remains contingent upon their unique consumption preferences. In sum, owners of factors specific to a particular industry will tend to seek protection for their industry and oppose protection for any other industry, whereas mobile factor owners will remain largely inactive.[7] Some authors have emphasized the importance of factor specificity in determining the intensity of actors' policy preferences on trade issues.[8] However, no one has explored the link between the mobility of investment capital and trade preferences.

In a number of major countries, notably the United States, the pronounced shift from individual to institutional ownership of financial assets, and the growth of highly liquid financial markets, have fostered the presumption that assets are foot-loose. Jeffry Frieden notes: 'Assets that are not specific at all are those that can easily be redeployed—demand deposits, financial assets more generally. Holders of completely liquid assets are indifferent to policy, for they can move their funds to whatever activity is earning the highest rate of return.'[9] This argument does not, however, adequately consider changes in the form of asset-holding, and hence changes in the perceived risk-profile of investors. This risk-profile is critical for determining the likelihood that owners of financial assets will mobilize for collective action. Some mobilize and others do not: factor mobility is only part of what defines investors' exposure to risk.

The framework of risk exposure has three elements: diversification versus concentration of returns to assets; the presence (or not) of investment insurance; and the transmission mechanism by which gains and losses from trade policy adjustments feed through to individual asset holders.

Diversification versus concentration. While at the industry and firm level there is evidence that production capital is not inter-sectorally mobile,[10] investors can avoid the worst consequences of being locked into a declining industry by diversifying their portfolios. Indeed, extensions to the Ricardo–Viner model relax the assumption that in the short run each person owns only one, or primarily only one, factor of production. The link between diversification and economic interests is simple: as investors reduce the proportion of their wealth tied up in a single firm or industry, their incentive to lobby on the industry's behalf is reduced. It is less painful to back a loser when the maximum expected loss is small relative to total wealth.

Individuals who are diversified to the point where their endowment of factor shares matches the national endowment should prefer free trade to protection of any kind. Such an endowment would, however, entail diversification both across factor inputs and within each factor. That is, an individual's portfolio would be a microcosm of the nation's endowment of, say, land, labour, and capital (or more exhaustively, human, physical, knowledge and capital resources, and infrastructure[11]), and for any particular factor, ownership across industries would reflect the nation's comparative mix. Although it is unlikely that any one individual's or institution's factor endowment would constitute a perfect microcosm of the national factor endowment, for a particular factor such as capital, an individual could well own a sufficiently diversified portfolio to warrant a preference for free trade.

Insurance. Alternatively, an individual could enjoy sufficient insurance on his asset portfolio such that, under limited circumstances, losses are absorbed by the insurer and not by the individual. Standard trade theory maintains that free trade benefits all, as long as losers are provided with adequate compensation. The provision of insurance to cover losses on assets may then be viewed as a form of compensation.

Transmission mechanisms and property rights. The preferences of investors will also depend upon the transmission of income, which varies with the form of investment (i.e. the form of the property rights). Property rights in developed countries are usually assumed to be well defined and unproblematic, and are a prerequisite for a market economy. Such property rights (1) assign exclusive ownership rights to each property; (2) allow owners the right to claim the residual income accruing to their assets; and (3) allow owners the right to determine the use of assets, including the restructuring, sale, or lease of property. In other words, (1) and (2) define the form of the residual claim (ownership) while (3) shapes the decision-making process available to owners (control). True property owners (residual claimants) must ultimately pay for mistakes, bad judgement, or bad luck; they also stand to reap the rewards of diligence, foresight, and good luck. Consequently, owners have the incentive to monitor the firm's behaviour, and to sustain or increase profitability. Property rights thus create economic interests, and thereby policy preferences.

We argue that property rights of financial investments are not, in fact, so well defined in developed countries,[12] and hence factor ownership is less transparent. Moreover, failure to explore ambiguities in property rights results in a misspecification of the economic interests underpinning political conflicts over trade policy. Several reasons explain this development. First, the rights themselves, which constitute a claim on the capital of firms, are mobile in the sense that an investment can be costlessly (or nearly costlessly) transferred from a firm (or sector) that loses from a policy shift to one that gains. This could occur if, for instance, the equity market is expected to be sufficiently liquid to allow a holding to be liquidated (which in turn is dependent on the size of the holding). Second, individual investors strive to achieve a degree of portfolio diversification, thereby diluting their interest in a particular firm or industry. Third, the rights are held in an indirect form. This could be because they are held by banks that translate the right into a deposit contract, or by institutional investors who issue pension or insurance contracts or act as a simple intermediary in the case of mutual funds or unit trusts.

Consider the case of IBM in 1989. Approximately 50 per cent of IBM stock was held by 653 institutional investors; 16 per cent was held by the top twenty pension funds plus ten of the largest investment managers.[13] Who might be said to own these IBM shares—the institutions or the individuals who invested? Rather than having a well-defined owner who has control over the use of the assets, a chain of factor ownership is created with the introduction of institutional intermediation. Each link in the chain may be seen as holding a unique ownership claim; and each property-owner possesses a unique and possibly dissimilar trade-policy preference. Property-rights theory assumes that owners possess the requisite information to exercise control. If, however, owners are not privy to the requisite information, control becomes limited, if not impossible. Consequently, the political cleavage(s) predicted by the specific-factors model are unlikely to materialize. We develop this argument below, but to summarize, poorly defined property rights—in particular resulting from institutional intermediation—distort the political manifestation of conflicts of economic interest between gainers and losers from trade policy.

2. FINANCIAL INTERMEDIATION AND THE RISK-PROFILE OF INVESTORS

Financial Intermediation and the Trade-Policy Preferences of Individual Investors

Differences in the contractual relationship between individual savers and financial intermediaries reflect differences in the 'investment-contract demand' of individuals, which will in turn have a bearing on the formation of trade-policy preferences among those individuals. Contracts written between institutions and individual policy-holders, investors, or depositors differ significantly between the different types of financial intermediaries. We focus on five common forms of financial intermediation: mutual funds, pension funds, life insurance, private trusts and endowments, and bank deposits. Three broad characteristics of investing shape the formation of interests among investors: (1) the relationship between the return on the institutions' assets and payments to investors, depositors, and policy-holders; (2) the extent to which individuals expect that their investments are insured (or guaranteed) against the institution defaulting; and (3) the share of individuals' factor income represented by investments (which includes, but is not limited to, the extent of portfolio diversification within asset holdings) (see Table 9.1).

The relationship between the earnings of financial institutions and the returns they pay to individuals is the 'income link'. It covers two properties of the contractual relationships: the directness of the earnings relationship and the transparency of financial institutions' assets to individual investors. Where the earnings relationship is direct (i.e. the income of the institution is passed through directly to individuals) the assets of the institution will normally be transparent to owners. In such cases the income link will be stronger and individuals will find it easy to monitor the financial intermediary, and to form trade-policy preferences. Individual investors are thus more likely to hold strong interests in firms in which the institution invests. Mutual funds and private trusts or endowments exhibit strong income links because returns are directly linked to the income of the fund, trust, or endowment. Private trusts and endowments are more transparent, but this has more to do with the concentration of individuals' savings in such trusts (i.e. it has more to do with the third characteristic considered below).

At the other extreme, banks have the weakest income link both because there is a weak connection between the return on banks' assets and payments on deposit contracts, and because banks have low levels of asset transparency.[14] The bank depositor delegates to the bank the task of monitoring loans. Banks have a cost advantage in monitoring, because the alternative is either gross duplication of effort or free-rider problems where no lender monitors.[15] Banks also act as silent monitors of companies to which they lend. The assumption that banks act as a screen preventing information about companies going into the public domain, and hence to bank depositors, suggests that companies believe they derive more value from limiting the flow of information than from helping depositors to associate with and advocate company interests.[16] Bank intermediation creates a problem of information asymmetry: the contract between depositor and lender is not complete, and at least part of the property right—i.e. the individual's interest in the companies in which the bank invests—is not well defined.

Part of the solution to information asymmetry lies in the extent to which the individual investor expects a guarantee to cover unanticipated losses resulting from inability to monitor the financial intermediary.[1] We will call this the 'insurance component'. A priori, we should expect an inverse relationship between the strength of the income link and the strength of the insurance component

TABLE 9.1. *Individual investors: influences on policy preferences*

	Mutual fund	Pension fund
Part A: Form of contract with financial institutions		
1. Income link: Link between earnings of the institution and returns to investors or depositors	Direct link. e.g. Returns on equity mutual funds are directly related to equity market performance. Transparency of fund investments usually high.	No direct link. In traditional 'defined-benefit' pensions no direct link exists: but growth of 'defined-contribution' pensions creates a stronger link. Limited disclosure of investments.
2. Insurance component: investment guarantee scheme/ expectation of government support.	No industry scheme: government support unlikely.	Limited insurance via legal action: possibility of government support through moral suasion of pensioners.
3. Factor concentration component, share of factor returns invested.	Variable, but usually not high.	Variable: expected to be high in old age.
Part B: Incentives for individual investor to monitor institutional inter-		
4. How strong is the incentive to monitor based on link between earnings & returns (from row 1).	Strong: High transparency of investments.	Weak for defined-benefit pension plans; stronger for defined-contribution plans.
5. Is the incentive to monitor limited by insurance? (from row 2).	No.	No formal guarantee scheme: Pensioners may be expected to use moral suasion.
6. Do collective action problems exist in monitoring? (from row 3).	Large numbers of fund-holders, holding small stakes will tend to free-ride.	Fund-holders with small stakes will free-ride (as age increases free-riding should diminish).

TABLE 9.1. *Cont.*

Life insurance	Private trust/endowment	Banks
No direct link. Long life of policies before income is realized and difficulty of with-drawal. Limited dis-closure of investments.	Direct link. Returns directly linked to performance of trust investments. Usually high level of disclosure of investments.	No direct link. Returns to depositors and earnings of banks not directly linked. Limited disclosure of investments.
Formal insurance schemes often based on pooled industry-wide insurance.	No industry scheme; government support highly unlikely.	Industry scheme almost always available; government functions as lender of last resort in some circumstances.
Variable: may be expected to be high for surviving dependents or in old age.	Frequently large (beneficiaries do not diversify across trusts).	Variable—but usually not high.

mediaries and form strong trade-policy preferences

Weak: benefits are often defined. Long life and illiquidity of policies.	Very strong: high transparency of investments.	Weak: limited transparency of investments.
Industry guarantee scheme usually available: limited expectation of public bail-out (more so where insurance com-panies are subject to public supervision).	No.	Yes: Potential for moral hazard created by deposit protection and likelihood of public bail-out. Also, public supervision is expected to substitute for monitoring.
Fund-holders with small stakes will free-ride.	No obvious problems (small *n*).	Large numbers of depositors holding small stakes will tend to free-ride.

across different forms of financial intermediation. When the income link is both strong (returns to savers are directly linked to the intermediary's earnings) and predictable (there are few unanticipated shocks for investors), there is less need for insurance. In banking there is commonly a contingent or insurance contract, often in the name of the government (although in many countries costs may fall on other banks via pooled guarantees) either through a deposit insurance scheme (although this may at times be supplemented by some form of lender-of-last-resort intervention), a policy of requiring a competitor to purchase a troubled bank, or direct public ownership of banks. The effectiveness of insurance provision depends, however, on the extent to which depositors and investors understand the insurance they receive. Debate exists as to whether the public always realizes that deposits are insured. There is an interesting contrast here between the United States and Germany. In the former, banks advertise their federal insurance coverage, whereas in Germany the advertising of deposit insurance is prohibited.[17]

Table 9.1 shows that generally there is an inverse relationship between the income link and the insurance component. Banks enjoy the strongest insurance and the weakest income link, while mutual funds and private trusts and endowments have strong income but weak insurance links. Pension funds and life insurers are somewhere in the middle, with an insurance component that may, for instance, depend upon the unpredictable moral suasion power of pensioners.[18]

The third characteristic of the relationship between individuals and financial intermediaries is the 'factor-concentration component', the share of individuals' factor income represented by investment through a particular type of financial intermediary. We expect this component to be complementary to, rather than a substitute for, the income link and insurance component. As Table 9.1 summarizes, the factor-concentration component is greatest in private trusts and endowments, because beneficiaries typically have few other sources of income on the same scale. In contrast, banks have the weakest factor-income component, because bank deposits are typically a small source of overall income. Mutual funds, pension funds, and life-insurance companies fall somewhere in the middle: pension funds have a special characteristic because the factor-income dependence is expected to increase significantly in old age.

We can use the framework of Table 9.1 to speculate on the strength of interest formation across the forms of financial intermediaries. The sign for the strength of influence is positive for the income link and factor-concentration component, and negative for the insurance component. For instance, beneficiaries of private trusts and endowments are predicted to have the strongest interest due to their strong income link and factor concentration and weak insurance component. In contrast, bank depositors will have the weakest interest because of the weak income link and factor concentration combined with strong insurance. Mutual funds, pension funds, and life insurance fall in the middle, although it would be inadvisable to propose a rank order based on such a highly stylized presentation.[19]

Financial Intermediation and the Trade-Policy Preferences of Financial Intermediaries

Information imperfections affect not only the form of investment but also the relationship between financial intermediaries and corporate borrowers, the distribution of information between them, and hence the coincidence of preferences on trade policy. It is frequently argued that the long-term relationships observed in a bank-oriented system such as that in Germany mitigate informational problems and create a close bond between banks and companies. The private nature of such information flows, and the consequent illiquidity of bank claims on companies, ties banks more closely to borrowing companies, thereby making banks more powerful advocates of their borrowers' interests.[20] The corollary is that the bond between individual savers and companies is much weaker because banks are able to create long-term stable financing for companies by removing the threat that individual savers will disrupt the market for investment by unexpectedly leaving the market when they face sudden liquidity constraints.

Our interest lies not only in loans but also in equity held by banks, particularly in Germany, where banks commonly hold equity stakes in major firms. Equity holdings commit banks to firms: by holding equities banks become residual claimants, increasing the link between the returns to the company's business and those to the bank.[21] An equity holding reinforces the bank's influence over the firm, whilst the firm gains by the long-term relationship.[22]

For the other categories of financial institutions, the income link depends as much on other characteristics—the presence of insurance and portfolio diversification or asset concentration—as on the nature of the information flows from borrowers. In theory the stronger (weaker) the insurance the less (more) likely the financial intermediary is to monitor the borrower, and hence participate in advancing policy preferences. Thus a mutual fund or private trust or endowment with no insurance protection should be a strong monitor of companies and should participate in advocating their interests. In contrast, a bank with substantial insurance protection should be a weak monitor and policy-preference advocate. This is a simple moral-hazard problem: where banks have incomplete contracts they do not bear the full consequences of their own inaction. In practice, the position is not so simple, because for almost all insurance schemes the insured are the depositors and not the shareholders and managers of banks. This is one important tool available to the authorities when writing insurance contracts to limit moral hazard, and should strengthen banks' links to borrowers.

A more important influence is the ability of financial intermediaries' to diversify their portfolios (which parallels the earlier discussion of the factor-concentration component for individual savers). A diversified financial intermediary will have no strong incentive to advance the preferences of a particular company or industry (e.g. an import-competing company) where this conflicts with the interest of another company in which it invests (e.g. an export-oriented company).

3. INVESTMENTS AND INTERESTS IN THE UNITED STATES AND GERMANY

The United States

In the 1980s and early 1990s, two seemingly independent trends converged in the policy domain of the United States: institutionalization of investment, and 'competitiveness mania'.

Competitiveness mania. In the past few years, academics,[23] 'pop internationalists',[24] and the popular press have spilled much ink comparing the US to the 'competitively advantaged' countries of Germany and Japan (recent evidence notwithstanding[25]). Another group of authors have cited the myopia of American investors as contributing to a perceived decline in US international competitiveness.[26] They find an inherent mismatch between the short-term profit-maximization interests of American investors and managers and the longer-term investment and planning needs of a strategically competitive national economy. The leading proponent of changes in the system of corporate governance is Michael Porter who argues: 'The American system creates a divergence of interests among shareholders, corporations, and their managers that impedes the flow of capital to those corporate investments that offer the greatest payoffs. *Just as significant, it fails to align the interests of individual investors and corporations with those of the economy and nation as a whole*'.[27] (our emphasis). As far as the role of government is concerned, 'Governments do not control national competitive advantage; they can only influence it', especially 'through such devices as capital market regulations, tax policy, and antitrust laws.'[28] Porter argues for a more stable, long-term system of capital ownership, thereby creating interests (particularly among investors) that are associated less with simply owning capital or labour and more with the specific industries in which they invest or work. Implicit in Porter's argument is that investors should also become less diversified. Porter is thus encouraging factor-owners (especially asset-holders) to exercise control over their property-ownership rights (i.e. to aggressively monitor the firms in which they invest) while holding strictly in reserve the ultimate mechanism of exit through selling their shares.

For the investor, Porter prescribes concentration of assets; for the firm, he prescribes specialization of production (with diversification advisable only through closely related activities[29]); and at the national level, he equivocates. On the one hand, Porter maintains that certain types of factors of production—namely, advanced, specialized factors (e.g. highly educated personnel, or infrastructure with specific properties relevant to a limited range of industries)—are most important for gaining competitive advantage, and that government efforts to create these specialized factors may succeed if they are closely aligned with industry.[30] He thus imposes a hierarchy on factors of production in terms of their contribution to competitive advantage. On the other hand, he rejects a hierarchy of industries, asserting that 'Most industries are, or will become, high-technology or knowledge-intensive industries'.[31]

The growth of institutional investors.   At the end of 1990, institutional investors controlled 20.5 per cent of total financial assets outstanding in the US economy.[32] Between 1950 and 1989, the share of pension-fund assets allocated to equities jumped from 6 to 40 per cent.[33] Institutional ownership of the equity of US corporations rose from 8 per cent in 1950 to 38 in 1981 and 53 per cent in 1990.[34] Over 300 of the top 1,000 American corporations are now more than 60 per cent owned by institutional investors.[35] In 1988 the level of institutional ownership was 82 per cent for General Motors, 74 for Mobil, 70 for Citicorp, 86 for Amoco, and 71 per cent for Eli Lilly and Co.[36] At the end of 1989 the top fifty institutions in the US owned 27 per cent of stock-market capitalization ($925 bn.): half of this was owned by the thirteen largest institutions.

Individual institutions have grown quickly. For example, CalPERS (California Public Employees' Retirement System) has more than $56 bn. of assets invested in publicly traded US securities, and the New York State pension funds together control about $100 bn. of assets.[37] Demographic trends alone ensure that pension-fund ownership will rise. This trend was already evident in the 1980s, when stock owned by public and private pension funds rose from 18.6 per cent of stock-market capitalization in 1980 to 28 per cent in 1990. Mutual funds were also growing rapidly throughout the 1980s, with equity holdings rising from $38 bn. (2.5 per cent of market capitalization) in 1980 to $200 bn. in 1986 (6.5 per cent of market capitalization), and around $350 bn. in September 1992 (10 per cent of market capitalization).[38] The other side of the coin is that private investors have been net sellers of equity: between 1984 and 1989 US households sold 38 per cent of their equity holdings, amounting to $500 bn.[39]

The effect of the institutionalization of investment on trade preferences.   Criticisms of corporate governance in the United States concern the rapid growth over the last thirty years of institutional investment, and the decline of large, supposedly stable, individual investment holdings. To assess the implications of these changes for trade preferences, we examine Porter's argument that institutionalization has increased the mobility of investment capital (i.e. reduced asset specificity) to the point where investors ignore forecast long-term returns. We use our three-component model to assess whether institutions are diversified to the extent that their holdings in any given firm have become so diluted that free-riding is rational. The critics of American investment policies and corporate governance argue that institutional investors (1) do not take an active interest in overseeing managers of firms because they are (2) transient owners more intent on trading than owning shares, and because (3) their ownership share is too diversified (hence individual holdings are too small) to warrant anything other than rational apathy, thereby creating free-rider problems for any investor seeking to take the lead. We examine these three arguments in turn.

1. The view that American corporate owners are strangled by their own passivity is not universally endorsed. Some authors point to institutions, notably public pension funds, showing a greater willingness either to hold large stakes themselves or to form groups to hold such stakes.[40] The 'Wall Street Rule (or Walk)'—where institutional investors vote with their feet and sell their shares in (exit) a poorly performing firm rather than voice their concerns to management—is said to be on the wane. The evidence of institutional activism is, however, anecdotal at best, and certainly not yet suggestive of a widespread trend. Indeed much of the press coverage of activism is generated by one institution, CalPERS, which commands attention on account of its size.[41]

2. The transience of investment argument is easier to verify: the average holding period of stocks in the US has declined from more than seven years in 1960 to about two years in the early 1990s. This has fuelled the debate over the existence of a conflict between short-term interests and long-term investment. Porter highlights an apparent paradox of the American system: institutions entrusted with funds for extremely long periods resort to active trading and short holding periods.[42]

3. Diversification of investment portfolios has undoubtedly increased in the last twenty years. The evidence suggests that major US institutions often hold between 2 and 3 per cent of the stock of large corporations.[43] Porter cites the case of CalPERS, which in 1990 reportedly held stock in more than 2,000 US companies.[44] Two reasons appear to explain the pattern of diversification. First, legal restrictions apply: disclosure requirements limit holdings above 5 per cent, and, more severely, insider trading rules apply to holdings above 10 per cent. These laws are part of what some

commentators argue is an overly restrictive US regulatory structure.[45] Second, indexation of investments has become an accepted and cheap fund-management strategy. Almost one-third of equity investments held by US institutional funds are indexed.[46] It is almost self-evident that holding stakes in all of the Standard and Poor's 500 severely limits the capacity of institutions both to monitor those corporations and to lobby on their behalf.[47]

Critics of excessive diversification argue that a reduction in the number of stocks held by institutions would not lead to a commensurate increase in exposure to risk through concentration.[48] Reducing the number of stocks held in a portfolio may contribute to greater institutional activism in corporate governance, thus improving internal management productivity, which may ultimately increase the competitiveness of American industry. But as long as they remain diversified, albeit with a smaller number of holdings (say 20 as opposed to 200), institutions will not have an incentive to lobby on trade policy. To expect institutions to lobby actively on trade-policy issues on behalf of firms in which they invest requires them to forsake the principle of diversification, not just reduce the number of holdings. But any argument for a deliberate concentration of institutional holdings contradicts the legal consensus (for instance, on the interpretation of the prudent-man rule, whereby institutional investors are obliged to act responsibly in handling the assets of their customers).[49] Most important of all, a policy of deliberate concentration would require a willingness by investors to forgo the reduction in risk associated with a diversified portfolio. However, most investors expect institutional intermediaries to spread risks, they do not seek to create or acquire trade interests.

In sum, any prescription for improving America's competitiveness by overhauling the structure of corporate governance will not easily deliver a cure when it comes to sharpening trade-policy preferences. Creating commitment through asset specificity will not of itself create competitively advantaged industries with share-owners strongly advocating the trade preferences of firms, unless there are accompanying, and unlikely, changes in the legal system and in the expectations of investors who have used institutional investment as a more efficient route to portfolio diversification.

Germany

Five features of bank oriented financial systems are distinctive of the German scene: (1) depositors have very limited information about the relationship between a bank and its major borrowers; (2) depositors therefore have an agency problem in monitoring banks (although they may solve the problem by relying on a combination of public supervision, deposit-insurance schemes, assumptions on lender of last resort and too-big-to-fail policies among the authorities, and the publications of rating agencies); (3) in contrast, the banks themselves generally have private information; (4) such information contributes to making bank exposures illiquid, thereby reinforcing the shared interest of banks and borrowers; and (5) the incentive for banks to advocate the interest of borrowers is potentially strong unless their exposures[50] are highly diversified.

Traditional versus revisionist assessments of German banking. The traditional story of German banking suggests that, through a combination of direct holdings of equity capital and substantial proxy-voting powers, German banks exercise tight control over German corporations. German banks have been described by John Zysman as 'prefects' in the German system of organized capitalism.[51] Moreover 'The power of the German banks in industrial affairs rests on two pillars: their market power over the sources of finance for industry, and their legal right to own substantial stock in corporations and to exercise proxy votes for other shareholders.'[52]

The revisionist view stems from Zysman's observation that 'Few existing studies attempt to show the extent of banks' prefectural and tutorial roles or to examine the consequences.'[53] More recently, empirical tests of the traditional assumptions of German bank power have been attempted.[54] Four findings of this work are notable. First, 'shareholdings in industry, presence on supervisory boards and proxy-voting rights increasingly do not indicate the power of banks in Germany,'[55] Second, 'Arms-length market relationships between banks and firms are increasingly replacing traditional co-operative or non-market relationships'.[56] Major firms have achieved more autonomy from banks: for instance, German industrial restructuring in the 1980s was more decentralized, with the banks supporting rather than leading.[57] Third, the state has quietly expanded its role in economic governance (particularly at the regional level). Fourth, the growth of competition among German banks for the business of large German companies has severely circumscribed the scope for non-market relationships between banks and companies.

We noted earlier that the traditional idea of long-term relationships between banks and the firms in which they invest, as well as the illiquid nature of those investments, means that banks could be powerful advocates of the interests of those firms. Below we consider five elements of the revisionist interpretation of German banking in order to determine whether it affects the interest formation of banks.

1. First, we consider banks' shareholdings. Few German corporations use the stock market, and those that do raise only a small proportion of capital by issuing exchange-listed securities.[58] This reflects the continued presence of significant legal restrictions in Germany which limit firms' access to equity finance.[59] The rapid growth of German industry in the last quarter of the nineteenth century is often regarded as in part dependent on the rise to prominence of major so-called universal banks which could mobilize the substantial financing needs of an economy pursuing the earlier industrialized powers, notably the UK and US. The size of the demand for finance, and the information problems this created for prospective lenders to major firms, cemented the role of banks as intermediaries. The revisionist view argues that German banks no longer dominate German industry though large holdings of equity capital. Various calculations suggest that German banks own between 5 and 10 per cent of German industrial share capital.[60] Declining ownership has been evident since the mid-1970s, and therefore pre-dates the introduction of regulations to limit bank ownership. In the ten years to 1986, the number of German corporations in which banks jointly held 10 per cent or more equity ownership fell from 129 to 86. In 1976 the ten largest private banks in West Germany held 4.5 per cent of the nominal capital of all publicly traded firms, but by 1986 this figure was 3.2 per cent.[61] The number of firms in which banks controlled more than 25 per cent of the shares—a blocking minority—was 86 in 1976 and only 45 in 1986.[62] Of the 50 largest firms in West Germany, the private banks held more than 25 per cent of shares in only two.[63] Deutsche Bank, the largest among the private banks, has reduced the

number of large holdings in firms and has announced its intention to cease acquiring large new holdings.

2. The large German banks effectively control many corporations through extensive proxy-voting powers.[64] Among the 100 largest Aktiengesellschaften (AGs are the largest corporations in Germany) the combined bank vote (direct plus proxy holdings) exceeded 50 per cent in thirty.[65] Moreover, the big three German banks (Deutsche Bank, Dresdner Bank, and Commerzbank) accounted for 26 of the 41 corporations where the voting strength of banks exceeded 25 per cent.[66]

Under the proxy voting system banks will have more voting control in firms with more small shareholders.[67] Thus proxy-voting powers diminish the interest, and hence the trade-policy preferences, of small shareholders. Banks normally have certain trust obligations to monitor management if they are acting in a proxy capacity for small shareholders, but such a duty does not extend to advancing trade preferences on behalf of small shareholders. For firms where the bank has a direct shareholding of its own, proxy-voting powers will, if anything, reinforce the trade preference of the bank. Moreover, banks can reinforce this position through the system that allows them to loan proxy rights to each other.[68] But in cases where the bank is voting proxies in a company in which it has no direct interest, it is unlikely that the bank will have a strong incentive to advance trade preferences. We conclude that proxy-voting powers can in some circumstances reinforce the trade preferences of banks; but where the bank has no strong interest through direct ownership of equity, and the individual owners have surrendered much of their interest by signing away their voting rights, the proxy system cannot augment the sum of trade preferences.

3. The boardroom activism of German banks is traditionally viewed as reflecting their strong economic interests. From here it is a small leap to the argument that German banks supervise corporate management in a close and intensive fashion. Such activism, or exercise of voice, is predictable in so far as the relatively undeveloped German stock market creates illiquid bank holdings.[69] But revisionist authors have questioned the power of German banks to control corporate managements on behalf of shareholders. Edwards and Fischer, and Esser question the numerical strength of banks on supervisory boards of corporations, and the ability of

supervisory boards to monitor managements.[70] Bank representation on the supervisory boards of the hundred largest firms fell to 7 per cent of board members by 1989. Perhaps even more striking is the behaviour of Deutsche Bank, which has voluntarily decided to relinquish its chairmanships of supervisory boards of German corporations, positions which are generally believed to wield the greatest influence and capacity for monitoring.[71] Another line of attack on the traditional theory of bank control questions the capacity of supervisory boards to exercise control over corporate policy which is the responsibility of the Executive Board (*Vorstand*).[72]

4. The revisionists argue that in the last twenty years Germany has become a highly competitive banking market, and that the power of traditional bank–firm relations has been eroded. In a competitive market there is more scope for large firms to be independent and to play banks off against each other. Increased competition has led to a greater homogeneity among German banks and an equalization of their market shares, although the savings banks are still restricted geographically and have limits on their ability to take equity positions.

5. The traditional model of German banking emphasizes the involvement of the banks in industrial policy. The competitive bargaining relationship between banks and industry[73] avoids either a strong state role in industrial policy or heavy reliance on private capital-market forces. One of the distinctive features of the traditional interpretation is the role of the banks in industrial restructuring and corporate rescues: 'there are clear instances in which banks have taken industrial matters into their own hands and the evidence, though scanty, suggests that bank involvement is a central component of the private collective management of industrial change.'[74] This has led to a stylized view of German bank–industry relations which has the banks co-ordinating the activities of industry and government on industrial issues.[75] Yet, as Zysman notes, none of the traditionalist studies offered 'an implicit argument as to how the banking system affects the choice of firms and government in industrial development and adjustment.'[76]

The evidence on bank involvement in industrial restructuring does point to a long-run pattern of change over the last thirty years. Through the mid-1970s West German governments insisted that industrial problems would be tackled by the private sector (including the banks) rather than by state intervention. In its successive crises in 1962–3 and 1967, the steel industry 'preferred intervention by banks rather than the state as a way of limiting the politicization of the industry. The banks had strong financial incentives to intervene, whereas the state had an ideological stake in avoiding overt intervention.'[77] The result was a bank-led rationalization of the steel industry, increasing the two largest German steel firms' share of production from 23 per cent in 1960 to 52 per cent ion 1984. When the steel industry was in trouble in the late 1970s and 1980s the response was different. The federal government became increasingly involved 'in negotiations for the restructuring of the industry because neither the banks nor the state governments were capable of handling it alone'.[78] A similar pattern has prevailed in the electronics industry.[79] In the German car industry the pattern has likewise been one of a growing involvement of the federal and state governments in setting the rules for industrial restructuring, but as a partner of not a substitute for the banks.[80]

Another important aspect has been the growing emphasis on regional policy which involves a partnership with banks, and an emphasis on the regional focus of many German banks. Most important from the perspective of trade-policy preferences, regional banks, which have been growing in terms of market share, have encouraged local economic growth by developing relationships with local firms.[81] A greater regional emphasis by at least the second or third tier of German banks is likely if anything to strengthen their trade preferences by creating interests which are strongly associated with a local economy.

The trade preferences of German banks: An application of the three-component model. A quick review of the evidence for the traditionalist and revisionist interpretations of German banking leaves an important question in relation to prospective changes in the pattern of trade preferences of German banks. Does the prospect of more autonomous firms (reflecting fewer large bank shareholdings, fewer bank-appointed members of supervisory boards, and more competition among the banks themselves), and a more active public-sector involvement, change the incentive for banks to form trade preferences and for firms to rely on banks as intermediaries lobbying government on their behalf? This question can be put into the context of a breakdown in the ordered hierarchy of German economic institutions. Katzenstein and others have argued that German interest-groups have traditionally been 'large, centralized, and encompassing. The "peak associations" of business and labor, in particular, have been central actors'. Labour and capital have existed largely peacefully under 'codetermination', supported by a dense network of para-public institutions. The established model of German interest-group behaviour is illustrated by the metal industries, where the trade union (IG Metall) and employers' organization (Gesamtmetall) represent the entire industry and focus on common interests rather than the diverse interests of firms and industries. Moreover, because the German federal constitution gives only national trade associations 'consultative or semi-official status', the government 'forces the centralization of interest representation'.[82] The result is that the peak associations for employers and labour are pro free trade.

We can only provide a partial answer to the question of the impact of change in Germany on the preference formation of banks. We do not, for instance, have sufficient information to assess the role of the banks within what Katzenstein terms the para-public institutions that 'provide the key for a relatively quiet process of policy formulation and implementation'.[83] Under the traditional model of German bank–industry relations, which seems to have survived in most important respects until at least the mid-1970s, the major banks are likely to have had industrial interests through shareholdings and board seats which spanned a wide range of the German economy. In this respect the banks can be likened to the so-called peak organizations of business and labour, and most probably contributed to earning West Germany the reputation as the most liberal (and pro free trade) large country member of the European Community.[84] However, important features of the evidence supporting the revisionist case point to a change in the pattern of trade-policy preferences. Industries such as coal-mining, steel, and shipbuilding, which have received substantial subsidies since the late 1970s, 'fall almost completely outside the institutional framework supporting freer trade.'[85] All three industries are heavily concentrated regionally and all have benefited from greater government intervention in reconstruction. We can therefore see some evidence of a change in the pattern of interest-group activity in Germany. But whether this change is mirrored in the behaviour of German banks is not revealed by the revisionist studies of German banking.

Turning to our three-component model, little direct evidence is available for either the degree of diversification of German bank exposures across sectors or the lobbying activities of the banks on behalf of firms. The stock ownership of German firms is certainly more concentrated than for large US firms. Among the 400 German corporations traded on German stock exchanges in 1988, around 300 possessed a (mostly non-bank) controlling shareholder or shareholder group. More recent estimates suggest that, although the number of publicly traded companies in Germany has risen to around 600, 90 per cent of these have a controlling shareholder.[86] Share ownership in Germany is therefore sufficiently concentrated to leave owners with distinct incentives to adopt firms' trade preferences. However, a more important issue for the banks is the form of ownership links (property rights) and the concentration of banks' own portfolios (diversification).

There are three principal types of ownership links for German banks: the exercise of proxy voting rights on behalf of shareholders; loans; and direct equity holdings. With proxy voting, the contract between shareholder and bank does not give the bank a direct financial interest in the performance of the firm—the bank's responsibility to the share-owners is to vote the shares not to lobby for political action. Loans are obviously a major part of the business of German banks, and it is reasonable to believe that the large German banks have traditionally held loan-books with highly diversified holdings of exposures across the German economy. Unlike US mutual funds, diversification may not blunt the incentive to lobby on behalf of a particular firm since loan contracts have a bounded outcome—i.e. a bank can do no better than receive the contracted payments—whereas equity holdings have potentially unlimited gains. While a US mutual fund might expect protectionism in one industry to reduce the returns on holdings in other industries, a German bank may conclude that protectionism would not damage the likelihood of loans being serviced by firms in other industries.

By selling a portion of their large equity holdings banks are becoming more concentrated in their residual holdings. This pattern of greater concentration is supported by the evidence that banks, particularly in the second and third tiers, have become more regionally concentrated, and have entered into understandings with state governments which have led to closer relationships with local firms. We therefore conclude tentatively that German banks are currently in a position to be more forceful advocates of the trade preferences of the firms in which they invest both as a result of a movement towards greater concentration of equity ownership and some evidence of greater regional concentration. Moreover, the signs of movement towards a more pluralist approach to trade and industrial policy among German business and labour representatives supports the idea that banks, too, may be taking a more partisan approach to the advocacy of preferences.

Finally, we predict that German bank depositors are at least as likely to have weak preferences as their counterparts in the US. German bank depositors are well protected by deposit insurance. Moreover, the income link in Germany that runs between the earnings of the bank on its investment portfolio and the returns to depositors has until very recently been obscured by the prevalence of hidden reserves which act as a buffer and smooth the income of banks.[87] Finally, the proxy-voting rights system means that individual small shareholders (who will typically also be bank depositors) will have substantially diminished interests in the firms in which they invest.

4. CONCLUSION

Trade theorists and finance theorists make interesting bedfellows. In this chapter we have brought together strands of these two literatures in order to expose deficiencies in trade theory. These deficiencies arise from a mistaken belief that to predict trade preferences—and hence, to predict coalition formation—the fundamental question is whether factors are specific or mobile. Whereas trade theory may predict the direction of trade preferences (free trade or protection), it falls short of specifying the strength of these preferences. Without understanding the strength of preferences, prediction about how these preferences may organize into coalitions to influence policy will at best be shaky and at worst be wrong. We focused on one factor of production—investment capital (particularly financial assets)—to demonstrate the importance of assessing the risk exposure of individual investors. We drew upon three components to gauge the riskiness of financial assets: the income link; the insurance component; and the concentration of factor returns component. We applied our framework of analysis (as summarized in Table 9.1) to two countries, the United States and Germany.

The application of our framework to the US and Germany cautions against over-simplistic conclusions about a policy agenda to restore national competitiveness. We do not, for instance, find that individual Germans are more likely to hold their savings in a form that promotes a strong identity with the trade-policy preferences of German firms. If anything, they are less likely to form strong preferences than individual Americans (whose preferences are also likely to be weak) despite the periodic use of Germany as a role-model for fostering national competitiveness. Moreover, when it comes to comparing German banks with American institutions, our conclusion that the former have more concentrated holdings, and hence a stronger likelihood to act on their preferences, is a cautious one. More evidence is required on the behaviour of German banks in the area of trade-policy lobbying.

Our response to the competitiveness debate in the US is more categorical. If the enactment of trade policies designed to restore national competitiveness depends on the active involvement of investors—both individuals and institutions—as Porter and others have suggested, then financial intermediation would need to be restructured such that information asymmetries are minimized; financial-insurance provisions are sufficiently ambiguous to avoid moral-hazard problems; and a reliance on portfolio diversification is replaced with an acceptance that investing in firms involves sharing the market risks facing those firms, all of which would radically alter how investors assess their exposure to risk.

NOTES

1. A. L. Hillman, *The Political Economy of Protection* (London and New York: Harwood Academic Publishers, 1989); S. P. Magee, W. A. Brock, and L. Young, *Black Hole Tariffs and Endogenous Policy Theory: Political Economy in General Equilibrium* (Cambridge: Cambridge University Press, 1989); R. E. Baldwin, *The Political*

Economy of U.S. Import Policy (Cambridge, Mass: MIT Press: 1985).

2. P. Evans, D. Rueschmeyer, and T. Skocpol (eds.), *Bringing the State Back In* (Cambridge: Cambridge University Press, 1985); S. Krasner, *Defending the National Interest: Raw Materials Investments and U.S. Foreign Policy* (Princeton, NJ: Princeton University Press, 1978).

3. See A. L. Hillman, 'International Trade Policy: Benevolent Dictators and Optimizing Politicians', *Public Choice*, 74 (1992), 1–15. C. Schonhardt-Bailey, 'A Model of Trade Policy Liberalization: Looking Inside the British "Hegemon" of the Nineteenth Century', Ph.D. thesis (Los Angeles, 1991) applies the political-support-maximizing approach to explain British trade policy in the last century.

4. K. Shepsle and B. Weingast, 'Structure-Induced Equilibrium and Legislative Choice', *Public Choice*, 37 (1981), 503–19.

5. R. E. Caves, J. A. Frankel, and R. W. Jones, *World Trade and Payments: An Introduction*, (New York: Harper Collins, 6th edn., 1993), 136–9; 146–9.

6. Arye Hillman as kind enough to bring this to our attention.

7. Hillman, *Political Economy*, 104.

8. J. E. Alt, and M. Gilligan, 'The Political Economy of Trading States: Factor Specificity, Collective Action Problems, and Domestic Political Institutions', paper presented at the American Political Science Association Annual Meeting (Washington, DC, 1993); W. Mayer, 'Endogenous Tariff Formation', *American Economic Review*, 74 (1984), 970–85; C. Schonhardt-Bailey, 'Specific Factors, Capital Markets, Portfolio Diversification, and Free Trade: Domestic Determinants of the Repeal of the Corn Laws', *World Politics*, 43 (1991), 545–69; J. A. Frieden, *Debt, Development, and Democracy: Modern Political Economy and Latin America, 1965–1985* (Princeton, NJ: Princeton University Press, 1991).

9. Frieden, *Debt*, 21.

10. Although Stephen Magee, 'Three Simple Tests of the Stolper-Samuelson Theorem', in P. Oppenheimer (ed.), *Issues in International Economics* (London: Oriel Press, 1980), has provided some indirect evidence based on the constancy of free-trade lobbying between capital and labour which leads him to conclude that both factors are specific to their sector, one of the few direct tests of the behaviour of capital has been made by G. M. Grossman and J. A. Levinsohn, 'Import Competition and the Stock Market Return to Capital', *American Economic Review*, 79 (1989), 1065–87). They measure the responsiveness of returns to capital in a number of US industries over 1974–86 to shocks in the prices of competing imports.

11. M. E. Porter, *The Competitive Advantage of Nations* (London: Macmillan, 1990), 74–6.

12. Here we build upon M. L. Weitzman and C. Xu's discussion of a continuum of property rights, along which societies may fall, 'Chinese Township Village Enterprises as Vaguely Defined Cooperatives', *Journal of Comparative Economics* (forthcoming).

13. The average 1989 institutional holdings of the top 50 corporations ranked by stock-market value was also 50%. The corresponding average for the top 1,000 companies was 48% (C. K. Brancato, 'The Pivotal Role of Institutional Investors in Capital Markets', in A. W. Sametz (ed.), *Institutional Investing: The Challenges and Responsibilities of the 21st Century* (New York: Business One Irwin, 1991).

14. D. W. Diamond, 'Financial Intermediation and Delegated Monitoring', *Review of Economic Studies*, 51 (1984), 393–414. See also Y. Chan, 'On the Positive Role of Financial Intermediation in Allocation of Venture Capital in a Market with Imperfect Information', *Journal of Finance*, 38 (1983), 1543–68; E. P. Davis, 'Theories of Intermediation, Financial Innovation and Regulation', *National Westminster Bank Quarterly Review*, (1983), 41–53; H. Leyland and D. Pyle, 'Informational Asymmetries, Financial Structure and Financial Intermediation', *Journal of Finance*, 32 (1977), 371–87.

15. Diamond, 'Financial Intermediation', 393.

16. J. Bisignano, 'Banking in the European Community: Structure, Competition, and Public Policy', in G. G. Kaufman (ed.), *Banking Structures in Major Countries* (Norwell, Mass.: Kluwer Academic Publishers, 1992), 158–9.

17. E. Baltensperger and J. Dermine, 'European Banking, Prudential and Regulatory Issues', mimeo, paper presented at the INSEAD Conference on European Banking after 1992, (Fontainbleau, 1989); cited in Bisignano, 'Banking', 221.

18. 'Defined-benefit' pension plans (where employers bear the risk of providing a pre-defined pension) have been losing ground to 'defined-contribution' pension plans (where individuals bear the risk of an uncertain value for the pension pay-out). Defined-contribution plans are closer to mutual funds in having a stronger income link–weaker insurance component profile than defined benefit plans.

19. The evidence suggests, however, that mutual fund investors show little interest in the composition of boards of fund managers, and often do not have the right to vote for them. See E. F. Fama and M. C. Jensen, 'Separation of Ownership and Control', *Journal of Law and Economics*, 26 (1983), 301–25.

20. For instance, see J. Cable, 'Capital Market Information and Industrial Performance: The Role of West German Banks', *Economic Journal*, 95 (1985), 118–32.

21. A. B. Frankel, and J. D. Montgomery, 'Financial Structure: An International Perspective', *Brookings Papers on Economic Activity*, 1 (1991), 293.

22. Davis ('Theories of Intermediation', 45) notes that 'commitment is a form of "implicit contract"—the nature of the agreement to provide credit (by the lender) and to remain a customer (by the borrower) cannot be specified formally.' (See also C. Mayer, 'New Issues in Corporate Finance', *European Economic Review*, 32 (1988), 1167–88.)

23. A summary edited volume presenting the arguments for free trade (A. O. Krueger), bilateralism (R. W. Dornbusch) and managed trade (L. D'Andrea Tyson) is R. Z. Lawrence and C. L. Schultze (eds.), *An American Trade Strategy: Options for the 1990s* (Washington, DC: Brookings Institution, 1990). Caves, Frankel, and Jones, (*World Trade and Payments*, 234–82) offer a more balanced exposition of managed trade and industrial policy. See also P. R. Krugman (ed.), *Strategic Trade Policy and the New International Economics* (Cambridge and London: MIT Press, 1986); J. D. Richardson, 'The Political Economy of Strategic Trade Policy', *International Organization*, 44 (1990), 107–35; and I. M. Destler, *American Trade Politics: System Under Stress*, (Washington, DC: Institute for International Business, 2nd edn., 1992).

24. P. R. Krugman ('What Do Undergrads Need to Know About Trade?', *American Economic Review*, 83 (1993), 23–6) coins this phrase to criticize the works of M. Crichton (*Rising Sun* (New York, 1992)), L. Thurow (*Head to Head* (New York: William Morrow, 1992)), and R. Reich (*The Work of Nations* (New York: Knopf, 1991)).

25. A recent study by McKinsey Global Institute (*Manufacturing Productivity* (Washington, DC, 1993)), debunks common perception by finding that labour productivity for manufacturing as a whole is higher in the US than in Germany and Japan.

26. See, for example, M. E. Porter, 'Capital Disadvantage: America's Failing Capital Investment System', *Harvard Business Review*, 70 (1992), 65–82; and B. S. Black, 'Institutional Investors and Corporate Governance: The Case for Institutional Voice', *Continental Bank: Journal of Applied Corporate Finance*, 5 (1992), 19–32.

27. Porter, 'Capital Disadvantage', 66.

28. Porter, 128, 617.

29. Ibid. 604–6.

30. Ibid. 81.

31. Ibid. 624.

32. C. K. Brancato, and P. A. Gaughan, 'Institutional Investors and Capital Markets: 1991 Update', Center for Law and Economic Studies Institutional Investor Project (New York, 1991).

33. Brancato, 'Pivotal Role', 35–6.
34. Ibid. 18; J. C. Coffee, Jr., 'Liquidity Versus Control: The Institutional Investor as Corporate Monitor', *Columbia Law Review*, 91 (1991), 1277–1368, 1298.
35. Among companies in the top 1000, 30 per cent have institutional levels above 60 per cent (Coffee, 'Liquidity versus Control', 1291; and A. F. Conard, 'Beyond Managerial Capitalism: Investor Capitalism?', *University of Michigan Journal of Law*, 88 (1989), 117, 132).
36. J. C. Coffee, Jnr., 'Liquidity versus Control'.
37. L. Pollack, 'Investor Activism via Professionally Managed Special-Purpose Funds', in Sametz, *Institutional Investing*, 287. Of the total assets controlled by pension funds in the US, corporate pension funds control one half, public pension funds one third, and the balance is held by union pension funds and the funds of non-profit entities (Coffee, 'Liquidity Versus Control', 1292).
38. B. Black, 'Shareholder Passivity Re-examined', *Michigan Law Review*, 89 (1990), 520–608. Investment flows into mutual funds in the first nine months of 1993 totalled $200 bn.—representing a 13 per cent increase in total mutual fund assets ('Only Perform', Investment Management Survey, *The Economist*, 27 Nov. 1993, 4).
39. J. O. Light, 'The Privatization of Equity', *Harvard Business Review*, 67 (1989), 62–3.
40. See, for example, recent stories about CalPERS: 'Return of the Active Shareholder', *The Economist*, 30 Jan. 1993, 18–19; 'A Fund in Wolf's Clothing?', *The Economist*, 30 Jan. 1993, 82; 'American Corporate Governance: Shareholders Call the Plays', *The Economist*, 25 Apr. 1993, 117–20. See also Coffee, 'Liquidity Versus Control', 1288.
41. It is ironic that both sides cite CalPERS as a case in point to illustrate both excessive diversification and nascent activism.
42. Porter, 'Capital Disadvantage', 80.
43. These figures are probably underestimates because they rely on the incomplete coverage of SEC filing data.
44. Porter, 'Capital Disadvantage', 69.
45. Black, 'Institutional Investors', 20.
46. Indexation is commonly defined as 'a passive investment strategy whereby an investor holds a portfolio of securities that serves as a proxy for the market as a whole (such as the Standard and Poor's 500). Such investors seek not to beat the market, but to match it' (Coffee, 'Liquidity Versus Control', 1290).
47. Coffee and Rock have noted the powerful competitive and cost reasons why institutions cannot afford to devote resources to monitoring companies or lobby on their behalf. They assume that either there are few benefits from lobbying or monitoring, or that any benefits which

might accrue would be dispersed among other free-riding institutions ("Coffee, 'Liquidity Versus Control', 1341; E. Rock, 'The Logic and (Uncertain) Significance of Institutional Shareholder Activism', *Georgetown Law Journal*, 79 (1991), 474).

48. B. Black, 'Institutional Investors and Corporate Governance', *Continental Bank Journal of Applied Corporate Finance* (1991), 19. See also M. Roe, 'Political and Legal Restraints on Ownership and Control of Public Companies', *Journal of Financial Economics*, 27 (1990), 17–41.

49. This is illustrated by the version of the prudent-man rule found in the 1974 ERISA legislation.

50. For the sake of convenience we combine debt and equity positions under the term 'exposure'.

51. J. Zysman, *Governments, Markets, and Growth: Financial Systems and the Politics of Industrial Change* (Ithaca, NY: Cornell University Press, 1983), 260.

52. Ibid. 261.

53. Ibid. 265. See also H. Oberbeck, and M. Baethge, 'Computer and Pinstripes: Financial Institutions', in P. J. Katzenstein (ed.), *Industry and Politics in West Germany: Toward the Third Republic* (Ithaca, NY: Cornell University Press, 1989), 279–80.

54. J. Edwards, and K. Fischer, 'Banks, Finance and Investment in West Germany Since 1970', Centre for Economic Policy Research Discussion Paper No. 497 (London: CEPR, 1991); R. Deeg, 'The State, Banks and Economic Governance in Germany', paper presented at the 1992 Annual Meeting of the American Political Science Association, Chicago, Ill.; J. Esser, 'Bank Power in West Germany Revised', *West European Politics* 13 (1990) 17–32.

55. Esser, 'Bank Power', 29.

56. Deeg, 'State', 3.

57. See Katzenstein, *Industry and Politics*; J. A. Hart, *Rival Capitalists: International Competitiveness in the United States, Japan, and West Germany* (Ithaca, NY: Cornell University Press, 1992).

58. Germany has seven regional stock exchanges (in Frankfurt, Dusseldorf, Munich, Stuttgart, Berlin, Hanover, and Bremen). Frankfurt and Dusseldorf account for around 75% of turnover. 425 German corporations are presently listed on German stock markets. In contrast, the same figure for UK companies on the London Stock Exchange is 1,950. In 1991, turnover on the stock exchanges in Germany equalled around 7% of German GNP, compared to about 25% for the US: R. J. Pozdena and V. Alexander, 'Bank Structure in West Germany', in Kaufman, *Banking Structures*, 566; 'Learning to Love Equity', *The Economist*, 3 July 1993, 75.

59. A law dating from 1896 prohibits a firm from dealing on the stock exchange or bond markets for a year after its registration. As Jeffrey Hart observes, there is effectively a one-year probationary period for firms during which they must rely on banks for financing: Hart, *Rival Capitalists*, 187.

60. Based on portfolio statistics collected by the Deutsche Bundesbank (Depotstatistik), Jeremy Edwards, and Klaus Fischer (Edwards and Fischer, 'Banks', 26–8) calculate that in 1984 and 1988 banks held 7.6% and 8.1% respectively of outstanding German shares. Adding in securities managed by investment funds (which have to be placed in the custody of a depot-bank—and the funds are generally owned by their depot-banks) the figures for direct holdings rise to 10.3% and 11.6% respectively.

61. Deeg, 'State', 8; Esser, 'Bank Power', 23–5.

62. One caveat is that some of the reduction in holdings may have been achieved by banks placing part of their holdings in related group companies: Deeg, 'State', 10.

63. The two firms are Daimler-Benz and Karstadt (a major retailer). Of the 500 largest firms, the private banks held more than 25% of equity in 13 cases in 1986: Deeg, 'State', 9, citing F.-J. Arndt, 'Macht der Banken gegen Macht der Fakten—Anmerkungen zu einer DGB-Publikation', *Die Bank*, 12 (1986), 641–3.

64. Under the Depotstimmrecht law small investors can leave their shares in a custody account at a bank and sign over both the discretionary investment authority and the exercise of proxy-voting rights for a 15-month period: Frankel and Montgomery, 'Financial Structure', 285.

65. In a further eleven it exceeded 25%—sufficient to block certain important decisions at shareholders' meetings.

66. Edwards and Fischer, 'Banks', 26–8.

67. This proposition is confirmed by Steven Kaplan, who finds a positive correlation between a measure of bank control and a measure of the dispersion of shareholders (S. N. Kaplan, 'Top Executives, Turnover and Firm Performance in Germany', NBER Working Paper No. 4416 (Cambridge, Mass.: NBER, 1993), 15.

68. Zysman, *Governments*, 264.

69. Coffee, 'Liquidity Versus Control', 1304.

70. Edwards and Fischer also argue that although the banks control the equity-voting rights of many large German corporations, the same proxy-voting system allows the management of banks to control the banks themselves. The proxy votes held by each of the big three banks at its own shareholder meetings are: Deutsche Bank (47.2%), Dresdner Bank (59.3%), and Commerzbank (30.3%). Hence the banks are not bound to act solely in the interests of their shareholders either: Edwards and Fischer, 'Banks', 43–6.

71. Coffee, 'Liquidity Versus Control', 1305–6.
72. Esser, 'Bank Power', citing U. Jurgens, and G. Lindner, 'Zur Funktion und Macht der Banken', *Kursbruch*, 36 (1974), 121–60.
73. Katzenstein, 'Stability and Change in the Emerging Third Republic', in Katzenstein, *Industry and Politics*, 349.
74. Zysman, *Governments*, 260.
75. Ibid. 265.
76. Ibid.
77. Hart, *Rival Capitalists*, 192.
78. Ibid. 198.
79. Katzenstein, 'Stability and Change', 341.
80. Hart, *Rival Capitalists*, 188.
81. C. S. Allen, 'Corporatism and Regional Economic Policies in the Federal Republic of Germany: The "Meso" Politics of Industrial Adjustment', *Publius: The Journal of Federalism*, 19 (1989), 147–64.
82. Zysman, *Governments*, 253.
83. Katzenstein, 'Industry', 12.
84. F. D. Weiss, 'Domestic Dimensions of the Uruguay Round: The Case of West Germany in the European Communities', in H. R. Nau (ed.), *Domestic Trade Politics and the Uruguay Round* (New York, 1989), 70.
85. Weiss, 'Domestic Dimensions, 79.
86. Coffee, 'Liquidity Versus Control', 1302–3; D. Demougin, and H.-W. Sinn, 'Privatization, Risk-Taking, and the Communist Firm', NBER Working Paper No. 4205 (Cambridge, Mass.: NBER, 1992), 29.
87. In 1989 Dresdner Bank disclosed hidden reserves equal to about 30% of capital. Only following the implementation of the European Community Bank Accounts Directive, which must be adopted for 1993 full-year accounts, will German banks be required to disclose details of provisions against potential losses.

10

The Internal Balance of Power and Relative Economic Decline

HUGH WARD

In his editorial introduction to a volume on the economic decline of ancient empires, Carlo Cipolla stresses how the political rigidity of such societies blocked the necessary changes on the supply side: 'Change hurts vested interests . . . Conservative people and vested interests cluster around obsolete institutions, and each element supports the other powerfully. Innovating minorities are bound to see their efforts frustrated by this combination.'[1] This passage suggests social immobilism—where no group has the resources to force through change against combinations of other interests—an internal balance of power. The idea that blocking coalitions are inimical to growth is common to both the left and the right on standard cases of relative economic decline such as Britain, the US, and the former Soviet Union.[2] In this chapter I will attempt to make this idea more precise. Existing treatments have not made use of formal theory, making it difficult to derive testable hypotheses. My argument rests upon an analogy between an internal balance of power within a society and a system of states in which a balance of power exists. I draw upon recent game-theoretic analyses of the international balance of power which are both analytically rigorous and applicable, with some modifications, to the problem of relative economic decline.[3] Within my model, leaders of distributive coalitions play a zero-sum game, seeking to maximize their security of tenure of leadership and their power. Coalition formation in this zero-sum game may result in Pareto-inferior outcomes in the positive-sum growth game played between groups, blocking coalitions emerging which result in the failure to take advantage of growth opportunities. Although institutions are often created because certain individuals and groups have particular ends in mind, they also come to define interests and to provide power resources. Institutions are seen here as the structural context of growth politics, shaping and being shaped by individual and group action.

Although the balance-of-power idea has been represented in the literature on economic growth, recent discussion in political science has centred around Mancur Olson's *The Rise and Decline of Nations*.[4] Olson believes that in stable political systems more and more latent groups will eventually solve their collective-action problem and organize politically.[5] As the number of organized groups grows, economic inefficiencies generating barriers to growth typically become worse. It is seldom rational for organized interests to promote growth, since the benefits of growth are non-excludable and largely leak away to others in society, while the associated costs of growth promotion are borne by the group itself.[6] The exceptions to this rule arise when groups are encompassing, organizing a large fraction of the relevant public. However, there is a tendency for groups to remain exclusive rather than attempting inclusively to organize the public.[7] In contrast it is often rational for groups to seek a larger slice of the existing social cake by rent-seeking from government: all the benefits flow to group members; but the costs (in terms of static efficiency losses in the economy and growth) associated with monopoly powers, protection from international competition, tax breaks, control over entry into professions by professional associations, and other economic distortions are largely borne outside the group.[8] While groups may sometimes co-operate together to make society more efficient and faster growing, inter-group bargaining is time-consuming and costly, the more so the larger the number of organized groups.[9] Olson's model suggests that an empirical correlation ought to exist between political stability and low growth: more groups will have organized and successfully sought monopoly rents from government; and inter-group agreement will be more difficult to achieve. Olson argues that this accounts for relatively slow growth in stable countries such as Britain and high post-war growth in Japan and Germany, where organized interests were destroyed under fascism and during the occupation by the Allied Powers.[10]

The extensive critical commentary upon Olson's book has centred on testing the correlation between growth and stability, and upon the fit between Olson's argument and particular cases. Olson's formal argument has received far less attention, although it has a number of problems.[11] Throughout his work Olson ignores the possibility that political entrepreneurs may fail to act in the interests of groups they establish. It is quite plausible that leaders will have personal interests which conflict with those of members.[12] It is often argued that the separation of ownership from control in corporations gives a great deal of autonomy to managers, because it is difficult for shareholders to act collectively to control them. Political entrepreneurs organizing workers, social classes, and regional or religious groups often have a great deal of autonomy for the same reason. Moreover, the option of exiting from the organization may be impossible because of the lack of any alternative organization or because of legally enforced closed shops or quasi-closed shops.[13] The fact that Olson ignores this problem is important. To see why, consider two groups A and B, the stronger being A and the weaker being B. Suppose that the costs to A's membership of using its power to impose costs of growth on B mean that they would each prefer a voluntary cost-sharing agreement with B. Suppose that given that their security of tenure is guaranteed, leaders have the secondary aim of maximizing their personal power. A's leader would sometimes prefer to use the group's power to impose the whole costs of growth on the other group, for to defeat B would be to increase her personal power. Although the members of A may dislike this solution, they may be able to do little about it, and the fact that some gains in terms of growth are achieved may further reduce their motivation to overthrow their leader.

From this perspective, then, while the underlying growth game may be positive-sum for the mass of the citizenry, the actual politics of growth often more closely resembles a zero-sum game played by leadership élites, in which outcomes facilitating growth are a side effect of élite pursuit of security of tenure and power in a world they see as a zero-sum power game. The degree of internal support from group members is important, and this might plausibly be assumed to fall if there is a continued failure to take growth opportunities, even if the membership cannot get rid of its leaders easily. Even this effect is irrelevant so long as group support generally decays at the same rate so that leaders' relative holdings of resources are unaffected. My assumption that leaders have absolute control of group resources so long as costs associated with economic growth are not imposed on members probably over-simplifies in order to facilitate analysis. However, I regard it as more realistic than Olson's assumption.

Olson's model emphasizes the number of organized groups and, in effect, provides a theoretical rationale in stable political systems for linking slow growth with political overload by special inter-ests.[14] In contrast, slow growth in my model is a function of the distribution of power across group leaders. Moreover, my model suggests an alternative explanation of the correlation between sta-bility and low growth in terms of the movement towards a balance-of-power equilibrium. Although Olson sometimes talks of distributional struggles, he does not take seriously the idea that organized and unorganized groups may be too weak, or may lack sufficient allies, to prevent others imposing the costs of growth on them.[15] Resolution of inter-group conflict is seen as taking place through consensual bargaining or group lobbying.[16] The way in which power is down-played surely does violence to the actual pol-itics of growth.[17] Not only may the state threaten or bribe groups to make them co-operate, but groups may use their power to evade the costs of growth while attempting to ensure that others bear the costs. In liberal democracies much group activity will centre on the state and the party system, with groups working to take away oth-ers' monopoly powers, to reduce their real incomes, to reallocate productive resources under their control, and so on. In other sys-tems overt coercion is often more significant. If group leaders have a great deal of autonomy, whether they use their group's power defensively or to force another group to bear the costs of growth may depend on whether they stand to gain in terms of power or security of tenure, rather than upon the effects of growth on the well-being of their group members. In comparative perspective, then, the relative economic decline of some countries may have to do with differences in the way power is distributed and in élite per-ceptions of their self-interest.

As Russel has argued, Olson, and the literature which sets out to test his position, has ignored the case of the military-industrial complex, which has often been a powerful actor in the growth game.[18] There is an extensive empirical literature which suggests that military expenditure is inimical to growth in advanced indus-trial societies: via its effects on investment; through creating shortages of skilled manpower; and because of the diversion of entrepreneurial effort into the area of soft military contracting.[19] It is crucial that any attempt to test Olson's thesis cross-nationally should take this question seriously. The successor states to the Axis powers defeated in the Second World War, particularly Japan, have had low levels of military spending and good growth records, their military-industrial complexes having been broken up.[20] Moreover, these countries generally score low on scales which attempt to proxy democratic sclerosis, the assumption being made that a combination of fascism and occupation destroyed many pre-existing organized special interests. This leads to the suspicion that correlations between growth rates and measures of sclerosis may actually be capturing the effects of low military spending by the successor states to the Axis powers, on the one hand, and continued higher military spending among the wartime Allies, particularly the US and the UK, on the other. Moreover, the case of the military-industrial complex bears upon my main thesis here: the relative immunity of military spending to cuts is often explained by the power of the military-industrial complex and the interests of the associated military, political, and industrial élites in power and personal tenure of office. More generally, I treat state managers in the same way as other group leaders. Key bureaucrats and politicians seek to protect the interests of their particular coalition, which, like the military-industrial complex, may span the divide between state and civil society. Elected politicians also act as leaders of voter coalitions constituted by economic and other interests. State managers, too, are only interested in growth because it affects their tenure of office and personal power.

Olson applies his size principle which states that, other things being equal, a group is less likely to act in such a way as to promote growth (either in an active way or by foregoing rent-seeking) the smaller the overall fraction of the total benefits it might generate which would be enjoyed by its own members. If groups are often driven to act by others' use of power, there is no good reason to believe that this would be true. Indeed, I show below that the existence of an internal balance of power in which no group can be made to bear the costs of growth does not depend at all on the number of groups. Let us suppose, though, that at least some group action in relation to growth is voluntary. As I suggested above, Olson argues that bargaining costs associated with achieving inter-

group co-operative agreements increase with the number of organized interests in society. However, the number of groups involved
in a particular bargain is often small and unrelated to the overall
number of organized groups in society. For instance, in the paradigm case of bargaining between employers and unions over technological change in the work process, the number around the table
is hardly likely to increase just because sexual and linguistic minorities, fundamentalist religious groups, and so on, have become organized. A general increase in group organization need not imply that
more groups are involved in deciding economic issues, either at the
national or the sub-national level.

Olson argues that the benefits of acting to promote growth
largely leak away elsewhere unless the group is highly inclusive.
This argument assumes that growth is an impure public good, non-
excludable but with divisible benefits. If we focus on the overall
picture in society, there is some sense in this assumption. However,
changes which may promote growth often generate non-excludable
and indivisible benefits for some groups involved in state-level bargaining. For instance, neo-Schumpeterian analysis of innovation
frequently stresses synergistic interaction between different companies and sectors rather than the short-term competitive advantages
a firm gets by adopting new technologies.[21] There are possibilities
of skill and personnel interchanges; methods adopted by others are
often copied with their approval; the new techniques can be
adapted to other product lines and industrial processes; the generation of positive expectations in the sector creates all-round benefits, even the slowest adaptors gaining via sub-contracting to the
most innovatory firms; and the unit costs of the technology itself
fall if a successful innovative swarm of companies forms around
the technology. Now many of these benefits are indivisible: the fact
that one firm and its workforce enjoy them does not leave less for
others to enjoy. Moreover, such benefits are likely to be of far
greater importance to those in the sector or industry than general
considerations about effects on the rest of society, including
growth. The general arguments for the size principle which Olson
offers have come in for a good deal of criticism. In particular,
where non-excludable but indivisible public goods are concerned
contributions do not generally fall as the numbers of possible contributors increases.[22] Thus, public-goods theory provides no general grounds for believing that innovation will be more heavily

resisted in an industry with more fragmented union structures or a larger number of firms; or that more encompassing national peak organization of capital and labour will promote innovation. In other areas, to the extent to which growth-promoting action also supplies indivisible and non-excludable benefits, there is no reason to suggest that just because a relevant group is small that it is less likely to contribute.

The sort of co-operative deal-making Olson portrays is sometimes important, although I believe that Olson's account of it is flawed. By excluding such deal-making, the balance-of-power model ignores what are sometimes important processes. The question of the relative importance of co-operation and conflict in a certain context can only be settled empirically. Olson's thesis has been tested by comparing growth-rates cross-nationally and by comparing growth between different states in the US.[23] Although this literature throws up some indications that the balance of power matters to growth, no attempt has been made to test Olson's model against a balance-of-power model. In Section 3 of this chapter, a non-recursive causal model is estimated for a cross-sectional data-set covering eighteen OECD countries in the 1970s. The results largely support the balance-of-power model.

1. THE BALANCE-OF-POWER MODEL

Although I have already briefly outlined the balance-of-power model, more specific assumptions need to be made if insights from Niou and Ordeshook's work on the international balance of power are to be drawn upon. The growth game is pictured as taking place through time and as consisting of distinct rounds: periods of time during which a particular conflict occurs about how to allocate the costs of growth. Consider a round in which there are n ($n \geqslant 2$) organized groups playing the growth game. Assume that during this round total power resources in society are fixed, that resources are infinitely divisible, and transferable without loss between groups. The i-th group's power resources will be denoted by r_i.

Let C and C' be two coalitions. (A single group is a notional coalition here.) Let $r(C)$ be the sum of the resources of the groups in coalition C. Then C can defeat C' if and only if $r(C) > r(C')$.[24] If C defeats C', the leaders of groups in C may choose either to impose the costs of growth upon some group or groups in C', thus destroying the groups and their resources; or to transfer control of resources in groups in C' to leaders of groups in C. Either way, defeated leaders lose tenure. I assume that undefeated groups cannot be made to bear any costs of growth. It is a necessary condition for growth to occur in some round that at least one group should be defeated.

The assumption that groups which have costs of growth imposed on them cease to play the growth game reflects, albeit in extreme form, the more realistic idea that a major political defeat means that groups usually cease to be of much overall importance to political conflicts about growth. It might be objected that in reality groups loaded with growth costs in the past might be further burdened in the future, especially as they are now outside the growth game. While this is sometimes plausible, there are probably diminishing returns from repeated cost imposition. Again my assumption reflects this in a stark but analytically convenient form. If the reality is one of gradually diminishing returns to repeatedly hitting already defeated groups, there might still be some growth after a balance-of-power equilibrium has been reached in which no group currently in the growth game can be defeated, but this would gradually taper off. Notice that it is not sufficient for growth that some group can be defeated, for defeated groups may be taken over by victorious leaders, instead. Resource transfer is not unrealistic, although in reality it seldom takes place without some losses. For example, general unions which have promoted technical change along with management often take over the residual membership of small craft unions weakened by de-skilling. Where a group is taken over and incorporated in another group its new leader then has incentives to protect it, for imposition of growth costs would mean possible loss of tenure. The way in which general unions go on to provide some cover for craftsmen they have incorporated is an example, although it also illustrates that incorporated members are unlikely to have exactly the same status as the original members, as assumed here.

Group leaders are seen as primarily interested in securing continuing tenure for themselves. Security of tenure is guaranteed only if the group is not defeated. Let r and r' be two distributions of resources over the leaders. Then a more precise statement of the assumption about leadership motivation is that the i-th leader prefers r to r' if $r_i > r'_i$ provided she can ensure that no r'' results from r in the current or in a future round of the growth game in which $r''_i = 0$.[25]

Supposing that the i-th group survives a round of the growth game, members' support for their leader changes in the following way: if growth occurs in the last round and the group's resources at the end of the round are r_i, its resources at the beginning of the next round are r_ip, where $p > 1$; if the growth opportunity is not taken, resources at the beginning of the next round are r_iq, where $I > q > 0$. Thus leaders will not always choose to take over defeated groups: given that their security is ensured, they maximize resource holdings and this means that they have to compare the resources they can gain by taking over another group to the loss of support among their membership which they would suffer if this results in growth being foregone. Other things being equal, it is more likely that the costs of growth would be imposed on weak groups: because they have fewer resources, the gains from incorporating them within victorious groups are lower.

In the growth game leaders form, or threaten to form, coalitions to force another group or coalition of groups to bear the costs of growth. A coalition or group can potentially defeat another coalition or group if it has more resources. However, a group which is threatened with defeat can take counter-measures. Its leader might form a defensive coalition to mobilize enough resources to prevent her group bearing the costs of growth. Another possibility is that a group or coalition might buy off hostile advances by transferring resources. In the process of jockeying between groups not all logically possible coalition structures and distributions of political resources are likely to be observed: group leaders must have some reason for sticking with any current coalition partners. In a balance of power, any threat to form a new coalition which is an improvement on the status quo for the leaders of the groups involved can be met by a viable counterthreat. (For formal definitions of viable threats, counter-threats, and system stability see the Appendix.) This would take the form of some alternative coalition which could feasibly act so as to leave at least some leaders of groups in the first coalition worse off than in the status quo. Such a threat and counter-threat pair cancel out, and situations in which any threat can be met by a counter-threat are defined as balance-of-power equilibria.

Niou and Ordeshook prove that a balance of power exists if and only if resources are distributed in such a way that each country (in our case each group), in combination with at least one set of partners, forms a coalition that is minimal-winning. Any group which is not essential to the game, in the sense that it does not belong to at least one such coalition, is vulnerable to defeat. On analogy with the classical dynamics of the international balance of power, a key feature of the growth game is political jockeying to prevent any single group from coming to control more than half the resources and becoming hegemonic. This gives incentives to groups to come to the aid of others: their own defeat would rapidly follow the emergence of a hegemon, for a hegemon can defeat all other groups combined. Allowing for this, Niou and Ordeshook show that essential groups can always mount a counter-threat to any viable threat.[26] Suppose there is a balance-of-power equilibrium in some round. So long as each leader's resources erode at the same rate due to the non-occurrence of growth, exactly the same equilibrium will occur in the next round. This is because if all resource holdings fall in fixed proportion, the set of minimal-winning coalitions, and thus the set of essential groups, remains the same. Once a balance of power has been achieved it will persist round after round and there will be no growth. It follows from Niou and Ordeshook's results that a balance-of-power equilibrium—and hence slow growth—may exist for any number of groups greater than or equal to two, depending only on the distribution of resources. To the extent to which coercion is an important aspect of the growth game, this result challenges Olson's size principle.[27]

Suppose we start in a round in which some group(s) is (are) inessential, so that there is not an internal balance of power. Inessential groups can be defeated, leading either to growth or to a transfer of their resources to other leaders. Either way a shift in resource holdings usually occurs among remaining groups. As a consequence, some surviving groups essential in the last round of the game may no longer be so in the next round. Niou and Ordeshook's results applied to the case in hand show that this dynamic leads, via the round-by-round elimination of inessential groups, to a balance-of-power equilibrium. In this equilibrium one group has half the resources, the remaining resources being distributed among the rest. The other equilibrium of the game is that in which one group is initially hegemonic and destroys or incorporates all other groups in the first round. We would expect growth to slow down if the long-run equilibrium was of the first sort: eventually all the groups which are inessential are defeated and only groups which are strong enough to protect themselves survive.[28] The implications of the second sort of long-term equilibrium for growth are ambiguous. However, the initial conditions under which such an equilibrium would eventually be arrived at are surely empirically implausible—at least in liberal democracies. Therefore, an alternative to the Olsonian explanation of slow growth in mature, stable democracies is that such systems eventually reach an internal balance of power after the elimination of all inessential groups.

2. POLITICAL SCLEROSIS, THE BALANCE OF POWER, AND RELATIVE ECONOMIC DECLINE IN ADVANCED INDUSTRIAL SOCIETIES

Albeit in highly abstract form, the process of building and breaking up alliances, defending and attacking, and seeking out weak groups in society implicit in the balance-of-power model is a more adequate description of the politics of growth in advanced capitalist societies in the last 20 years than Olson's bargaining model. This claim can be illustrated by comparing the account the two models give of the Swedish case. Sweden, while it is stable politically, had a good growth record up to the 1970s. This appears at odds with Olson's argument. However, Olson suggests that the unions in Sweden organized a high fraction of the workforce under the umbrella of one peak organization. Because the membership of these peak organizations stood to gain a large fraction of the collective gains from growth, there was less incentive to block growth-promoting social change and to make gains by externalizing costs onto other groups. Similarly, the peak organizations of business were relatively encompassing and less of a barrier to growth.[29] This explanation is suspect on theoretical grounds. Olson's model cannot explain the failure of Sweden's economic miracle in the 1970s, a period in which interest-group membership became, if anything, more encompassing.[30]

In contrast to the Olsonian picture, in which power asymmetries receive little attention, the post-war success of the Swedish economy rested heavily on the ability of organized labour, in conjunction with the Social Democrats who controlled the state mechanism, to impose the costs of growth on certain groups in society against their resistance. First, the active labour-market policy imposed costs of restructuring onto workers and businesses in declining sectors of the economy, by using the economic power of the state to steer economic development into new sectors.[31] Secondly, high wage-rates pushed the costs of restructuring onto employers by forcing capital to invest in productivity increases to remain competitive.[32] Finally, costs were also shifted onto small businesses and farmers, one token of this being the breakdown of the coalition between the Social Democrats and the Centre Party.[33]

The Swedish economy gradually slowed down in the 1970s as it moved towards a situation in which further change was blocked. Labour no longer had the power to push through its proposals for economic democracy against the resistance of business, workers who suffered from the effect of earlier restructuring, and the growing strength of the white-collar unions. In the 1970s the Social Democrats alternated in power with a right-wing coalition, and neither left nor right has achieved firm control. I interpret this as a balance of power between the coalition of the left and the coalition of the right, with poor growth performance being a consequence of the failure coherently to pursue a path to increased growth. Esping-Anderson and Friedland argue that 'In the present tug-of-war over Sweden's economic future, the white collar "middle strata" hold the key to whatever solution will ultimately emerge.'[34] If, as this quotation suggests, both capital, blue-collar labour, and white-collar labour are now essential groups, Sweden has become a stalemated system. This may account for the slowdown of the Swedish economy in the 1970s and 1980s. Although the discussion here has been very brief, the balance-of-power model is better able to explain a case which is anomalous within Olson's paradigm.

The cross-national comparative work of Esping Anderson and Friedland shows that the balance-of-power model has plausibility across a range of advanced capitalist countries in the post-war period. Operating within a framework which suggests that coalition formation between social groups is crucial to growth, these authors ascribe the general slow-down in the advanced capitalist economies of the 1970s and 1980s to an emergent balance of power in the struggle over income shares. This syndrome is exhibited to varying degrees because, in some of the systems, either the left or the right retains allies with whom they are powerful enough to prevail against weak groups in society. The emerging pattern is that of a balance of power where neither the left nor the right can prevail.[35] The 1970s was a period of severe stress for the major capitalist economies, encompassing the oil price shock of 1973–4, the onset of stagflation, great political and economic pressure on institutions such as the welfare state, and major changes in technology. Other authors have also noted that adaptation to these circumstances was more successful when either the left or the right dominated, but less successful when neither could prevail.[36] In countries with an extensive and cohesive union movement and domination of electoral politics by the social democratic left, a form of corporatist hegemony often developed in which organized labour, organized business, and the state all participated. This allowed successful adaptation to crisis. Lange and Garrett argue that left electoral domination was essential to this strategy, because it gave credibility to state promises to maintain welfare expenditure and to promote investment if they limited wage demands in return.[37] Corporatism was not the only available road to success: Schmidt and also Lange and Garret argue that successful adaptation took place in political systems dominated by a coalition of the right.[38] Where either corporatist or market-based hegemony existed, a majority coalition existed which was powerful enough to ensure that inessential groups could be made to bear the costs of adaptation to the crisis of the 1970s. In contrast, some societies exhibited a balance of power in which adaptation was hindered by blocking coalitions, leading to high degrees of conflict and the fragmentation of social effort.

To focus purely on electoral politics is to ignore parts of the dynamics of social power which are crucially important to growth. Nevertheless, electoral outcomes are significant and may act as a proxy for the underlying distribution of power across the major social blocks in society. If the balance-of-power argument is correct, one would expect that the rate of economic growth would be low where neither the left nor the right can consistently prevail electorally and higher when either one or the other dominated. In order to test this argument empirically I constructed a scale to measure the ideological complexion of the executive in eighteen OECD countries in the 1970s.[39] For each nation I examined each distinct government. I multiplied the duration of the government in months by the number of ministerial portfolios held by each party to get a score in portfolio-months for each party. (If a party held no portfolios or was outside the governing coalition it scored zero.) I then summed the score for each party across every government, ending up with a total score in portfolio-months. I made the assumption that each party's power was equal to its own total score divided by the sum of the total scores of all parties. This procedure gives a figure between 0 (for a party never in office) to 1 (for a party continually in office in the 1970s which shared power with no coalition partners). Using existing internationally comparable judgemental scales placing the parties on a numerical scale from zero for far left to 10 for far right, I calculated a summary measure of the ideological complexion of each nation's governments during the period concerned.[40] This was the sum, taken across all parties, of party-power scores multiplied by their ideological position on the left–right spectrum. This summary measure can be thought of as the resultant of the pressures exerted by parties, allowing for party ideologies and weighting for party power. A score of 0 indicates that a far-left party monopolized the executive for the whole of the 1970s; a score of 10 indicates that a far-right party monopolized the executive for the whole of the 1970s. A balance of power between left and right is indicated by a score near five, the midpoint of the scale.[41]

If we examine the relationship between the average rate of growth of real gross domestic product in the 1970s (GROWTH) and the overall ideological complexion of governments (IDEOL), the impression is that the relationship is as predicted by the balance-of-power model—see Fig. 10.1.[42] The slowest-growing countries tended to have scores around 5 on the ideology scale; the fastest-growing countries tended to have either high or low scores. Notice that it is difficult to account for this relationship within Olson's framework. For Olson, governments in democracies are highly open to successful lobbying by rent-seeking groups, and there is no reason to suspect that this effect would be more pronounced if neither the left nor the right dominated.

If a quadratic equation is fitted to the data, both the variable

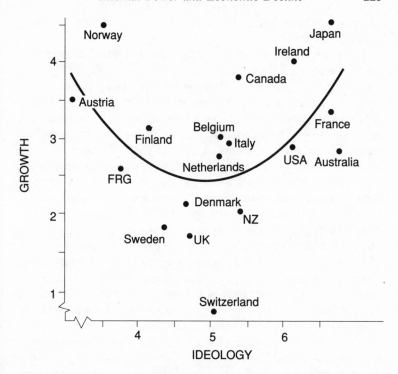

FIG. 10.1 The relationship between economic growth and executive ideology in the 1970s

IDEOL and its squared value are significant at the 90 per cent (0.1) level. The quadratic equation is also plotted on Fig. 10.1, the minima being associated with a value of IDEOL very close to 5, as predicted theoretically. The U-shaped quadratic relationship in Fig. 10.1 suggests that as the IDEOL scores depart further and further in either direction from 5, growth tends to become higher at a rate proportional to the square of the deviation. It will be convenient in further analysis to exploit this by creating a new variable IDEOLD^2 by subtracting 5 from the ideology score of each country and then squaring the result. A score of 0 on IDEOLD^2 indicates the likely existence of an internal balance of power. The theoretical maximum score of 25 on IDEOLD^2 indicates that it is unlikely that there is an internal balance of power. The prediction is that

GROWTH will be an increasing linear function of IDEOLD^2, allowing for other influences.

There are several objections to the idea that scores of near 0 on IDEOLD^2 are always a proxy for a balance of power. In the US, gridlock develops when the relative strengths of voting blocks is such that the President's party does not control Congress. Some political systems cannot be adequately characterized in terms of a single left–right dimension. Moreover, the regional, ethnic, religious, and other cleavages which cross-cut the left–right dimension may be important to economic growth, for they may generate groups and associated political parties which aim to block changes harmful to their members' interests. In plural societies of this sort politics often takes the form of what Lijphart calls consensus democracy. The following situations occur in the ideal-type consensus democracy: the system is truly multi-party, with some form of proportional representation and groups created by major social cleavages being well organized at legislative level either within parties or as parties; coalition governments are the norm and coalitions are often inclusive, controlling more legislative votes than would be necessary to be minimum-winning; relations between executive and legislature are balanced in power terms, the executive dominance seen in majoritarian systems being absent; power is regionally decentralized and dispersed to organs spanning the state–civil society divide; there is a tendency towards strong bicamerality, with each house being important.[43] The rationale of the system is to prevent majorities from harming minorities, thus institutionalizing the power of aggrieved groups to block change.[44] The system gives a high degree of veto power to the major religious, ethnic, regional, and socio-economic groups through: representation in the governing coalition; the constraint of the executive by the legislature; the veto powers of major social blocks in regional assemblies and committees and commissions on which policy is made; constitutional protection of minorities; and blocking or delaying power exerted through the upper house. Consensus democracy is the institutional expression and structural reinforcer of a balance of power in society, created to protect the major power blocks and to prevent majority social coalitions remaining stable sufficiently long to endanger other groups. I would expect countries that approached the ideal-type of consensus democracy to have slower economic growth.[45]

Lijphart and Crepaz used factor analysis to create a compositive measure of consensus democracy over the period 1950 to 1980 for the same eighteen countries shown in Fig. 10.1.[46] A high score on CONSDEM indicates closeness to the consensus democracy ideal-type; a low score indicates closeness to the ideal-type majoritarian democracy. Belgium, Italy, the Netherlands, Switzerland, and Denmark all score highly on the CONSDEM scale and had centrist executives in the 1970s, with scores around 5 on the IDEOL scale. However, IDEOL and CONSDEM are picking up different variants of an internal balance of power: the UK, Canada, and New Zealand, countries with strongly majoritarian systems, also scored around 5 on the IDEOL scale as a result of the alternation in office of the two main parties; and Finland and Norway, which both score highly on the CONSDEM scale, had executives well to the left of centre in the 1970s, as measured on the IDEOL scale.[47]

Fig. 10.2 shows the bivariate relationship between GROWTH and CONSDEM. As expected theoretically, the correlation between these two variables is negative, albeit rather weak, as indicated by the slope of the fitted OLS regression line.[48] Of course it is inadequate to test the balance-of-power model by looking at the sorts of bivariate relationships shown in Figs. 10.1 and 10.2, since no account is taken of other variables which influence growth. (In the next section I discuss more defensible statistical models of growth.) I will continue to use IDEOLD^2 and CONSDEM as proxies for an internal balance of power. Much of the existing empirical work testing Olson's thesis uses a cross-sectional approach to examine liberal democracies within the OECD in the 1970s.[49] My empirical focus on the 1970s facilitated comparisons with the existing literature; allows lagged measures of some variables to be used to overcome estimation problems; and allows IDEOL and CONSDEM, which were constructed on data up to 1980, to be used in some equations.

3. DATA ANALYSIS

The starting-point is a standard economic model of growth. Growth ought to be a function of investment in both physical and human capital. To measure investment I used INV, the percentage of real GDP devoted to gross fixed capital formation in the 1970s.[50] I tested various measures of human-capital formation,

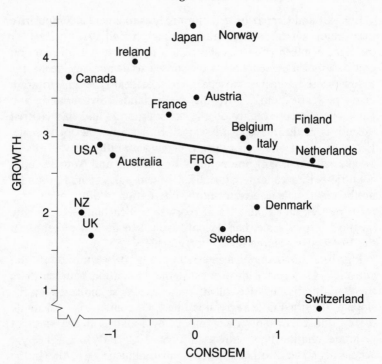

FIG. 10.2 The relationship between growth and consensus democracy in the 1970s

including measures of education spending, health spending, and overall spending on social welfare. Only education spending was significant, and the effect seemed to be more powerful after a lag.[51] This presumably reflects the time taken for those currently in education to achieve a significant economic role. Thus the proxy for human capital formation was EDUC(−1)—the average percentage of real GDP spent on education by government in the 1960s.[52] The 1970s was a period of slack capacity for most economies. On Keynesian grounds it would be expected that governments which ran budget deficits would have reinvigorated growth by taking up the economic slack, with the knock-on effect of increasing investment as business expectations improved. I included DEF, the average difference between government current expenditure as a percentage of real GDP and government receipts as a percentage of real GDP in the 1970s.[53] Garrett and Lange argue that the growth rate of countries highly dependent on imported oil suffered during the oil-price shock of the 1970s. To allow for this effect I included in the basic economic model the variable OILDEP—net oil imports as a percentage of total energy demand in the 1970s.[54]

There is an obvious potential for simultaneous-equation bias when GROWTH is regressed on INV and DEF: while economic growth depends on investment, investment is also likely to be higher when growth is stronger and business expectations are more positive; higher economic growth might either allow governments to run bigger deficits without running into capital-market constraints or might suppress their desire to continue to run deficits, because of the attendant risks of inflation.[55] I used the two-stage least squares (2SLS) version of the instrumental variables technique to overcome this estimation problem. The strategy is to construct instruments which are highly correlated with the endogenous variables in the growth equation but uncorrelated with the error terms. My procedure was to build a system of equations in which GROWTH, INV, and DEF were all endogenous. The 2SLS approach demands that all the variables to be treated as exogenous in the system of equations as a whole are used when constructing instruments to estimate a particular equation in the system. Before considering the results of estimating the growth equation I need to discuss the political variables used and the other equations in the system.

Choi constructed a proxy measure of political sclerosis on the assumption, derived from Olson's work, of a logistical development of sclerosis. After the date of transition to a modern political system, the number of organized groups increases, eventually approaching an upper limit. Choi also allowed for interruptions due to defeat in wars, the destruction of organized interests under fascist regimes, and revolutions.[56] For the moment I will take it that this variable CHOI measures political sclerosis. However, I will suggest below that it may also be regarded as a proxy for the existence of an internal balance of power. I assume that CHOI, CONSDEM, and IDEOL and IDEOL^2 (the two variables used to construct IDEOLD^2) are exogenous, testing the assumption below.

At first the equations I developed for INV and DEF were orientated towards allowing powerful instruments for these two variables to be used in estimating the growth equation. Where the desire is to construct powerful instruments, it is standard econometric practice to

use lagged values of endogenous variables.[57] Thus the equation for
INV included the lagged value INV(−1)—the percentage of real GDP
devoted to gross fixed capital formation for the period 1962 to
1969.[58] The equation for INV also included GROWTH and MIL—the
percentage of real GDP devoted to the military in the 1970s.[59] (The
rationale for including MIL was discussed above.) As equation 1 in
Table 10.1 shows, all coefficients were of the expected sign. The
equation for DEF included two variables: TAX—average central government taxes as a percentage of GDP in the 1970s; and DEF(−1)—
the lagged value of DEF for the period 1955 to 1965.[60] The estimates
for this equation are shown in equation 2 of Table 10.1. As might
be expected, the coefficient for TAX was negative and just significant
at the 90 per cent (0.1) level. To ensure the exogeneity of all the
instruments used in estimating the growth equation, equation 3 of
Table 10.1 for MIL simply included MIL(−1)—its lagged value for the
period 1960 to 1970.[61] Similarly, equation 4 of Table 10.1 for TAX
just included TAX(−1)—the lagged value of TAX for the period 1955
to 1965.[62] All equations in Table 10.1 were estimated using the 2SLS
procedure treating the variables CONSDEM, CHOI, IDEOL, IDEOL²,
OILDEP, TAX(−1), DEF(−1), INV(−1), EDUC(−1), and MIL(−1) as exogenous.

Equation 1 of Table 10.2 is the basic economic model of growth.
Like all other equations shown in this table it was estimated by
2SLS using the ten exogenous variables previously referred to as
construct instruments. All coefficients are of the expected sign.
EDUC(−1) is the only variable not significant at the 95 per cent
(0.05) level. Around 72 per cent of the variance in growth can be
explained in terms of the economic model alone.

Political conditions may undermine the effectiveness of investment in physical or human capital without affecting the amount of
such investment. The balance-of-power model suggests that the
lower the value of IDEOLD² the closer the situation is to internal
gridlock and the lower the effectiveness of overall investment. The
interaction term

$$\text{ID}^2\text{INVED} = \text{IDEOLD}^2 * (\text{EDUC}(-1) + \text{INV})$$

ought to have a positive coefficient if this is true. Similarly the balance-of-power model suggests that

$$\text{CDMINVED} = \text{CONSDEM} * (\text{EDUC}(-1) + \text{INV})$$

TABLE 10.1. *Other equations in the model (t-values in parentheses)*

	Equation					
	1	2	3	4	5	6
Dependent variable	INV	DEF	MIL	TAX	INV	EDUC
Constant	6.0634	6.5277	0.8881	7.7325	21.9514	1.2333
GROWTH	1.5461* (3.9766)	—	—	—	1.7405* (3.4231)	—
DEF	—	—	—	—	−0.4475* (−2.8514)	—
INV(−1)	0.6355* (5.0472)	—	—	—	—	—
EDUC(−1)	—	—	—	—	—	0.7516* (8.0926)
MIL	−0.6899† (−2.0310)	—	—	—	−1.5247* (−4.1181)	—
CHOI	—	—	—	—	—	0.0186* (2.5507)
DEF(−1)	—	0.9742* (5.8611)	—	—	—	—
TAX	—	−0.1268† (−1.7541)	—	—	—	—
MIL(−1)	—	—	0.5877* (4.7629)	—	—	—
TAX(−1)	—	—	—	0.9996* (3.7125)	—	—
Method of estimation	2SLS	2SLS	2SLS	2SLS	2SLS	2SLS
R^2	0.8723	0.7179	0.5875	0.4627	0.8047	0.8450
$\bar{R}^2$	0.8450	0.6803	0.5618	0.4291	0.7628	0.8244

* Significant at 95% (0.05) level in a 2–tailed test.
† Significant at 90% (0.10) level in a 2–tailed test.

will have a negative coefficient, since ideal-type consensus democracies are the institutional expression of internal gridlock. Finally, if CHOI is a proxy for political sclerosis and if Olson's thesis is correct, the interaction term CHINVED = CHOI*(EDUC(−1) + INV) ought to have a negative coefficient.

Equations 2, 3, and 4 in Table 10.2 show what happens when

each of these interaction terms is added to the economic model. In equations 2 and 3 the signs of the regression coefficients for the interaction terms are as expected on theoretical grounds from the balance-of-power model. ID²INVED is significant at the 95 per cent (0.05) level in equation 2. However, CDMINVED is not quite significant at the 90 per cent (0.10) level in equation 3. In equation 4 the coefficient of CHINVED is negative and significant at the 95 per cent (0.05) level, as Olson's model would suggest. Equation 5 includes all three interaction terms. This time ID²INVED and CHINVED are significant at the 90 per cent (0.10) level but CDMINVED is no longer significant even at this level. Accordingly, this variable was dropped in equation 6, the coefficients of the two remaining interaction terms being significant at the 90 per cent (0.10) level and having the expected signs.

Together with equations 1, 2, 3, and 4 in Table 10.1, equation 6 in Table 10.2 meets the rank and order conditions for identification of the overall system. Equation 6 improves on the economic model in equation 1: the R^2 value has increased from 0.7199 to 0.9186; and the adjusted R^2 value has increased from 0.6337 to 0.8742. The joint null hypothesis that an equation estimated using 2SLS methods is correctly specified and that the variables treated as exogenous in the overall system actually are so can be assessed using Sargan's chi-squared test. I carried out this test on equation 6 in Table 10.2 and the null hypothesis cannot be rejected, indicating that we can reasonably assume that there are no problems with this specification of the growth equation.

The provisional conclusion, based on equations in Table 10.2, is that there is empirical support both for the balance-of-power model and for Olson's model:

(1) The coefficient of ID²INVED is always positive and significant, indicating that the effectiveness of investment increases as we move further and further away from an internal balance of power.

(2) There is also a positive feedback path in the causal model from ID²INVED to GROWTH, for ID²INVED is positively related to GROWTH, GROWTH is positively related to INV, and INV is, in turn, positively, related to GROWTH. An internal balance of power indirectly reduces investment, with a second-order negative effect on growth.

(3) The coefficient for CDMINVED has the anticipated negative sign,

TABLE 10.2. *Growth equations (t-values in parentheses)*

	Equation					
	1	2	3	4	5	6
Constant	-2.9285	-2.0278	-3.8624	2.4634	0.4312	0.8479
EDUC(-1)	0.1760	0.3222*	0.2609†	0.3913*	0.4108*	0.3946*
	(1.4844)	(3.2516)	(2.1419)	(4.4287)	(4.8406)	(4.7144)
DEF	0.2285*	0.2618*	0.1932	0.1602*	0.1940*	0.2082*
	(3.6845)	(5.4395)	(3.1302)	(3.8687)	(4.0852)	(4.6274)
INV	0.2639*	0.1726*	0.2755*	0.1494*	0.1510*	0.1393*
	(5.5269)	(3.8882)	(6.0879)	(3.7854)	(3.8069)	(3.6988)
OILDEP	-0.0168*	-0.0141*	-0.0122†	-0.0320*	-0.0228*	-0.0242
	(-2.9790)	(-3.2375)	(-2.0633)	(-6.4967)	(-3.7753)	(-4.1244)
ID²INVED	—	0.0167*	—	—	0.0089616†	0.0103†
		(3.5802)			(1.8282)	(2.1770)
CHINVED	—	—	—	-0.002104*	-0.0012456†	-0.0012571†
				(-4.3718)	(-2.1038)	(-2.0986)
CDMINVED	—	—	-0.0111	—	-0.0037787	—
			(-1.7016)		(-0.8519)	
Method of estimation	2SLS	2 SLS	2SLS	2SLS	2SLS	
R²	0.7199	0.8501	0.7730	0.9010	0.9278	0.9186
R̄²	0.6337	0.7877	0.6784	0.8598	0.8772	0.8742

* Significant at 95% (0.05) level in a 2-tailed test.
† Significant at 90% (0.10) level in a 2-tailed test.

indicating that an internal balance of power reduces the effectiveness of investment. Except in equation 3, where it is marginal, CDMINVED is clearly insignificant, so that the evidence is not compelling.

(4) The coefficient of CHINVED is always negative and significant, which may indicate that the effectiveness of investment is reduced in sclerotic political systems.

(5) There is an indirect negative feedback path from CHINVED to growth, since CHINVED is negatively related to GROWTH, and thus indirectly negatively related to the level of investment.

Before we accept that both the balance-of-power model and Olson's model are supported, a number of further questions need to be asked. First, it is possible that the political variables may affect growth because they directly or indirectly affect the amount of investment as well as its effectiveness in a way that equation 6 and the other equations in the system do not yet capture. Secondly, the political variables may have some influence on the budget deficit or its effectiveness. Each of these problems is now addressed.[63]

If IDEOLD^2, CONSDEM, or CHOI were affecting growth in some other way besides reducing the efficacy of investment, this might show up if these variables were included directly in the model with the interaction terms. I tried adding IDEOLD^2 to equation 2, CONSDEM to equation 3, and CHOI to equation 4, but in no case were the variables significant. These three variables were also added to equations 5 and 6 with the same result. Although this tends to indicate that the significant effects of the political variables are captured by the interaction terms, it is still possible that they affect the level of investment in some way.

To assess this possibility I first added the variables IDEOLD^2, CONSDEM, and CHOI in turn to equation 1 in Table 10.1 for INV. Nothing was added to the model in terms of explanatory power, and each variable proved insignificant. However, there is a potential problem with this procedure. Equation 1 in Table 10.1 includes the lagged value for investment in physical capital, INV(-1). The rationale was to allow a powerful instrument for INV to be employed when estimating the growth equation. However, if the balance-of-power model is correct, in the absence of a major political shock balance-of-power equilibria should persist through time. INV(-1) could also be effected by the existence of a balance of power at time $t - 1$; and the inclusion of INV(-1) in the equation for INV might mean that if proxies for the balance of power were also included in the equation, they would seem insignificant because INV(-1) was also picking up the balance-of-power effect. The same might also hold in relation to the proxy for sclerosis, CHOI. If INV(-1) is dropped, a satisfactory alternative equation for investment can be constructed on the basis of GROWTH, DEF, and MIL, as shown in equation 5 of Table 10.1. DEF was negatively and significantly related to INV, as accounts of the crowding out of investment by government budget deficits might suggest. Adding the three political variables in turn to this equation threw up no indication that they were impacting directly on INV: in each case the variables were insignificant and the explanatory power of the model was not improved by their inclusion. There is no evidence to suggest that an internal balance of power or political sclerosis directly reduces the level of INV.

The variable used to measure human-capital formation is EDUC(-1). Since IDEOLD^2 is based on data for the 1970s, I could not directly test whether this proxy for an internal balance of power related in any way to EDUC(-1). Since any cross-sectional research design is premissed upon the assumption that equations are stable through time it is appropriate to seek a relationship between EDUC—the average percentage of GDP spent on education by central government in the 1970s—and other political and economic variables in the model. Just as in relation to physical-capital formation, the issue is whether to include the lagged value of the dependent variable in the equation. When EDUC(-1) is included, it is possible to build an equation for EDUC in which the political variable CHOI is significant and has a positive coefficient—see equation 6 in Table 10.1. Neither of the other two political variables is significant if it is added to this equation. However, if EDUC(-1) is dropped from equation 6, CHOI becomes non-significant, and the other two political variables are also easily non-significant if they are added to the equation.[64] An Olsonian account might suggest that educational special interests are able to oversupply education in sclerotic systems. This is consistent with the positive coefficient of CHOI in equation 6 of Table 10.1.[65] However, this result is only plausible if there is also a good theoretical rationale for including EDUC(-1) in the model, and the very high t-value of this variable in equation 6 of Table 10.1 suggests that it may well be blanketing out other influences, suggesting a misspecification problem and a biased estimate of the effect of CHOI.

I considered the possibility that the political variables somehow reduced the efficacy of budget deficits. However, interaction terms designed to capture such effects were not significant when added to equations 5 or 6. I was unable to find a satisfactory equation for DEF which did not include DEF(−1), and it is quite plausible that there is a causal relationship here, since deficits incurred at an earlier time generate interest payments which may increase future deficits. I tried adding CHOI, CONSDEM, and IDEOLD^2 in turn to equation 2 of Table 10.1, but in each case the coefficient was insignificant, even at the 90 per cent (0.1) level. On the basis of this, I conclude that the political variables do not interact with or directly affect the size of the budge deficit, as measured by DEF.

Finally, I examined whether the political variables had indirect effects on growth via direct effects on TAX and MIL, through causal pathways including INV and DEF. When I added CHOI, CONSDEM, and IDEOLD^2 in turn to equation 4 in Table 10.1 for TAX, each proved insignificant.[66] Both IDEOLD^2 and CONSEDEM were insignificant at the 90 per cent (0.1) level when added in turn to equation 3 in Table 10.1 for MIL. When CHOI was added to this equation, however, its regression coefficient was positive, with a t-value of 1.6956, which is almost significant at the 90 per cent (0.1) level. This result suggests that political sclerosis may be associated with higher military spending, and thus with lower investment and lower growth. However, care is needed in making this interpretation. I created a dummy variable DEFEAT, which took on the value 1 for Japan, Italy, Austria, and the Federal German Republic and 0 otherwise. When both CHOI and DEFEAT were added to equation 3 in Table 10.1, CHOI became insignificant and of trivial importance, while DEFEAT had a negative coefficient and was significant at the 90 per cent level when CHOI was dropped. One way of interpreting this is that defeat in World War II involved the dismantling of the military industrial complexes of the four countries concerned. It is difficult to account for the growth-retarding effects of the military-industrial complex unless its power effectively to block reduced military expenditure is allowed for, so that these results hardly support Olson's analysis of these four cases.

To summarize: (1) there is no evidence that an internal balance of power directly reduces the amount of investment; (2) there is no evidence that the size or effects of the budget deficit are influenced by any of the political variables; and (3) there is some evidence that political sclerosis may increase investment in education, with a positive knock-on affect on growth. Even allowing for the possible positive causal pathway between CHOI and GROWTH via EDUC, the overall effect of CHOI on growth is negative when the negative causal pathway between CHOI and GROWTH via CHINVED is allowed for. The overall effect of sclerosis may be to reduce growth.[67] Taking account of all the causal pathways examined there is a positive relationship between ID^2INVED and GROWTH, indicating that an internal balance of power slows growth. CONSDEM, the other proxy for an internal balance of power, could not convincingly be shown to have any impact, although there was some evidence that it may have reduced the efficacy of overall investment and investment levels. This is disappointing. However, given that the CONSDEM scores were constructed using factor analysis, they may well measure the consensus democracy trait with low precision, and I feel that we should not totally reject the idea that consensus democracy is linked to low growth at this stage.

We might still conclude, then, that both Olson's model and the balance-of-power model receive some empirical support. Before finally accepting this conclusion we need to determine what CHOI is actually measuring. CHOI has usually been taken as a proxy for institutional sclerosis. However, the balance-of-power model shows that unless one group is initially hegemonic (which I argued is unlikely) there will be a gradual evolution towards a balance-of-power equilibrium, as non-essential groups are defeated. It is reasonable to assume that this process would also be disrupted by events such as defeat in war, fascism, and social revolution. Thus it could be the case that CHOI is another proxy for the existence of an internal balance of power; and that the negative overall causal pathway from CHOI to growth supports the balance-of-power model rather than Olson's model. Weight is given to this idea by the fact that the correlation of CHOI with IDEOLD^2 is significant at the 90 per cent (0.1) level and negative in value at –0.4846. Thus older political systems (as measured by CHOI) are significantly more likely to have a low score on IDEOLD^2, indicating an internal balance of power. Given the fact that a balance of power is the most plausible long-term equilibrium of the growth game, this correla-

tion seems to me to be sufficiently robust to suggest substance
rather than statistical artefact. The correlation between CHOI and
the other proxy for an internal balance of power, CONSDEM, is
−0.2534. While this correlation is not significant, the fact that it is
negative again suggests that CHOI may be a proxy for an internal
balance of power.

The statistical evidence alone cannot settle the issue of whether
CHOI is an adequate proxy for sclerosis. But Olson's argument that
the presence of more organized groups makes it harder to envisage
collective action to obtain growth is badly flawed. In the light of
this finding, I think that the burden of proof now falls on Olson
and his followers to generate an adequate explanation for the negative link between CHOI and GROWTH. In the absence of such an
explanation, we could either interpret this link as further evidence
for the balance-of-power model or we could ignore is altogether,
on the grounds that no adequate theoretical rationale is available.

3. CONCLUSION

It is implausible that any single model will be able to account for
all historical and current cases of relative economic decline or all
the relevant features of the social processes involved. Nevertheless,
the balance-of-power model seems to provide a more coherent and
empirically better supported account of relative growth rates in the
1970s than Olson's model. The sort of cross-national statistical
testing carried out here obviously needs to be supplemented by
more detailed comparative case-studies of the politics of growth
before it can convincingly be claimed that the balance-of-power
model provides a better description of the politics of growth. The
Swedish case discussed above is suggestive, but not conclusive, and
the interpretive issues in relation to the 1970s cannot be settled in
a single chapter! Rather than take these concerns further here, this
conclusion explores theoretical issues surrounding the perspective
I advocate.

John Hall has argued that the sorts of power stand-offs discussed here were characteristic of a number of economically stagnant civilizations and societies, whereas social flexibility has often
gone with openness to co-operative deal-making.[68] Hall's work
suggests that as social dynamism begins to wind down, the growth

game increasingly comes to resemble the zero-sum world portrayed by the balance-of-power model. However, in dynamic societies such as those of early modern Europe—especially Britain—it may be more like a positive-sum co-operative game. This raises the important issue of whether the balance-of-power model can explain the initial shift in world-view towards a zero-sum, conflictual conception of economic life. Moreover, co-operative deal-making between groups is clearly important in dynamic societies and the balance-of-power model does not capture this. I believe Olson's account of collective action is theoretically flawed, but a satisfactory model might need to integrate insights from both the balance-of-power perspective and from collective-action theory.

Macro-sociological arguments such as those of Hall also suggest that the religious, ideological, and cultural roots of gridlock were important in such cases as China, India, and the Roman Empire. These arguments are rather difficult to square with the notion that gridlock is an epiphenomenon of the distribution of the sorts of powers which can reasonably be characterized as zero-sum. In the *realpolitik* world pictured here all coalitions are possible. While politics sometimes makes strange bedfellows, certain coalitions will typically be ruled out by ideology, culture, or history, and this needs to be allowed for. Much recent commentary on the left, especially on the case of Britain, has drawn on Gramsci's work to explain relative economic decline in terms of the failure of any of the competing hegemonic projects in existence to become truly hegemonic.[69] Gramsci himself argued that building hegemony involves inter-group deal-making and material concessions of the sort emphasized here.[70] Yet, as Gramsci—and particularly neo-Gramscians—stress, it involves more than that: the hegemonic group or coalition is also able to impose and gain acceptance for its intellectual and moral vision. While the processes captured by the internal balance-of-power model are significant today in countries such as Britain, I believe that a more comprehensive analysis would also require an account of the ideological dimensions of hegemony, something notoriously difficult to address within a rational-choice perspective.

APPENDIX: FORMAL DEFINITIONS OF VIABLE THREAT, COUNTER-THREAT, AND SYSTEM STABILITY

$\mathcal{C} = (C_1, \ldots, C_n)$ is a coalition structure which partitions the groups into a set of n disjoint coalitions, including the notional empty coalition $\emptyset$ and the grand coalition of all groups, S; $(r, \mathcal{C})$ is a proposal consisting of a distribution of resources over the groups, r, and a coalition structure, $\mathcal{C}$; $g(C,C^*) = r(C^*)$ are the resources that coalition C can secure if it defeats C^*, assuming that C and C^* are disjoint. Then, we define threat, counter-threat, and viable counter-threat in the following way:

Threat: $(r', \mathcal{C}')$ is a threat by C against C' with respect to (r,S), the current status quo, if and only if:

    (1) $C, C' \varepsilon \mathcal{C}'$;
    (2) $r(C) > r(C')$;
    (3) $r'_i = 0$ for all $i \varepsilon C'$;
    (4) $r'_j > r_j$ for all $j \varepsilon C$.
    $(r', \mathcal{C}')$ is a threat against i if $i \varepsilon C'$.

Counterthreat: $(r'', \mathcal{C}'')$ is a counterthreat to $(r', \mathcal{C}')$ by $K \subseteq C' \cap C''$ if and only if:

    (1) either $C \subseteq C^*$ or $C \cap C'' = \emptyset$, where $C'', C^* \notin C''$;
    (2) $(r'', \mathcal{C}'')$ is a threat to C^*;
    (3) r''_i is preferred to r'_i for all $i \varepsilon C''$.

$(r'', \mathcal{C}'')$ is a viable counterthreat for $i \varepsilon K$ if and only if there is no $\tilde{C} \subseteq C'' - \{i\}$ such that C has a threat, $(\tilde{r}, \tilde{\mathcal{C}})$ against C^* or $C^* + \{i\}$ with $\tilde{r}_j$ preferred to r_j'' for all $j \varepsilon \tilde{C}$.

The set of groups, S, and a distribution of resources over the set of groups such that $r_i > 0$ for each group in S will be called system stable if no group or coalition of groups can be defeated by some other group or coalition of groups. System stability exists if and only if for each group i, and for every threat against i, i has a viable counter-threat.

NOTES

1. C. M. Cipolla (ed.), *The Economic Decline of Empires* (London: Methuen, 1970), 11. Roberto Unger has also argued that flexibility of

social practices translates into economic and military power. See his *Plasticity Into Power: Comparative-Historical Studies on the Institutional Conditions of Economic and Military Success* (Cambridge: Cambridge University Press, 1987).

2. On the US see, for example, L. C. Thurow, *The Zero-Sum Society* (Harmondsworth: Penguin, 1981), ch. 1; on the Soviet Union see M. I. Goldman, *USSR In Crisis* (New York: Norton, 1983), 182; on Britain see, for example, B. Fine and L. Harris, *The Peculiarities of the British Economy* (London: Lawrence and Wishart, 1985), where the main groups are seen as industrial capital, financial capital, the state, and organized labour.

3. See, in particular, E. M. S. Niou and P. C. Ordeshook, 'A Theory of the Balance of Power in International Systems', *Journal of Conflict Resolution*, 30 (1986), 685–715. Another interesting analysis is R. H. Wagner, 'The Theory of Games and the Balance of Power', *World Politics*, 38 (1985/6), 546–75. Many of Wagner's results parallel those of Niou and Ordeshook.

4. M. Olson, *The Rise and Decline of Nations* (New Haven, Conn.: Yale University Press, 1982).

5. Ibid. 38–41.

6. Ibid. 41–7.

7. Ibid. 47–53; 66–9.

8. Ibid. 58–65.

9. Ibid. 53–9, 63.

10. Ibid., ch. 4.

11. There is now an extensive critical literature on Olson's thesis. For collections of papers see: D. C. Mueller (ed.), *The Political Economy of Growth* (New Haven, Conn.: Yale University Press, 1982); the symposium on Olson's thesis in *International Studies Quarterly*, 27 (1983); the special issue on Olson's thesis in *Scandinavian Political Studies*, 9 (1986). Two critiques of the underlying rational-choice logic of Olson's argument are: B. E. Pasch and P. J. Sorenson, 'Organisational Behaviour and Economic Growth: A Norwegian Perspective', *Scandinavian Political Studies*, 9 (1986), 51–63; D. Cameron, 'Distributional Coalitions and Other Sources of Economic Stagnation', *International Organisation*, 42 (1988), 561–603, esp. pp. 564–80. For relevant empirical studies see n. 23.

12. M. Laver, *The Politics of Private Desires* (Harmondsworth: Penguin, 1981), ch. 3.

13. The best-known analysis of the exit option is A. Hirschman, *Exit, Voice and Loyalty* (Cambridge, Mass: Harvard University Press, 1970).

14. M. Crozier, S. P. Huntingdon, and S. Watanuki, *The Crisis of*

Democracy: Report to the Trilateral Commission on the Ungovern-ability of Liberal Democracies (New York: New York University Press, 1975); A. King, 'Overload: Problems of Governing in the 1970s', *Political Studies*, 23 (1975), 283–96; J. Douglas, 'The Overloaded Crown', *British Journal of Political Science*, 6 (1976), 483–505.

15. e.g. Olson, *Rise and Decline*, 47.

16. Ibid. 53–5.

17. S. Bowles and J. Eatwell, 'Between Two Worlds: Interest Groups, Class Structure, and Capitalist Growth', in Mueller (ed.), *Political Economy*, 299; Cameron, 'Distributional Coalitions', 565.

18. A. Russel, 'Olsonian Age Versus Militarism: The Case Against Olson's Account of Relative Economic Decline', unpublished M.A. thesis (Essex, 1989). The literature on the economic effects of military expen-diture is extensive, but see the following: R. Smith, 'Military Expenditure and Capitalism', *Cambridge Journal of Economics*, 1 (1977), 61–76; R. Smith, 'Military Expenditure and Investment in OECD Countries', *Journal of Comparative Economics*, 4 (1980), 19–32; A. Cappelan *et al.*, 'Military Spending and Economic Growth in OECD Countries', *Journal of Peace Research*, 21 (1984), 375–87; S. Chan, 'The Impact of Defence Spending on Economic Performance: A Survey of Evidence and Problems', *Orbis*, 29 (1985), 403–33.

19. R. de Grasse, *Military Expansion Economic Decline: The Impact of Military Spending on U.S. Economic Performance* (Armonk, NY: Sharpe, 1983); M. Chalmers, *Paying For Defence: Military Spending and British Decline* (London: Pluto, 1985).

20. D. C. van Raemdonck and P. F. Diehl, 'After the Shooting Stops: Insights on Post-War Economic Growth', *Journal of Peace Research*, 26 (1989), 121–48; Cameron, 'Distributional Coalitions', 581–8.

21. See, for example, C. Freeman, J. Clark, and L. Soete, *Unemployment and Technical Innovation* (Westpoint, Conn.: Greenwood, 1982). Compare this with Olson's gestures towards Schumpeterian analysis of technical change: Olson, *Rise and Decline*, 61–6.

22. A good summary of the main points is M. Taylor, *The Possibility of Cooperation* (Cambridge: Cambridge University Press, 1987), 9–13. On the inapplicability of the size principle to some indivisible goods see J. Chamberlin, 'Provision of Public Goods as a Function of Group Size', *American Political Science Review*, 68 (1974), 707–16.

23. Relevant empirical work includes: K. Choi, 'A Statistical Test of Olson's Model', in Mueller (ed.), *Political Economy*, P. Whiteley, 'The Political Economy of Economic Growth', *European Journal of Political Science*, 11 (1983), 197–213; E. Weede, 'Catch-up Distributional Coalitions and Governments as Determinants of

Economic Growth or Decline in Industrialised Democracies', *British Journal of Sociology*, 37 (1986), 194–220; G. Garrett and P. Lange, 'Performance in a Hostile World: Economic Growth in Capitalist Democracies, 1974–1982', *World Politics*, 38 (1985/6), 517–45; P. Lange and G. Garrett, 'The Politics of Growth: Strategic Interaction and Economic Performance in Advanced Industrial Societies 1974–1980', *Journal of Politics*, 47 (1985), 793–807; V. Gray and D. Lowery, 'Interest Group Politics and Economic Growth in the US States', *American Political Science Review*, 82 (1988), 109–31; S. Wallace and J. T. Turner, 'Explaining Differences in State Growth: Catching up versus Olson', *Public Choice*, 51 (1990), 201–13; J. E. Lane and S. Ersson, *Comparative Political Economy* (London: Pinter, 1990), ch. 8; F. G. Castles and S. Dowrick, 'The Impact of Government Spending Levels on Medium-Term Economic Growth in the OECD, 1960–85', *Journal of Theoretical Politics*, 2 (1990), 173–204.

24. Also assume that if for three disjoint coalitions C, C', and C'', if C attacks C' and C' attacks C'', when $r(C) > r(C') > rC'')$, then C defeats C', leaving C'' undefeated. This reflects the idea that weak coalitions can take advantage of conflicts between stronger ones.

25. Besides having choices about what they do to defeated groups, leaders can act aggressively to secure resources from other groups or negotiate to secure resources from other groups. If both options lead to outcomes between which a leader is indifferent under this criterion above, they prefer to negotiate.

26. Niou and Ordeshook, 'Balance of Power', 701.

27. Compare this result with the classic argument that the possibilities of an international balance of power are linked to the number of pertinent nations in M. Kaplan, *System and Process in International Politics* (New York: Wiley, 1957).

28. Niou and Ordeshook, 'Balance of Power', 707. The proof that a balance of power is an equilibrium if no group is initially hegemonic needs to be amended to allow for the assumption that the resources of defeated groups on which the costs of growth are imposed are destroyed at the end of the round, as assumed here. However, this makes no difference, as far as I can see, so long as leaders take this possibility into account when calculating their best moves. A balance of power on this account is an unstable equilibrium: some slight miscalculation or slight shift in resources could tip the balance in a way that would make a single group dominant. Olson's model is unable to explain cases in which a spurt of relatively rapid growth occurs without any major system shock in what was a relatively stagnant economy. The internal balance-of-power model here might make sense of such phenomena: what was a balance of power 'flops over' cata-

strophically into a situation in which one group is hegemonic. Compare this idea with Riker's argument that the decline of empires may result from miscalculations made when paring down their alliances to minimal-winning form, resulting in their becoming defeatable: see W. H. Riker, *The Theory of Political Coalitions* (New Haven, Conn.: Yale University Press, 1962), 212–16.

29. Olson, *Rise and Decline*, 53.
30. Cameron, 'Distributional Coalitions', 588; A. Gustafsson, 'Rise and Decline of Nations', *Scandinavian Political Studies*, 9 (1986), 35–49.
31. G. Esping-Andersen and P. Friedland, 'Class Coalitions in the Making of Western European Economics', in M. Zeitlin (ed.), *Political Power and Social Theory*, iii (Greenwich, Conn.: JAI Press, 1982), 19–20.
32. Ibid. 20–1.
33. Ibid. 21, 38–9.
34. Ibid. 25.
35. Ibid. 42.
36. M. G. Schmidt, 'The Welfare State and the Economy in Periods of Economic Crisis: A Comparative Study of Twenty-Three OECD Nations', *European Journal of Political Research*, 11 (1983), 1–26, 13; Garrett and Lange, 'Performance'. It has also specifically been argued that growth was higher in the 1970s when the left dominated. See Whiteley, 'Political Economy'; Lange and Garrett, 'Politics of Growth'. This second argument has been disputed: see R. W. Jackman, 'The Politics of Economic Growth in The Industrial Democracies, 1974–80: Leftist Strength or North Sea Oil', *Journal of Politics*, 49 (1987), 242–56; Lane and Errson, *Political Economy*, 203.
37. Garrett and Lange, 'Performance', 544.
38. Schmidt, 'Welfare State'; Garrett and Lange, 'Performance'.
39. The political data were drawn from J. E. Lane, D. McKay, and K. Newton, *Political Data Handbook OECD Countries* (Cambridge: Cambridge University Press, 1991), pt. 2.
40. The most comprehensive set of cross-nationally comparable ideological scales which I could find appeared in F. G. Castles and P. Mair, 'Left-Right Political Scales: Some "Expert" Judgements', *European Journal of Political Research*, 12 (1984), 73–88. Switzerland and Japan were not included. The scale for Switzerland was from H. H. Kerr, 'Swiss Party System: Steadfast and Changing', in H. Daalder (ed.), *Party Systems in Denmark, Austria, Switzerland, The Netherlands and Belgium* (London: Pinter, 1987). I could not locate any scale for Japan. As the liberals were in office throughout the 1970s it sufficed to place them, and I assigned a score of 6.6. Results are not sensitive to this placement as long as the Liberals are located to the right of centre.

Although the data on governing coalitions was available up to 1985, the ideological scales pertained to the 1970s. This was one reason for my choice of time-period.

41. The only similar scale I am aware of is Schmidt's rank order on a five-point scale of the overall ideological complexion of the eighteen governments in the countries concerned in the 1970s—see his 'Welfare State'. Treating this scale as an interval measure, its correlation with my scale is 0.8597.

42. The figures for growth are from Lane *et al.*, *Political Data Handbook*, 61 and are year-to-year averages.

43. A. Lijphart, *Democracies: Patterns of Majoritarian and Consensus Government in Twenty-one Countries* (New Haven, Conn.: Yale University Press, 1984), 23–31; id., and M. L. Crepaz, 'Corporatism and Consensus Democracy in Eighteen Countries: Conceptual and Empirical Linkages', *British Journal of Political Science*, 21 (1991), 235–56, 236.

44. Lijphart, *Democracies*, 21–3.

45. The idea of consensus democracy bears a family resemblance to Lijphart's ideas about consociationalism. Lane and Errson have argued that there is no clear empirical evidence that consociationalism affects growth, although their proxy for consociationalism has a negative and significant coefficient—see their *Comparative Political Economy*, 203.

46. Lijphart and Crepaz, 'Corporatism', 239.

47. CONSDEM is not highly or significantly correlated with IDEOLD², the correlation being 0.1933. It might also be suggested that if CONSDEM were negatively related to growth this is the result of the instability of governments in the multi-party coalitions of consensus democracy. However, CONSDEM has a very low correlation with a measure of government durability, and my research indicates that government durability itself is unimportant.

48. The correlation is −0.18, and the *t*-value −0.7239.

49. Some tests of Olson's thesis use a pooled cross-section/time series research design: see Gray and Lowery, 'Interest Group Politics'; Castles and Dowrick, 'Impact of Government Spending'. In principle this ought to allow greater precision in estimation by increasing the number of observations. However, this was precluded here because IDEOL had to be calculated over reasonably long time-periods to get meaningful results and this meant that few successive cross-sections could have been taken within an overall time-frame in which it would be reasonable to assume stability of coefficients and within which lagged values of some variables could be used.

50. OECD, *Historical Statistics 1960–1984* (Paris: OECD, 1984), 154.

51. Compare this to Castles and Dowrick, 'Impact of Government Spending', 196, which reports results indicating that education is not significant although social transfer payments are. Some authors suggest that a positive relationship exists between overall government expenditure and growth. See D. Cameron, 'On the Limits of Public Economy', *Annals of the American Association for Political and Social Science*, 459 (1982), 46–62; Castles and Dowrick, 'Impact of Government Spending', 192. Others have argued the opposite way: see Weede, 'Catch Up'.

52. Lane *et al.*, *Political Data Handbook*, 99, averaging the figures for 1970, 1975, and 1980.

53. Ibid. 105, averaging the figures for 1970, 1975, and 1980. The data for New Zealand are missing since this country does not compile the relevant data. It was estimated by multiplying NZ government final consumption by OECD average total government outlays and dividing the product by OECD average government final consumption.

54. Garrett and Lange, 'Performance'. All figures are from this article except that for Switzerland, which is from IEA, *Energy Balances of the OECD Countries 1974/76* (Paris: IEA, 1976), and that for New Zealand, which is from UN Dept. of Economic and Social Affairs, *Supplement to the World Economic Survey 1975* (New York: UN, 1977). For New Zealand the figure is net imports of energy as a percentage of total energy consumption.

55. With the exception of Castles and Dowrick 'Impact of Government Spending', the empirical literature relating to Olson's work uniformly ignores this problem, although it frequently arises.

56. K. Choi, 'A Statistical Test of Olson's Model', in Mueller (ed.), *Political Economy*. This variable has been widely used by others as a measure of sclerosis. Lane and Ersson construct another proxy. Their institutionalization variable gives results which they say support Olson's position—see their *Political Economy*, 198–207. However this variable was not significant in the equations I ran for growth.

57. See, for example, P. Kennedy, *A Guide to Econometrics* (Cambridge, Mass.: MIT Press, 3rd edn., 1992), 139.

58. Lane *et al.*, *Political Data Handbook*, 101, taking the average of the values for 1970, 1975, and 1980.

59. OECD, *Historical Statistics*, 154. The particular lag taken can be chosen on the grounds of statistical power or convenience, as it was for this and other lagged instruments.

60. Lane *et al.*, *Political Data Handbook*; the lagged deficit figures are an average for 1955, 1960, and 1965—see p. 105; the tax figures are for central government, averaging the percentages for 1970, 1975, and 1980 on p. 73.

61. Ibid. 101, averaging the figures for 1955, 1960, and 1965.
62. Ibid. 73, averaging the figures for 1955, 1960, and 1965.
63. The way in which the interaction terms ID²INVED and CHINVED are set up effectively imposes the restrictions on the model that: an internal balance of power has the same impact on the effectiveness of physical and educational investment; and that political sclerosis, similarly, has the same impact on the effectiveness of physical and educational investment. I estimated a modified form of equation 6 in Table 10.2 in which ID²INVED and CHINVED were replaced by ID²INV = IDEOLD²*INV and CHINV = CHOI*INV. ID²INV had a positive coefficient significant at the 90% level (t=2.1331); and CHINV had a negative coefficient significant at the 95% level (t = −2.3915). All other variables remained significant with coefficients of the same sign as in equation 6. I then added ID²ED = IDEOLD²*EDUC and CHED = CHOI*EDUC. Neither variable was significant. However, the overall model was not identified and, not surprisingly, none of the other variables was significant either. While identification could have been achieved if I had then dropped ID²INV and CHINV, there is obviously a risk of misspecification. For what it is worth, though, if CHINVED and ID²INVED are replaced by CHED and ID²ED in equation 6, both have the anticipated sign but only ID²ED is significant at the 90% level, with all other variables except EDUC(−1) remaining significant. To summarize, I could not adequately test for separate effects of the two main political variables on the effectiveness of investment.
64. The relevant t-values were: CONSDEM t = 1.4238; CHOI t = 1.4355; IDEOLD² t = −0.9126.
65. It might be suggested that this relationship is merely an artefact due to sclerotic systems having had more time to grow, and thus having higher GDP per capita, and spending more on the superior good education as a consequence. The correlation between CHOI and GDP75 (GDP per capita in 1975 measured in dollars) is 0.3765, which gives some support to this. However, GDP75 is non-significant if added to equation 6 in Table 10.1, employing GDP75 as an extra instrument. Some have used variables like GDP75 as a proxy for the catch-up effect that poorer countries grow faster because they copy technology and institutions from richer countries—see e.g. Weede, 'Catch-up'. I found no support for this. GDP75 had a negative coefficient but a t-value of − 0.3939 if added to the growth equation, equation 6 in Table 10.2, treating GDP75 as an extra exogenous variable, and other coefficients and t-values remaining almost stable.
66. There is some evidence that left-wing governments are associated with higher taxes. Adding IDEOL to the tax equation gave it a negative coefficient and a t-value of −1.54.

67. Allowing for feedback between GROWTH and INV and the consequent feedback between CHINVED and GROWTH, the overall path coefficient is −0.0307.

68. J. A. Hall, *Powers and Liberties: The Causes and Consequences of the Decline of the West* (London: Penguin, 1986), 22–3.

69. e.g. B. Jessop, K. Bonnett, S. Bromley, and T. Ling, *Thatcherism* (Cambridge: Polity, 1988).

70. A. Gramsci, *Selections From the Prison Notebooks* (London: Lawrence and Wishart, 1973), 161.

11

Rationality, Revolution, and Reassurance

MARK WICKHAM-JONES

1. INTRODUCTION

The orthodox rational-choice account of revolutionary behaviour is that 'rationality requires inaction'.[1] The free-rider conclusion is entailed by a series of assumptions: actors are end-orientated and selfish; the large number required for successful revolutions creates co-ordination problems; and the non-excludable benefits mean backsliding from putative agreements is probable. Revolutionary participation has thus been typified as an *n*-person Prisoners' Dilemma with a dominant strategy of non-cooperation.

The orthodox rational-choice account provides a logical and coherent explanation of why revolutions are rare. The problem, of course, is that it does not provide an account of why they sometimes do occur. The orthodox model is too negative, too pessimistic, and too hopeless in the conclusion it reaches.

In this chapter, I argue that the strong conclusion of the orthodox account assumes restrictive postulates. By relaxing, in turn, key assumptions, revolution can be explained. The assumptions relaxed are: first, the end-orientated nature of the benefits of revolutionary participation; second, the selfish motivations of participants; third, the isolated and non-iterated nature of collective-action decisions; and fourth, the non-excludable gains of participation. Without departing from the rational-choice framework, the partial relaxation of these assumptions allows for rational revolutionary participation. It does not suggest that revolutions

I am very grateful to Brian Barry, Christopher Bertram, John Broome, Keith Dowding, Patrick Dunleavy, Vernon Hewitt, Desmond King, and Albert Weale for their comments on this chapter.

are routine and uncomplicated. Potential revolutionaries face formidable obstacles. Participative benefits and altruism are unlikely to provide sufficient motivations, so reciprocity and excludable benefits (Olson's 'selective incentives') remain important components of successful action. Partial relaxation suggests that there is no single determinant of rational behaviour. Different institutional settings yield different solutions to collective-action problems.[2] To understand participation we need to understand the institutional context in which relevant actors make their choice. Orthodox models pay little attention to institutional or cultural settings. Drawing on the work of Michael Taylor, a reconstructed rational-choice account emerges which shows multiple solutions to the collective-action problem of revolution.[3] Two problems loom for such an account: what is the role of norms in guiding revolutionary action? And what is the relationship of reciprocity to the excludable benefits? I conclude that despite the importance of other factors, excludable benefits remain an important motivation. Even when institutions are factored into the account of revolution, Olson's original solution remains powerful.

2. THE ORTHODOX ACCOUNT

Allen Buchanan presents revolutionary action as an *n*-person Prisoners' Dilemma (see Fig. 11.1). Of the four possible outcomes, the most desirable for an individual is *Y*, where he or she gets the benefits of revolution (*B*) without the costs (*C*). The second best is *W*, where an individual has to contribute, an outcome preferable to *Z*, where the revolution does not get off the ground. The worst possible outcome is *X*. Here the individual does not get to enjoy any of the benefits of the revolution but pays the costs. As *Y* > *W* and *Z* > *X*, the structure represents a Prisoners' Dilemma where non-participation dominates.

Shaw presents the argument in a similar fashion.[4] Revolutionary participation can be represented as:

$$J = BP - C + L.$$

The individual's decision to join, *J*, depends upon the benefits that revolution brings, *B*, multiplied by the probability, *P*, that he or she is decisive in the success of the revolution, subtracting the costs

		All other potential revolutionaries	
		Participate	Don't Participate
Individual revolutionary	Participate	*W* (*B–C*)	*X* (*–C*)
	Don't participate	*Y* (*B*)	*Z* (0)

Fig. 11.1 Preferences for the potential revolutionary

of action, *C*, including the possibility of punishment, the resources invested, and the wages foregone.[5] Mueller and Shaw do not assume that benefits are entirely material and include an extra factor, *L*, representing the participative benefits of revolution, the personal pleasures of action and the feelings of solidarity with others that revolutionary struggle engenders. Without *L*, revolutionary participation depends upon $C < BP$, but given the tiny size of *P* that is unlikely.

Does orthodox rational choice have a solution for free-riding? In smallish or 'intermediate' groups Olson believes that tactical agreement is possible, but in large groups such as classes, co-ordination cannot overcome free-riding. Here Olson argues that the provision of excludable private benefits, or selective incentives, is all that can make participation rational. These may be material or social (for example sanctions), but his concept of selective incentives is slippery.[6] Buchanan discounts this solution. It is difficult for a disorganized group, such as potential revolutionaries, to provide selective incentives. Whilst coercive sanctions may be possible, Buchanan claims that their capacity to mobilize individuals is weak.[7] His own solution is that successful revolutionaries should stress the moral claims they make and abandon cost–benefit analysis. Victorious revolutions will not be based on material objectives.[8]

Alternatively the public-good aspect of revolution is denied. In his survey of Chinese rebellions, James Tong claims that collective action was entirely motivated by private economic gains.[9] Bandits took part because the benefits were excludable, although participation was spurred on by economic hardship. Tong's account may explain banditry, but it is less applicable to abrupt actions, such as revolutions requiring mass participation. The individual gain from a revolution is likely to involve, in some way, the overthrow of an existing regime or system and its replacement by a new one (advantageously redistributing resources). Such redistributions are unlikely to be linked directly to participation. For example, classical Marxists claimed that proletarian revolution would bring benefits to the whole proletariat; peasant revolution likewise. Only a few participants are likely to gain post-revolutionary private benefits, such as power or money, directly related to their revolutionary role. Where reward and participation are not linked, the collective-action problem remains. Moreover, revolutionary success depends upon the actions of others. The potential contributor to a revolution must consider the likely decisions of others: individuals in such circumstances act strategically and not parametrically.[10]

3. THE BENEFITS OF REVOLUTIONARY ACTIVITY

In some accounts benefits are not end-orientated. Mueller's revolutionaries take part because of the participative benefits that action provides. Excludable and intangible pay-offs accrue immediately to participants.[11] Such benefits include the loyalty and solidarity of participating and the expression of a revolutionary identity. In this way participants derive benefits from fulfilling their principles. Rationality here is participatively or expressively orientated rather than instrumentally based.[12]

This conceptualization of rationality is expressed by Hirschman, who treats Olson's work with disdain.[13] He argues that people gain participative benefits, well above any costs (which he tends to regard as trivial), so free-riders 'cheat themselves first of all', and he claims that in many cases people will want to take part to get the full benefits of participation.[14] Hirschman suggests that rationale-choice theorists often misread the nature of costs as well. The desire to participate makes the orthodox account of costs into a benefit or an attainment. For example, Palestinians engaged in the Intifada may not have seen their actions as a cost but as inherently beneficial.[15]

The problem for the expressive account is that it seems to entail that participants do not care whether their action is successful in bringing about change. The problem for the orthodox account is that it finds it difficult to explain participation when success seems remote, as in the early years of the Intifada. Together the two accounts may help to explain the history of revolutionary movements. Someone seeking purely material gains may not join until some hope of success seems apparent. Those seeking participative benefits may join together sooner, though even here, participative benefits are 'step goods'.[16] A lone revolutionary will not experience feelings of solidarity and loyalty. However, the step for participative benefits comes well before the step for material benefits derived from success. Participation even without success in the ultimate goal of revolution would be rational. Consequently, the situation confronting an individual is not a Prisoners' Dilemma, it is an Assurance game, because mutual co-operation, with others who want participative benefits, pays the highest dividend. A potential participant needs assuring that a sufficient number participate to realize participative and expressive benefits. Collective action may remain difficult to achieve: an individual must be able to identify other participants and to co-ordinate action with them.

Whether or not this general solution of a wider definition of rational action is adequate to the specific case of revolutionary activity is uncertain. Buchanan concludes that in-process benefits will be inadequate because they do not explain how the collective action is launched initially.[17] Revolutionary activity may involve substantial costs which deter potential participants.[18]

The Motivation of Participants

Relaxing the self-interest assumption will not solve the revolutionary collective-action problem because success is still required:

regardless of whether I contribute or not, either enough others will contribute or they won't. If the former then my costs of contribution could do no good, while contributing a subtraction from the utility the group gains . . . If the latter then my costs are again a subtraction from the group's utility.[19]

The altruist's resources could always be better allocated. Consider a successful revolution which has adequate support. If an individual, who was not going to take part, switches at the last minute to support the revolution, the total costs sunk into mass action will rise but the total benefits remain static. In such circumstances the average pay-off to everyone, contributors and non-contributors included, falls. There are now an unnecessary number of people providing the public good. The more individuals who contribute to the revolution, the more group utility declines because unnecessary investment in the revolution is being wasted.

There are a number of objections to Buchanan's argument. There is the possibility, albeit remote, that an individual's contribution could be decisive.[20] Buchanan claims: 'in the case of concerted revolutionary action, a rational individual would regard the likelihood of his contribution occurring at a "threshold" as negligible'.[21] Chong notes that the step for some public goods may require unanimity—'all or nothing' goods require complete support—and points out that collective actions often involve a series of steps where an individual may be decisive at some stage.[22]

A more plausible objection to Buchanan concerns his calculation of group maximization. Whilst the unnecessary use of my resources will reduce overall group utility, it will only do so to the extent of my own loss. If I factor my utility equally with that of others, I may choose not to participate. However, if I factor it lower—as altruists are often thought to do—then I will contribute. Furthermore it is not certain that revolutions are a single-step good. Every extra participant in revolutionary action may increase the chances of a successful revolution. The expected average pay-off for the whole group will rise as the probability rises. Furthermore, the more participants the lower the individual costs that each must bear.[23]

Buchanan's claim that altruism does not explain participation rests on several factors. First, there must be only a minute threshold chance of being decisive in the success of the revolution. Second, the conception of group maximization must include the interests of the individual affected who is still concerned about the costs to him or herself. Third, there is little uncertainty or opportunity for individuals to co-ordinate their activities in the interest of the group. Last, his conception of revolution as a single-step good means an individual cannot improve the expected average pay-off. Relaxing any one of these conditions means that the group maximizer may well choose to take part. Relax all of them and the belief that altruists will join selfish individuals in free-riding cannot be sustained. Under these circumstances revolutionary action should not be regarded as a Prisoners' Dilemma in each and every possible interaction, but, in some situations at least, as an Assurance game. The problem for the group maximizer is co-ordination.[24]

Altruistic participation does not mean that revolutions become straightforward. They remain difficult to organize, the more so as the number required increases. The potential revolutionary will want sustained evidence of support before taking action. Besides mass altruism does not seem realistic. Individuals may usually be selfish.[25]

Iteration and Communication

Michael Taylor advances iteration as a solution to the Prisoners' Dilemma.[26] Although mathematically complex, the core of Taylor's argument is straightforward. In an iterated sequence, potential revolutionaries realize they are continually failing to organize or to develop their own solution. Taylor terms the solution 'conditional co-operation' because the crucial nature of participation is its conditionality—individuals will only participate if others reciprocate. In his study of protest in Japan, White argues that 'the villagers did not make their decisions in a social vacuum. Their decisions were "strategic"; that is, each individual's choices depended on his expectations about other people's decisions'.[27] Individuals co-operate, not from altruism, but because they calculate that this procedure will further their self-interest. To co-operate over time they must be prepared to wait for future benefits to materialize. This strategy is often called 'tit for tat'.[28]

Olson only accepts that conditional co-operation may occur in small and intermediate groups. By contrast, Taylor claims that size is not such a hindrance, partly because intermediate groups are able to log-roll into much larger ones. He maintains that most collective action 'succeeds in large groups because they are made up of intermediate groups'.[29] He calls this action an internal solution to the Prisoners' Dilemma, because the players themselves reach agreement on their own and without involving or presupposing changes to the dilemma.[30] What prevents individuals from breaking out of such conditional co-operation and opting for a free ride? According to Taylor, they know such defection will have disastrous repercussions. Because co-operation is conditional, if one steps out of line, then other peasants will follow: 'We might say there is a tacit "compact" amongst all the players which breaks down as soon as any one of them breaks ranks'.[31] Co-operation will unravel if people start to defect, and as such there are no long-term gains from defection.

This process is illustrated in Fig. 11.2 (adopted by Taylor from Schelling).[32] The figure indicates that the gains from participation (*P* curve) and defection (*D* curve) both depend upon the number of participants. The more who co-operate, the higher the gains are to both participants and defectors. At any one point defection is better than co-operation. But any defection will lead to further defections and any gains will swiftly be eroded. This approach suggests that there are only two stable positions: either all will participate (S^2) or all will defect (S^1).[33] Because S^2 is more desirable than S^1, individuals will strive for co-operation and will not step out of line by defecting. Chong gives an example in his account of non-violent mass protest: individuals participate because of the 'devastating consequences of a single defection'.[34]

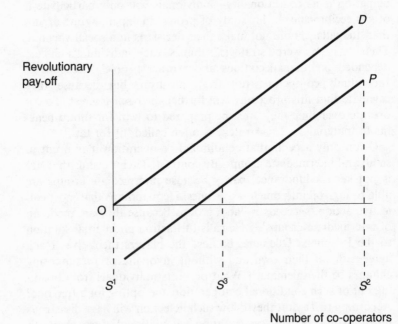

FIG. 11.2 Conditional co-operation as the basis for revolutionary action

Taylor believes there will be some defectors but a subset of participants may develop where individuals will acknowledge the conditional nature of their reciprocity. Co-operation may stabilize at S^3, where further defection will lead to collapse. In work with Hugh Ward, Taylor summarizes this point: 'there exist under certain conditions equilibria in which a subgroup of the players cooperate, each player's continued cooperation being dependent on the cooperation of all the other members of the subgroup. The stability of these conditionally cooperative minimal subgroups is broken by the defection of one player'.[35] Over time the pay-offs from conditional co-operation are much better than defection for successful participants.

Co-operation and Selective Incentives

There is an ambiguity in Taylor's argument. In *The Possibility of Cooperation* he is critical of Olson's analysis, concluding that 'Olson's *model*, then is rather unrealistic'.[36] But, while discussing his own internal solution, Taylor notes the possibility of an external one. An external solution changes the nature of pay-offs, thereby altering an individual's preference ordering and the nature of the game. Olson's selective incentives are a form of external solution, as they change the pay-offs by rewarding co-operators and punishing defectors. Taylor accepts that an external solution, through sanctions, may have a role to play, but argues that the internal solution is the more fundamental one. However in his discussion about revolutionary collective action, Taylor places much more emphasis on the use of sanctions.[37] In such circumstances there is an excludable and negative selective incentive to deter defection.

Fig. 11.3 illustrates that at any one point defection (D curve) is preferable to co-operation (P curve) until sanctions are developed. The effect of such sanctions is to lower the pay-offs from defection to a new curve (D^1) so that defection is now, at any point, no longer a rational strategy.

This solution is decentralized as it comes from society rather than from any centralized power-base and it does not require a state.[38] There might be a collective-action problem with such sanctions. If spontaneous, such as ostracizing someone or employing some other form of social rejection, then no decision about

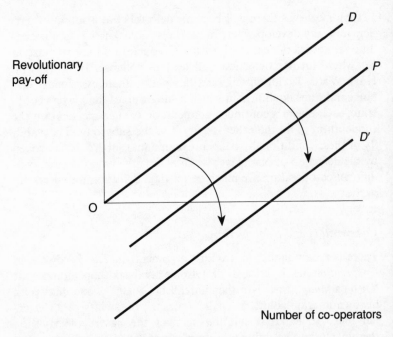

Fig. 11.3 Negative selective incentives facing the potential revolutionary

enforcement has to be reached. However, if sanctions require mechanisms of administration, the question of who carries them out remains unclear.[39] At what point does a group of revolutionaries who enforce punishments come to represent an emergent state? Taylor suggests that sanctions would be spontaneous and informal. He says that 'the cost of applying such sanctions is typically slight'.[40] He by-passes both the collective-action problem and the possibility of a state emerging from such sanctions.

These sanctions alter the non-excludable nature of revolution. There is an incentive not to free-ride in order to avoid social sanctions and punishments. Both critics and supporters of revolutionary activity look to such selective incentives. Critics often stress the coercive measures that revolutionaries employ to ensure complicity from potential supporters.[41] Elster refers to the public shaming of defectors and the use of pejorative terms such as 'scab'.[42] Others stress the positive benefits that revolutionaries might provide in order to clinch support from the wider population.[43] Taylor believes that the two mechanisms of conditional co-operation and selective incentives will work in tandem. One means that peasants worry about the potential consequences of their defection. The other means that they worry about the negative perceptions of free-riding.

Size, Community, and Entrepreneurs

Underpinning Taylor's discussion of conditional co-operation are three key variables: size, the existence of a community, and the role of political entrepreneurs.[44] He argues that conditional co-operation will be easier to ensure the smaller the group and the greater the sense of community.[45] A community may also provide an existing framework on which mass action can piggy-back. Communities provide an institutional basis for rational co-ordinated action to sustain co-operation. Political entrepreneurs or leaders work towards both of the mechanisms which Taylor argues foster co-operation. First, they provide an important co-ordinating role. They help communication and information flow and they guide the beliefs of individual actors. They spell out the conditional nature of what is going on. Tactically, political entrepreneurs can also focus on manageable issues and break up large tasks so that the participants are risking less by co-operating. Second, political entrepreneurs provide selective incentives—material and non-material. Revolutionary leaders may have material resources with which to win the support of peasants and they may also mobilize effective social sanctions. In his study of Vietnamese peasants, Samuel Popkin emphasizes the dual roles of political entrepreneurs: 'effective leaders may provide not only selective incentives; but by co-ordination of contributions, by manipulation of information, or by breaking up a large overall goal into numerous steps with critical thresholds, they may also elicit contributions not tied directly to selective incentives'.[46]

Such political entrepreneurs will have their own private incentives for taking part in revolutionary struggle and their position is less subject to free-riding than other potential revolutionaries. Leaders receive direct benefits from their participation.[47] Holding office in a post-revolutionary regime may depend on their role in bringing about the downfall of the old system. Political entrepreneurs may also gain immediate and future economic privileges from their participation in mass action. As well as these excludable benefits, political entrepreneurs know that their co-ordinating action will be important. Accordingly they have more chance of being decisive in promoting the success of the revolution.[48]

Reconstructed Rational Choice and Revolutionary Participation

Under Taylor's model, participants remain selfish and end-orientated. They are calculating individuals. But the problems of participation are analysed as an iterated game with communication between relevant individuals. They can discuss and negotiate the situation in which they find themselves. Some of the attributes of revolutions are excludable and the pay-offs are not solely material. Leaders are central figures in the organization of revolutionary activity.

An individual decision to join a revolution may be given as:

$$J = B^r + B^e - C$$

where B^r = expected benefits of the revolution and B^e = the selective incentives, material or social, which a community may provide. B^r is no longer discounted by the chance of being decisive because, under Taylor's argument, there is no chance that an individual will not be decisive. B^e includes a variety of items which are excludable. One has to participate to enjoy these, whether they are merely a lack of social sanctions or extra food. These can be further divided into present and future benefits. Selective incentives alone are not sufficient, but remain an important aspect of collective-action solutions.

4. CONCLUSIONS

The reconstructed rational-choice solution to revolutionary action has moved a long way from the orthodox pessimism. The role of expressive or participative benefits, the role of altruistic and group-orientated actors, the complex nature of the collective goods involving small to larger goals, the role of political entrepreneurs providing co-ordinative strategies, the use of social sanctions, and material and non-material selective incentives all help to explain how revolutionary action can occur. They do not provide a general model for all revolutions—a logarithm which can be substituted for historical analysis—but they do suggest that revolutionary action can be rational. The extent to which different elements of the revised account operate depends upon the institutions which exist in the society concerned. To a large degree the most recent discussions of revolutions by rational-choice writers concern the degree of independence of these institution-based elements from the standard rational-choice axioms.

Jon Elster is the most virulent of the rational-choice writers emphasizing the role of norms. He now thinks that 'cooperation is more likely to reflect a norm of fairness than a reaction mechanism in a self-interested equilibrium'.[49] Taylor accepts that his approach is not normless, but does not concede a central role for norms. Whilst norms may guide behaviour and help overcome free-riding problems, for Taylor they and the actions of the individuals abiding by them, must still be explained by essentially self-interested rationality.[50] What is not clear from Taylor's approach is the relationship between the internal and the external solutions. His internal solution allows for a substantial number of free-riders (those to the left of S^3 in Fig. 11.2), who exploit the others. Many have complained that there will be a rush by the rational to pre-commit to defection; how far do we require the external solution to stop such pre-commitment strategies? Carling has an ingenious, though ultimately puzzling, solution of 'vanishing police', who will punish free-riders, but since everyone knows the police will punish free-riders none will, and the police can vanish.[51]

Reassuring individuals that they will make a difference, using sanctions, and relying upon more human characteristics than the simplistic self-interest assumptions of the orthodox approach does explain revolutionary behaviour. The reconstructed rational choice is successful in its limited aims. How successful is still open to question: how far the norms of reciprocity and fairness can be explained within the approach and how far such institutions require sociological or social-psychological explanation remains moot. Ironically perhaps, without such alien additions, the reconstructed account gives a central role to the selective incentives of Olson's original argument. This is not to suggest that we have not progressed in the past thirty years. The diverse institutional contexts in which the preferences of actors develop and interact have become crucial in constructing explanations of mass action. The weakness of rational choice has been its failure to assess contextual information, making its conclusions premature and misleading. The task of rational choice is to provide such contextual information alongside its theoretical analysis.

NOTES

1. A. Buchanan, 'Rationality and Revolutionary Participation', *Philosophy and Public Affairs*, 9 (1979), 59–92, 66. See also M. Olson, *The Logic of Collective Action* (New Haven, Conn.: Yale University Press, 1971), 105; J. Elster, *Making Sense of Marx* (Cambridge: Cambridge University Press, 1985), 348; J. Coleman, *The Foundations of Social Thought* (Cambridge, Mass.: Harvard University Press, 1990), 482–3; and D. Mueller, *Public Choice II* (Cambridge: Cambridge University Press, 1990), 173–5.
2. E. Ostrom, *Governing the Commons* (Cambridge: Cambridge University Press, 1990).
3. M. Taylor, 'Rationality and Revolutionary Collective Action', in M. Taylor (ed.), *Rationality and Revolution* (Cambridge: Cambridge University Press, 1988).
4. W. Shaw, 'Marxism, Revolution and Rationality', in T. Ball and J. Farr (eds.), *After Marx* (Cambridge: Cambridge University Press, 1984), 12–35.
5. Mueller, *Public Choice II*, 173–5.
6. Olson, *Collective Action*, 61.
7. Buchanan, 'Rationality', 67–71.
8. Buchanan, 'Rationality', 73–6, 81.
9. J. Tong, *Disorder Under Heaven* (Stanford, Calif.: Stanford University Press, 1992), 76–96, esp. 87.
10. See D. Little, *Varieties of Social Explanation* (Boulder, Colo.: Westview, 1991), 51–2.
11. Buchanan, 'Rationality', 71–3 calls them 'in-process' benefits. See also D. Chong, *Collective Action and the Civil Rights Movement* (Chicago: University of Chicago Press, 1991), 73–8; K. Graham, *Karl Marx: Our Contemporary* (London: Harvester Wheatsheaf, 1992), 37–8.
12. Taylor, 'Rationality', 85–90, provides a critical discussion of such motivations.
13. Hirschman says 'Mancur Olson's idea of collective action just struck me as nonsensical. He argues for the impossibility, not the logic but the illogic of—collective action. According to him, collective action

should never happen since people act like rational actors: they always have a free ride and so on. Since my own experience of having participated in collective action was such that I found it very important, this construct of Olson's just struck me as obviously absurd': interview with Allen Swedberg, *Economics and Sociology* (Princeton: Princeton University Press, 1990), 159. Hirschman's own life demonstrates considerable collective action: he took part in the German Socialist Youth Movement in the early 1930s, the Italian and French resistance movements against fascism, and he has served in three armies (Republicans in Spain, French, and American): see L. Coser, *Refugee Scholars in America: Their Impact and their Experience* (New Haven, Conn.: Yale University Press, 1984), 163–8.

14. A. Hirschman, *Shifting Involvements* (Oxford: Blackwell, 1982), 87.
15. See D. Wheeler, 'Revolution by the Weak: Discursive Warfare, Symbolic Combat and the Palestinian Intifada', paper presented to the American Political Science Association, Chicago (3–6 Sept. 1992).
16. R. Hardin, *Collective Action* (Baltimore: Johns Hopkins University Press, 1982), 55–61.
17. Buchanan, 'Rationality', 72. Chong, *Collective Action*, 95, accepts the relevance of such benefits but doubts Hirschman's optimistic conclusion.
18. Chong, *Collective Action*, 82–9.
19. Buchanan, 'Rationality', 65.
20. J. White, 'Rational Rioters: Leaders, Followers and Popular Protest in Early Modern Japan', *Politics and Society*, 16 (1988), 35–70, 41–2.
21. Buchanan, 'Rationality', 65 n. 11.
22. Chong, *Collective Action*, 13–21. He draws on Samuel Popkin, 'Political Entrepreneurs and Peasant Movements in Vietnam', in Taylor (ed.), *Rationality and Revolution*.
23. G. A. Cohen, *History, Labour and Freedom*, (Oxford: Oxford University Press, 1988), 63.
24. In more recent work, Buchanan, 'Marx, Morality and History: An Assessment of Recent Analytical Work on Marx', *Ethics*, 98 (1987), 104–36, 114 n. 4, is less categorical about the rational decision of the group maximizer. He argues that 'even if the individual does not need to maximize her utility, by taking a free ride, she nonetheless may be unwilling to incur the costs of participation *unless* she has assurance that others will do so as well'.
25. Taylor, 'Rationality', 92, argues that 'scarcity and the coercive potential of the community tend to put the peasant in mind of his narrow self-interest and to leave little scope for such motivations as pleasure, genuine altruism (as opposed to reciprocity) beyond the household or moral self-interest'.

26. M. Taylor, *The Possibility of Cooperation* (Cambridge: Cambridge University Press, 1987).

27. White, 'Rational Rioters', 48.

28. R. Axelrod, *The Evolution of Cooperation* (New York: Basic Books, 1986). Formally, Axelrod's theory is less applicable than Taylor's because its focus is on two-person games.

29. Taylor, 'Rationality', 67. See also Hardin, *Collective Action*, 48–9.

30. Taylor, *Possibility of Cooperation*, 22. The possibilities open to the players, their preferences, and their beliefs remain those of the Prisoners' Dilemma.

31. Taylor, *Possibility of Cooperation*, 85. He notes other technical factors which will promote co-operation, concerning the relationship between the benefits from unilateral defection, those from successful co-operation, and the risks of unilateral co-operation. He also notes that effective monitoring must be possible.

32. T. Schelling, 'Hockey Helmets, Daylight Saving and Other Binary Choices', in his *Micromotives and Macrobehavior* (New York: Norton, 1978), 220.

33. Chong, *Collective Action*, 110. In effect, the collective good of participation comes close to being an 'all or nothing' good.

34. Chong, *Collective Action*, 30.

35. M. Taylor and H. Ward, 'Chickens, Whales and Lumpy Goods: Alternative Models of Public Goods Provision', *Political Studies*, 30 (1982), 350–70, 361.

36. Taylor, *Possibility of Cooperation*, 12.

37. Taylor, 'Rationality', 67 and 84. Selective incentives play an important role in his other work: see M. Taylor, *Community, Anarchy and Liberty* (Cambridge: Cambridge University Press, 1982), 83–94.

38. Taylor, 'Rationality', 22.

39. Buchanan, 'Rationality', 70.

40. Taylor, 'Rationality', 67.

41. Buchanan, 'Rationality', 67–8.

42. Elster, *Making Sense of Marx*, 363.

43. For example, see S. Popkin, *The Rational Peasant* (Berkeley, Calif.: University of California Press, 1979).

44. Taylor, 'Rationality', 67–70.

45. White, 'Rational Rioters', 46–9, notes the important role of the community in rebellion, and stresses the communications provided by local institutions. Chong, *Collective Action*, 36–7, argues that communities are an important provider of social selective incentives. Communities act as the basis for a tight identity-set, thus facilitating the formation of what P. Dunleavy, *Democracy, Bureaucracy and Public Choice* (London: Harvester Wheatsheaf, 1991) 54, 63–5, terms 'exogenous groups'.

46. Popkin, *Rational Peasant*, 257.
47. For a historical account, see M. Olson, 'Autocracy, Democracy and Prosperity', in R. Zeckhauser (ed.), *Strategy and Choice* (Cambridge: MIT Press, 1992), 137.
48. Tong, *Disorder Under Heaven*, 87.
49. J. Elster, *Nuts and Bolts in the Social Sciences* (Cambridge: Cambridge University Press, 1989), 133.
50. M.Taylor, 'Structure, Culture and Action in the Explanation of Social Change', *Politics and Society*, 17 (1989), 115–62, 136–7. See also R. Bates, 'Contra Contractarianism: Some Reflections on the New Institutionalism', *Politics and Society*, 16 (1988), 387–99, 398; and Popkin, *Rational Peasant*, 22.
51. A. Carling, *Social Division* (London: Verso, 1991), 398.

BIBLIOGRAPHY

ALDERMAN, G., *The Railway Interest* (Leicester: Leicester University Press, 1973).

ALLEN, C. S., 'Corporatism and Regional Economic Policies in the Federal Republic of Germany: The "Meso" Politics of Industrial Adjustment', *Publius: The Journal Federalism*, 19 (1989), 147–64.

ALLISON, G. T., *Essense of Decision: Explaining the Cuban Missile Crisis* (Boston: Little Brown, 1971).

ALT, J. E. and SHEPSLE, K. A. (eds.), *Perspectives on Positive Political Economy* (Cambridge: Cambridge University Press, 1990).

—— and GILLIGAN, M., 'The Political Economy of Trading States: Factor Specifity, Collective Action Problems, and Domestic Political Institutions', paper presented to the American Political Science Association (Washington, DC, 1993).

ANDERSON, C. R., 'Coping Behaviours as Intervening Mechanisms in the Inverted-U, Stress Performance Relationship' *Journal of Applied Psychology*, 61 (1976), 30–4.

ANDERSON, D., MARSLAND, D., and LAIT, J., *Breaking the Spell of the Welfare State* (London: Social Affairs Unit, 1981).

ARROW, K. J., *Social Choice and Individual Values* (New York: John Wiley, rev. edn., 1963).

D'ASPREMENT, C., JACQUEMIN, A., ERBSZEWICS, J., and WEYMARK, J., 'On the Stability of Dominant Cartels', *Canadian Journal of Economics*, 14 (1982), 17–25.

ATKINSON, A. B., 'Original Sen', *New York Review of Books*, 22 Oct. 1987.

AXELROD, R., *Conflict of Interest* (Chicago: Markham, 1970).

—— *The Evolution of Cooperation* (New York: Basic Books, 1984).

AYDELOTTE, W. O., 'Voting Patterns in the British House of Commons', *Comparative Studies in History and Society*, 5 (1963), 134–63.

—— 'Parties and Issues in Early Victorian England', *Journal of British Studies*, 5 (1966), 95–114.

—— 'The Country Gentlemen and the Repeal of the Corn Laws', *English Historical Review*, 82 (1967), 47–60.

—— *Study 521 (Codebook): 'British House of Commons 1841–1847'* (Iowa City: Regional Social Science Data Archive of Iowa, 1970).

AYDELOTTE, W. O., 'Members of the House of Commons 1841–47' (ESRC Archive, Essex University, 1970).

—— 'The Disintegration of the Conservative Party in the 1840s: A Study of Political Attitudes', in W. O. Aydelotte, A. G. Brogue, and R. W. Fogel (eds.), *The Dimensions of Quantitative Research in History* (Princeton, NJ: Princeton University Press, 1972).

—— 'Constituency Influence on the British House of Commons, 1841–1847;, in W. O. Aydelotte (ed.), *The History of Parliamentary Behavior* (Princeton, NJ: Princeton University Press, 1977).

BAGWELL, P. S., *The Railway Clearing House in the British Economy 1842–1922* (London: Allen and Unwin, 1968).

BAIN, J. S., *Barriers to New Competition* (Cambridge, Mass: Harvard University Press, 1956).

BALDWIN, R. E., *The Political Economy of U.S. Import Policy* (Cambridge: MIT Press, 1985).

BALTENSPERGER, E. and DERMINE, J., 'European Banking, Prudential and Regulatory Issues', paper presented at INSEAD Conference on European Banking After 1992 (Fontainebleau, 1989).

BARRY, B., *Sociologists, Economists and Democracy* (Chicago: University of Chicago Press, 2nd edn., 1978).

BARRY, N., *Welfare* (Buckingham: Open University Press, 1990).

BATES, R., 'Contra Contractarianism: Some Reflections on the New Institutionalism', *Politics and Society*, 16 (1988), 387–401.

BERNS, W. (ed.), *After the People Vote* (Washington, DC: American Enterprise Institute Press, 1992).

VON BEYME, K., *Political Parties in Western Europe* (Aldershot: Gower, 1983).

BISIGNANO, J., 'Banking in the European Community: Structure, Competition, and Public Policy', in G. G. Kaufman (ed.), *Banking Structures in Major Countries* (Norwell, Mass.: Kluwer Academic, 1992).

BLACK, B. A., 'Shareholder Passivity Re-Examined', *Michigan Law Review*, 89 (1990), 520–608.

—— 'Institutional Investers and Corporate Governance', *Continental Bank Journal of Applied Corporate Finance*, 5 (1991), 19–32.

BOWLES, S. and EATWELL, J., 'Between Two Worlds: Interest Groups, Class Structure, and Capitalist Growth', in D. C. Mueller (ed.), *The Political Economy of Growth* (New Haven, Conn.: Yale University Press, 1982).

BRAITHEWAITE, R. B., *Scientific Explanation* (Cambridge: Cambridge University Press, 1955).

BRAITHWAITE, W. J., *Lloyd George's Ambulance Wagon*, ed. H. N. Bunbury and R. Titmuss (Bath: Cedric Chivers, 1957).

BRAMS, S., KILGOUR, D., and ZWICKER, W., 'A New Paradox of Vote Aggregation', paper presented to the 89th Annual Meeting of the

American Political Science Association (Washington, DC, 2–5 Sept. 1993).

BRANCATO, C. K., 'The Pivotal Role of Institutional Investers in Capital Markets', in A. W. Sametz (ed.), *Institutional Investing: The Challenges and Responsibilities of the 21st Century* (New York: Business One Irwin, 1991).

—— and GAUGHAN, P. A., 'Institutional Investers and Capital Markets: 1991 Update', Center for Law and Economic Studies Institutional Invester Project (New York: Business One Irwin, 1991).

BRECHER, M. J., *Decisions in Crisis: Israel, 1967 and 1973* (Berkeley, Calif.: University of California Press, 1980).

—— and WILKENFELD, J., *Crisis, Conflict and Instability* (Oxford: Pergamon, 1989).

—— —— and MOSER, S., *Crisis in the Twentieth Century* (Oxford: Pergamon, 1988).

BRENNAN, G. and LOMASKY, L., *Democracy and Decision: The Pure Theory of Electoral Preference* (Cambridge: Cambridge University Press, 1993).

BROMLEY, D. W., *Economic Interests and Institutions* (Oxford: Blackwell, 1989).

BROWNE, E., FRENDEIS, J., and GLEIBER, D., 'An Events Approach to the Problem of Cabinet Stability', *Comparative Political Studies*, 17 (1984), 167–97.

—— —— —— 'The Process of Cabinet Dissolution: An Exponential Model of Duration and Stability in Western Democracies', *American Journal of Political Science*, 30 (1986), 625–50.

—— —— —— 'Contending Models of Cabinet Stability: A Rejoinder', *American Political Science Review*, 82 (1988), 939–41.

—— GLEIBER, D., and MASHOBA, C., 'Evaluating Conflict of Interest Theory: Western European Cabinet Coalitions, 1945–80', *British Journal of Political Science*, 14 (1984), 1–32.

BUCHANAN, J. M. and VANBERG, V., 'A Theory of Leadership and Deference in Constitutional Construction', *Public Choice*, 61 (1989), 15–27.

BUCHANEN, A., 'Rationality and Revolutionary Participation', *Philosophy and Public Affairs*, 9 (1979), 60–82.

—— 'Marx, Morality and History: An Assessment of Recent Analytical Work on Marx', *Ethics*, 98 (1987), 104–36.

CABLE, J., 'Capital Market Information and Industrial Performance: The Role of West German Banks', *Economic Journal*, 95 (1985), 118–32.

CAMERON, D., 'On the Limits of Public Economy', *Annals of the American Association for Political and Social Science*, 459 (1982), 46–62.

—— 'Distributional Coalitions and Other Sources of Economic Stagnation', *International Organisation*, 42 (1988), 561–603.

CAMPBELL, T., 'Optimal Investment and the Value of Confidentiality', *Journal of Financial and Quantitive Analysis*, 14 (1979), 913–24.

CAPPELAN, A., GLEDITSCH, N., and BJERKHOLT, O., 'Military Spending and Economic Growth in OECD Countries', *Journal of Peace Research*, 21 (1984).

CARLING, A., 'Liberty, Equality, Socialism', *New Left Review*, 171 (1988).

—— *Social Division* (London: Verso, 1991).

—— 'Analytical Marxism and Historical Materialism: The Debate on Social Evolution', *Science and Society*, 57/1 (1993), 31–66.

CASSING, J., MCKEOWN, T. J., and OCHS, J., 'The Political Economy of the Tarriff Cycle', *American Political Science Review*, 80 (1986), 843–62.

CASTLES, F. and DOWRICK, S., 'The Impact of Government Spending Levels on Medium-Term Economic Growth in the OECD, 1960–85' *Journal of Theoretical Politics*, 2 (1990), 173–204.

—— and MAIR, P., 'Left-Right Political Scales: Some "Expert" Judgements', *European Journal of Political Research*, 12 (1984), 73–88.

CAVES, R. E., FRANKEL, J. A., and JONES, R. W., *World Trade and Payments: An Introduction*, 6th edn. (London: Harper Collins, 1993).

CHALMERS, M., *Paying for Decline: Military Spending and British Decline* (London: Pluto, 1985).

CHAMBERLIN, J., 'Provision of Public Goods as a Function of Group Size', *American Political Science Review*, 68 (1974), 707–16.

CHAN, S., 'The Impact of Defence Spending on Economic Performance: A Survey of Evidence and Problems', *Orbis*, 29 (1985), 403–33.

CHAN, Y., 'On the Positive Role of Financial Intermediation in Allocation of Venture Capital in a Market with Imperfect Information', *Journal of Finance*, 38 (1983), 1543–68.

CHARLES, F. H. (ed.), *International Crises: Insights from Behavioural Research* (New York: Free Press, 1972).

CHOI, K., 'A Statistical Test of Olson's Model', in D. C. Mueller (ed.), *The Political Economy of Growth* (New Haven, Conn.: Yale University Press, 1982).

CHONG, D., *Collective Action and the Civil Rights Movement* (Chicago: University of Chicago Press, 1991).

CHRICHTON, M., *Rising Sun* (New York: Knopf, 1992).

CIPOLLA, C. M. (ed.), *The Economic Decline of Empires* (London: Methuen, 1970).

COFFEE, J. C., 'Liquidity Versus Control: The Institutional Invester as Corporate Monitor', *Columbia Law Review*, 91 (1991), 1277–1368.

COHEN, G. A. (1988), *History, Labour and Freedom* (Oxford: Oxford University Press).

COLEMAN, J., *The Foundations of Social Thought* (Cambridge: Harvard University Press, 1990).

CONRAD, A. F., 'Beyond Managerial Capitalism: Invester Capitalism?', *University of Michigan Journal of Law*, 88 (1989), 124–66.

COOPER, C. L., 'Executive Stress', *Human Resource Management*, 23 (1984), 395–407.

COSER, L., *Refugee Scholars in America: Their Impact and Their Experience* (New Haven, Conn.: Yale University Press, 1984).

COX, G. W., 'The Uncovered Set and the Core', *American Journal of Political Science*, 31 (1987), 408–22.

—— *The Efficient Secret: The Cabinet and the Development of Political Parties in Victorian England* (Cambridge: Cambridge University Press, 1987).

CROZIER, M., HUNTINGDON, S. P., and WATANUKI, S., *The Crisis of Democracy: Report to the Trilateral Commission on the Ungovernability of Liberal Democracies* (New York: New York University Press, 1975).

DAHL, R. A., 'Patterns of Opposition', in R. A. Dahl (ed.), *Political Oppositions in Western Democracies* (New Haven, Conn.: Yale University Press, 1966).

DAVIDSON, D., *Essays on Actions and Events* (Oxford: Clarendon Press, 1980).

DAVIS, E. P., 'Theories of Intermediation, Financial Innovation and Regulation', *National Westminster Bank Quarterly Review* (1983), 41–53.

DEACON, A., *In Search of the Scrounger*, Occasional Papers on Social Administration, No. 60 (London: G. H. Bell, 1976).

DEEG, R., 'The State, Banks and Economic Governance in Germany', paper presented to the American Political Science Association (Chicago, 1992).

DEMOUGIN, D. and SINN, H.-W., 'Privatization, Risk-Taking and the Communist Firm', NBER Working Paper No. 4205 (Cambridge, Mass.: NBER, 1991).

DEMSETZ, H., 'Towards a Theory of Property Rights', *American Economic Review*, 57 (1967), 347–59.

DIAMOND, D., 'Financial Intermediation and Delegated Monitoring', *Review of Economic Studies*, 51 (1984), 393–414.

—— and DYBVIG, P., 'Bank Runs, Deposit Insurance and Liquidity', *Journal of Political Economy*, 91 (1983), 401–19.

DODD, L. C., 'Party Coalitions in Multiparty Parliaments: A Game Theoretic Analysis', *American Political Science Review*, 68 (1974), 1093–117.

—— *Coalitions in Parliamentary Governments* (Princeton, NJ: Princeton University Press, 1976).

DORAN, G. and MAOR, M., 'Barriers to Entry into a Political System: A Theoretical Framework and Empirical Application from the Israeli Experience', *Journal of Theoretical Politics*, 3 (1991), 175–88.

DOUGLAS, J., 'The Overloaded Crown', *British Journal of Political Science*, 6 (1976), 483–505.

DOUGLAS, M., *How Institutions Think* (London: Routledge, Kegan and Paul, 1987).

DOWDING, K., *Rational Choice and Political Power* (Aldershot: Edward Elgar, 1991).

—— 'The Compatibility of Behaviouralism, Rational Choice and "New Institutionalism" ', *Journal of Theoretical Politics*, 6 (1994), 105–17.

—— and KIMBER, R., 'The Meaning and Use of "Political Stability" ', *European Journal of Political Research*, 11 (1983), 229–43.

DOWNS, A., *An Economic Theory of Democracy* (New York: Harper and Row, 1957).

DRYZEK, J. and GOODIN, R. E., 'Risk-sharing and Social Justice: The Motivational Foundations of the Post-War Welfare State', *British Journal of Political Science*, 16 (1986), 1–34.

DUNLEAVY, P., *Democracy, Bureaucracy and Public Choice* (Hemel Hempstead: Harvester Wheatsheaf, 1991).

—— and WARD, H., 'Exogenous Voter Preferences and Parties with State Power: Some Internal Problems of Economic Models of Party Competition', *British Journal of Political Research*, 4 (1981), 351–80.

DUVERGER, M., *Political Parties* (London: Methuen, 1964).

EDWARDS, J. and FISCHER, K., 'Banks, Finance and Investment in West Germany Since 1970', Centre for Economic Policy Research Discussion Paper No. 497 (London: CEPR, 1989).

EGGERTSSON, T., *Economic Behavior and Institutions* (Cambridge: Cambridge University Press, 1990).

ELIAS, N., *What is Sociology?* (London: Hutchinson, 1978).

ELLIS, C. H., *British Railway History 1830–1876* (London: Allen and Unwin, 1954).

ELLWOOD, D., *Poor Support* (New York: Basic Books, 1988).

ELSTER, J., *Ulysses and the Sirens* (Cambridge: Cambridge University press, 1979).

—— *Sour Grapes* (Cambridge: Cambridge University Press, 1983).

—— *Making Sense of Marx* (Cambridge: Cambridge University Press, 1985).

—— 'Introduction' to id. (ed.), *Rational Choice* (Oxford: Blackwell, 1986).

—— *Nuts and Bolts in the Social Sciences* (Cambridge: Cambridge University Press, 1989).

—— *The Cement of Society* (Cambridge: Cambridge University Press, 1989).

ESPING-ANDERSEN, G. and FRIEDLAND, P., 'Class Coalitions in the Making of Western European Economics', in M. Zeitlin (ed.), *Political Power and Social Theory*, iii (Greenwich, Conn.: JAI Press, 1982).

ESSER, J., 'Bank Power in West Germany Revised', *West European Politics*, 13 (1990), 17–32.

EVANS, P., Rueschmeyer, D., and Skocpol, T. (eds.), *Bringing the State Back In* (Cambridge: Cambridge University Press, 1985).

FAMA, E. F., 'What's Different About Banks?', *Journal of Monetary Economics*, 15 (1985), 29–40.

—— and JENSEN, M. C., 'Separation of Ownership and Control', *Journal of Law and Economics*, 26 (1983), 301–25.

FENNO, R., *The Making of a Senator: J. Dan Quayle* (Washington: Congressional Quarterly Press, 1989).

FEUCHTWANGER, E. J. *Gladstone*, 2nd edn. (London: Macmillan, 1989).

FIELD, S. L. and GROFMAN, B., 'Partial Single-Peakedness: An Extension and Clarification', *Public Choice*, 51 (1986), 71–80.

FISHER, I., 'The Debt-Deflation Theory of the Great Depression', *Econometrica*, 1 (1933), 337–57.

FINE, B. and HARRIS, L., *The Peculiarities of the British Economy* (London: Lawrence and Wishart, 1985).

FINEGOLD, D. and SOSKICE, D., 'The Failure of Training Policy in Britain: Analysis and Prescription', *Oxford Review of Economic Policy*, 4 (1988), 21–53.

FINN, D. and BALL, L., *Unemployment and Training Rights Handbook* (London: Unemployment Unit, 1991).

FOSTER, C., *Privatisation, Public Enterprise and the Regulation of a Natural Monopoly* (Oxford: Blackwell, 1992).

FRANKEL, A. B. and MONTGOMERY, J. D., 'Financial Structure: An International Perspective', *Brookings Papers on Economic Activity*, 1 (1991).

FRAZER, E. and LACEY, N., *The Politics of Community* (Brighton: Harvester Wheatsheaf, 1993).

FREEMAN, C., CLARK, J., and SOETE, L., *Unemployment and Technical Innovation* (Westpoint, Conn.: Greenwood, 1982).

FRIEDEN, J. A., *Debt, Development and Democracy: Modern Political Economy and Latin America, 1965–1985* (Princeton, NJ: Princeton University Press, 1991).

FURUBOTN, E. and PEJOVICH, S., 'Introduction: The New Property Rights Literature', in E. Furubotn and S. Pejovich (eds.), *The Economics of Property Rights* (Cambridge, Mass.: Ballinger, 1974).

GAMBETTA, D., *The Sicilian Mafia: The Business of Protection* (Cambridge, Mass.: Harvard University Press, 1993).

GARRETT, G. and LANGE, P., 'Performance in a Hostile World: Economic Growth in Capitalist Democracies, 1974–1982', *World Politics*, 38 (1985/6), 517–45.

GASH, N., *Politics in the Age of Peel* (Hassocks: Harvester, 2nd edn., 1977).

GERLICH, P., GRADNE, E., and MULLER, W. C., 'Corporatism in Crisis: Stability and Change of Social Partnerships in Austria', *Political Studies*, 36 (1988): 209–23.

GERTLER, M., 'Financial Structure and Aggregate Economic Activity', *Journal of Money, Credit and Banking*, 20 (1988), 559–96.

GILDER, G., *Wealth and Poverty* (New York: Basic Books, 1981).

GOLDMAN, M. I., *USSR in Crisis* (New York: Norton, 1983).

GOURVISH, T. R., *Mark Huish and the London and North Railway* (Leicester: Leicester University Press, 1972).

GRAFSTEIN, R., *Institutional Realism* (New Haven, Conn.: Yale University Press, 1992).

GRAHAM, K., *Karl Marx: Our Contemporary* (London: Harvester Wheatsheaf, 1992).

GRAMSCI, A., *Selections from the Prison Notebooks* (London: Lawrence and Wishart, 1973).

GRANITO, M., 'The Common Man, Linear Investment Rules, and an Agency Problem', in Sametz (ed.).

DE GRASSE, R., *Military Expansion Economic Decline: The Impact of Military Spending on US Economic Performance* (Armonki, NY: Sharpe, 1983).

GRAY, V. and LOWERY, D., 'Interest Group Politics and Economic Growth in the US States', *American Political Science Review*, 82 (1988), 109–31.

GROSSMAN, G. M., and LEVINSOHN, J. A., 'Import Competition and the Stock Market Return to Capital', *American Economic Review*, 79 (1989), 1065–87.

GURLEY, J. and SHAW, E., 'Financial Aspects of Economic Development', *American Economic Review*, 45 (1955), 515–38.

HALL, J. A., *Powers and Liberties: The Causes of and Consequences of the Decline of the West* (London: Penguin, 1986).

HALL, P., *Governing the Economy* (New York: Oxford University Press, 1986).

HALL, R. L., 'Participation and Purpose in Committee Decision Making', *American Political Science Review*, 81 (1987), 105–28.

HARDIN, R., *Collective Action* (Baltimore: Johns Hopkins University Press, 1982).

HARGREAVES-HEAP, S., *Rationality in Economics* (Oxford: Blackwell, 1989).

HARSANYI, J. C., 'Individualistic vs. Functionalist Explanation in the Light of Game Theory', in I. Lakatos (ed.), *Problems in the Philosophy of Science* (Amsterdam: Cambridge University Press, 1968).

HART, J. A., *Rival Capitalists: International Competitiveness in the United States, Japan and West Germany* (Ithaca, NY: Cornell University Press, 1992).

HAWKE, G. R., *Railways and Economic Growth in England and Wales 1840–1970* (Oxford: Clarendon Press, 1970).

HAWKSWORTH, M. E., *Beyond Oppression: Feminist Theory and Political Strategy* (New York: Continuum, 1990).

HECLO, H. and MADSEN, H., *Policy and Politics in Sweden* (Philadelphia: Temple University Press, 1987).

HERMAN, V. and POPE, J., 'Minority Governments in Western Democracies', *British Journal of Political Science*, 3 (1973), 191–212.

HILL, M., *Social Security Policy in Britain* (Aldershot: Edward Elgar, 1990).

HILLMAN, A. L., *The Political Economy of Protection* (London: Harwood Academic Publishers, 1989).

—— 'International Trade Policy: Benevolent Dictators and Optimizing Politicians', *Public Choice* 74 (1992), 1–15.

HIRSCHMAN, A., *Exit, Voice and Loyalty* (Cambridge, Mass.: Harvard University Press, 1970).

—— *Shifting Involvements* (Oxford: Basil Blackwell, 1982).

HOLSTI, O., 'Theories of Crisis Decision Making', in P. C. Lamer (ed.), *Diplomacy: New Approaches in History, Theory and Policy* (London: Free Press, 1979).

JACKMAN, R. W., 'The Politics of Economic Growth in the Industrial Democracies, 1974–80: Leftist Strength or North Sea Oil?' *Journal of Politics*, 49 (1987), 242–56.

JAFFEE, D. and RUSSELL, T., 'Imperfect Information, Uncertainty, and Credit Rationing', *Quarterly Journal of Economics*, 90 (1976), 651–66.

JANIS, I., *Groupthink*, 2nd edn. (Boston: Houghton Mifflin, 1982).

JENSEN, M. C. and MECKLING, W. H., 'Theory of the Firm: Managerial Behaviour, Agency Costs and Ownership Structure', *Journal of Financial Economics*, 3 (1976), 305–60.

JESSOP, B., BONNETT, K., BROMLEY, S., and LING, T., *Thatcherism* (Cambridge: Polity, 1988).

JORDAN, G., MALONEY, W., and McLAUGHLIN, A., 'Collective Action and the Public Interest Problem: Drawing a Line under Olson?', in P. Dunleavy and J. Stanyer (eds.), *Contemporary Political Studies 1994*, ii (Belfast: Political Studies Association, 1994), 519–43.

KAPLAN, M., *Systems and Process in International Politics* (New York: Wiley, 1957).

KAPLAN, S. N., 'Top Executives, Turnover and Firm Performance in Germany', NBER Working Paper No. 4416 (Cambridge, Mass.: NBER, 1993).

KATZ, M. B., *In the Shadow of the Workhouse* (New York: Basic Books, 1986).

KATZENSTEIN, P. J. (ed.), *Industry and Politics in West Germany: Toward the Third Republic* (Ithaca, NY: Cornell University Press, 1989).

KENNEDY, P., *A Guide to Econometrics* (Cambridge, Mass.: MIT Press, 3rd edn., 1992).

KERR, H. H., 'Swiss Party System: Steadfast and Changing', in H. Daalder (ed.), *Party Systems in Denmark, Austria, Switzerland, the Netherlands and Belgium* (London: Pinter, 1987).

KING, A., 'Overload: Problems of Governing in the 1970s', *Political Studies*, 23 (1975), 283–96.

KING, D. A., 'Political Centralization and State Interests in Britain', *Comparative Political Studies*, 21 (1989), 467–94.

—— 'Voluntary and State Provision of Welfare as Part of the Public-Private Continuum: Modelling the Shifting Involvements in Britain and the US', in A. Ware (ed.), *Charities and Government* (Manchester: Manchester University Press, 1989).

—— *The New Right: Politics, Markets and Citizenship* (London: Macmillan, 1987).

—— 'Citizenship as Obligation in the United States: Title II of the Family Support Act of 1988', in M. Moran and U. Vogel (eds.), *The Frontiers of Citizenship* (London: Macmillan, 1991).

—— 'The Establishment of Work-Welfare Programmes in the USA and Britain: Politics, Ideas and Institutions', in S. Steinmo, K. Thelen, and F. Longstreth (eds.), *The New Institutionalism* (Cambridge: Cambridge University Press, 1992).

—— and WALDRON, J., 'Citizenship, Social Citizenship and the Defence of Welfare Provision', *British Journal of Political Science*, 18 (1988) 415–43.

—— and WICKHAM-JONES, M., 'Social Democracy and Rational Workers', *British Journal of Political Science*, 20 (1990), 387–413.

KITSON CLARK, G., 'The Electorate and the Repeal of the Corn Laws', *Transactions of the Royal Historical Society*, 5th ser., 1 (1951), 109–26.

KRASNER, S., *Defending the National Interest: Raw Materials Investments and U.S. Foreign Policy* (Princeton, NJ: Princeton University Press, 1978).

KREPS, D., *Game Theory and Economic Modelling* (Oxford: Clarendon Press, 1990).

KRUGMAN, P. R. (ed.), *Strategic Trade Policy and the New International Economics* (Cambridge, Mass.: MIT Press, 1986).

—— 'What Do Undergrads Need to Know About Trade?', *American Economic Review*, 83 (1993), 23–6.

KYMLICKA, W., *Contemporary Political Philosophy* (Oxford: Oxford University Press, 1990).

LAMBERT, R. S., *The Railway King* (London: Allen & Unwin, 2nd edn., 1964).

LANE, J.-E. and ERSSON, S., *Comparative Political Economy* (London: Pinter, 1990).

—— —— *Politics and Society in Western Europe* (London: Sage, 1991).

—— McKAY, D., and NEWTON, K., *Political Data Handbook OECD Countries* (Cambridge: Cambridge University Press, 1991).

LANGE, P. and GARRETT, G., 'The Politics of Growth: Strategic Interaction and Economic Performance in Advanced Industrial Societies 1974–1980', *Journal of Politics*, 47 (1985), 793–807.

LAVER, M., 'Political Solutions to the Collective Action Problem', *Political Studies*, 28 (1980).

—— *The Politics of Private Desires* (Harmondsworth: Penguin, 1981).

—— 'Dynamic Factors in Government Coalition Formation', *European Journal of Political Research*, 2 (1974), 259–70.

—— and HUNT, W. B., *Policy and Party Competition* (London: Routledge, 1992).

LAVER, M. and SCHOFIELD, N., *Multiparty Government* (Oxford: Oxford University Press, 1990).

LAWRENCE, R. Z. and SCHULTZE, C. L. (eds.), *An American Trade Strategy: Options for the 1990s* (Washington, DC: Brookings Institution, 1990).

LEWIS, J., 'Back to the Future: A Comment on American New Right Ideas about Welfare and Citizenship in the 1980s', *Gender and History*, 3 (1991), 1–12.

LEYLAND, H. and PYLE, D., 'Informational Asymmetries, Financial Structure and Financial Intermediation', *Journal of Finance*, 32 (1977), 371–87.

LIGHT, J. O., 'The Privatization of Equity', *Harvard Business Review*, 67 (1989), 62–3.

LIJPHART, A., *Democracies: Patterns of Majoritarian and Consensus Government in Twenty-One Countries* (New Haven, Conn.: Yale University Press, 1984).

—— and CREPAZ, M. L., 'Corporatism and Consensus Democracy in Eighteen Countries: Conceptual and Empirical Linkages', *British Journal of Political Science*, 21 (1991), 235–56.

LITTLE, D., *Understanding Peasant China* (New Haven, Conn.: Yale University Press, 1989).

—— *Varieties of Social Explanation* (Boulder, Colo.: Westview, 1991).

LUBENOW, W. C., *The Politics of Government Growth: Early Victorian Attitudes Towards State Intervention 1833–1848* (Newton Abbot: David & Charles, 1971).

LUEBBERT, G., *Comparative Democracy: Policy Making and Governing Coalitions in Europe and Israel* (New York: Columbia University Press, 1986).

McCubbins, M. D. and Sullivan, T. (eds.), *Congress: Structure and Policy* (Cambridge: Cambridge University Press, 1987).

McKelvey, R. D., 'Intransitivities in Multidimensional Voting Models and some Implications for Agenda Control', *Journal of Economic Theory*, 12 (1976), 472–82.

—— 'General Conditions for Global Intransitivities in Formal Voting Models', *Econometrica*, 47 (1979), 1085–111.

—— 'Covering, Dominance, and Institution-Free Properties of Social Choice', *American Journal of Political Science*, 30 (1986), 283–314.

MacKeown, T., 'The Politics of the Corn Law Repeal', *British Journal of Political Science*, 19 (1989), 353–80.

McKibbin, R., 'The "Social Psychology" of Unemployment in Inter-war Britain', in R. McKibbin, *The Ideologies of Class* (Oxford: Clarendon Press, 1990).

MacKinnon, C., *Feminism Unmodified: Discourse on Life and Law* (Cambridge, Mass.: Harvard University Press, 1987).

McLean, I. S., *The Legend of Red Clydeside* (Edinburgh: John Donald, 1983).

—— *Public Choice: An Introduction* (Oxford: Basil Blackwell, 1987).

—— ' "The Politics of the Corn Law Repeal": A Comment', *British Journal of Political Science*, 20 (1900), 279–81.

—— 'Rational Choice and the Victorian Voter', *Political Studies*, 40 (1992), 496–515.

Magee, S. P., 'Three Simple Tests of the Stolper–Samuelson Theorem', in P. Oppenheimer (ed.), *Issues in International Economics* (Stocksfield: Oriel Press, 1980).

—— Brock, W. A., and Young, L., *Black Hole Tarriffs and Endogenous Policy Theory: Political Economy in General Equilibrium* (Cambridge: Cambridge University Press, 1989).

Maor, M., 'Barriers to Entry into a Political System', MA thesis (Tel Aviv, 1988).

—— 'The Dynamics of Minority Rule: Intra-Party Politics and Coalitional Behaviour in Western Europe', Ph.D. thesis (London School of Economics, 1992).

—— 'Intraparty Conflicts and Coalitional Behaviour in Denmark and Norway: The Case of "Highly Institutionalized" Parties', *Scandinavian Political Studies*, 15 (1992), 99–116.

—— *Political Parties: Comparative Approaches and the British Experience* (London: Routledge, 1995).

—— and Smith, G., 'Government–Opposition Relationships as a Systemic Property', paper presented at ECPR joint sessions of workshops (Leiden, 1993).

—— —— 'On the Structure of Issues', in T. Bryder (ed.), *Party Systems,*

Party Behaviour and Democracy (Copenhagen: Copenhagen Political Studies Press, 1993).

MARCH, J., *Decisions and Organizations* (Oxford: Blackwell, 1988).

—— and OLSEN, J., 'The New Institutionalism: Organizational Factors in Political Life', *American Political Science Review*, 78 (1984), 734–49.

MARSHALL, T. H., 'Citizenship and Social Class', in *Citizenship and Social Development* (New York: Doubleday, 1964).

MAYER, C., 'New Issues in Corporate Finance', *European Economic Review*, 32 (1988), 1167–88.

MAYER, W., 'Endogenous Tarriff Formation', *American Economic Review*, 74 (1984), 970–85.

—— 'New Issues in Corporate Finance', *European Economic Review*, 32 (1988), 1167–88.

MAYHEW, D. R., *Congress: The Electoral Connection* (New Haven, Conn.: Yale University Press, 1974).

MEAD, L., *Beyond Entitlement: The Social Obligations of Citizenship* (New York: Free Press, 1986).

MERTON, R. K., *Social Theory and Social Structure* (New York: Free Press, 1957).

MILLER, D., *Market, State, and Community* (Oxford: Clarendon Press, 1989).

MILLER, N. R., 'A New Solution Set for Tournaments and Majority Voting: Further Graph-Theoretical Approaches to the Theory of Voting', *American Journal of Political Science*, 24 (1980), 68–96.

—— GROFMAN, B. and FIELD, S. L., 'The Geometry of Majority Rule', *Journal of Theoretical Politics*, 1 (1989), 379–406.

VON MISES, L., *Human Action: A Treatise on Economics* (London: William Hodge, 1949).

MISHKIN, F., 'The Household Balance Sheet and the Great Depression', *Journal of Economic History*, 38 (1978), 918–37.

MODIGLIANI, F. and MILLER, M., 'The Cost of Capital, Corporation Finance and the Theory of Investment', *American Economic Review*, 48 (1958), 261–97.

MOON, J. D., 'The Moral Basis of the Democratic Welfare State', in A. Gutmann (ed.), *Democracy and the Welfare State* (Princeton, NJ: Princeton University Press, 1988).

MUELLER, D. C., *Public Choice II* (Cambridge: Cambridge University Press, 1990).

—— (ed.), *The Political Economy of Growth* (New Haven, Conn.: Yale University Press, 1982).

MURRAY, C., *Losing Ground* (New York: Basic Books, 1984).

NAGEL, J. H., 'Populism, Heresthetics and Political Stability: Richard Seddon and the Art of Majority Rule', *British Journal of Political Science*, 23 (1993), 139–74.

NATIONAL GOVERNORS' ASSOCIATION, *Job-Oriented Welfare Reform* (Washington, DC: NGA, 1987).

NICHOLSON, M., *The Scientific Analysis of Social Behaviour: A Defence of Empiricism in Social Science* (London: Frances Pinter, 1983).

—— *Rationality and the Analysis of International Conflict* (Cambridge: Cambridge University Press, 1992).

—— 'Stress and the Rational Decision Maker', *Journal of Conflict Processes*, 1 (1992), 17–25.

NIEMI, R. G., 'Why So Much Stability? Another Opinion', *Public Choice*, 41 (1983), 361–70.

NIOU, E. M. S. and ORDESHOOK, P. C., 'A Theory of the Balance of Power in International Systems', *Journal of Conflict Resolution*, 30 (1986), 685–715.

NOELLE-NEWMAN, E., *The Spiral of Silence* (Chicago: Chicago University Press, 1987).

NORTH, D., *Structure and Change in Economic History* (New York: W. W. Norton, 1981).

NORTH, R. C., HOLSTI, O. R., ZANINOVICH, M. G., and ZINNES, P. A., *Content Analysis* (Evanston, Ill.: Northwestern University Press, 1963).

OBERBECK, H. and BAETHGE, M., 'Computer and Pinstripe: Financial Institutions', in P. J. Katzenstein (ed.), *Industry and Politics in West Germany: Towards the Third Republic* (Ithaca: Cornell University Press, 1989).

OKIN, S., *Justice, Gender and the Family* (New York: Basic, 1989).

OLSON, M., *The Logic of Collective Action* (Yale: Yale University Press, 1971).

—— *The Rise and Decline of Nations* (New Haven, Conn.: Yale University Press, 1982).

—— 'Autocracy, Democracy and Prosperity', in R. Zechkhauser (ed.), *Strategy and Choice* (Cambridge: MIT Press, 1992).

ORDESHOOK, P. C., *Game Theory and Political Theory* (Cambridge: Cambridge University Press, 1986).

—— *A Political Theory Primer* (London: Routledge, 1992).

OSTROM, E., *Governing the Commons* (Cambridge: Cambridge University Press, 1990).

PAGE, B., *Choices and Echoes in American Elections: Rational Man and Electoral Democracy* (Chicago: University of Chicago Press, 1978).

VAN PARIJS, P., *Evolutionary Explanation in the Social Sciences: An Emerging Paradigm* (Totowa, NJ: Rowman and Littlefield, 1981).

—— 'The Evolutionary Explanation of Beliefs', in W. Callebaut and R. Pinxton (eds.), *Evolutionary Epistemology* (Boston: W. Reidel, 1987).

PARKER, H., *The Moral Hazards of Social Benefits* (London: Institute of Economic Affairs, 1982).

PARRIS, H., *Government and the Railways in the 19th Century* (London: Routledge, 1965).

PASCH, B. E. and SORENSON, P. J. 'Organisational Behaviour and Economic Growth: A Norwegian Perspective', *Scandinavian Political Studies*, 9 (1986), 51–63.

PIERSON, P., 'When Effect Becomes Cause: Policy Feedback and Political Change', *World Politics*, 45 (1993), 595–628.

POLLACK, L., 'Invester Activism via Professionally Managed Special-Purpose Funds', in A. W. Sametz (ed.), *Institutional Investing: The Challenges and Responsibilities of the 21st Century* (New York: Columbia, 1991).

POPKIN, S., *The Rational Peasant* (Berkeley: University of California Press, 1979).

—— 'The Political Economy of Peasant Society', in J. Elster (ed.), *Rational Choice* (Oxford: Basil Blackwell, 1986).

—— 'Political Entrepreneurs and Peasant Movements in Vietnam', in M. Taylor (ed.), *Rationality and Revolution* (Cambridge: Cambridge University Press, 1988).

PORTER, M. E., *The Competitive Advantage of Nations* (London: Macmillan, 1990).

—— 'Capital Disadvantage: America's Failing Capital Investment System', *Harvard Business Review*, 70 (1992), 65–82.

PORTER, R., 'Optimal Cartel Trigger Price Strategies', *Journal of Economic Theory*, 29 (1983), 313–38.

POSNER, R. A., 'Oligopoly and Antitrust Laws: A Suggested Approach', *Stanford Law Review*, 21 (1969), 1562–1606.

POZDENA, R. J. and ALEXANDER, V., 'Bank Structure in West Germany' in G. G. Kaufman (ed.), *Banking Structures in Major Countries* (Norwell, Mass.: Kluwer Academic Press, 1992).

PRZEWORSKI, A., *Capitalism and Social Democracy* (Cambridge: Cambridge University Press, 1985).

van RAEMDOCK, D. C. and DIEHL, P. F., 'After the Shooting Stops: Insights on Post-War Economic Growth', *Journal of Peace Research*, 26 (1989), 121–48.

RAWLS, J., *A Theory of Justice* (Oxford: Oxford University Press, 1971).

REICH, R., *The Work of Nations* (New York: Knopf, 1991).

RICHARDSON, J. D., 'The Political Economy of Strategic Trade Policy', *International Organization*, 44 (1990), 197–35.

RIKER, W. H., *The Theory of Political Coalitions* (New Haven, Conn.: Yale University Press, 1962).

—— *Liberalism Against Populism* (San Francisco: W. H. Freeman, 1982).

—— 'Political Theory and the Art of Heresthetics', in A. W. Finifter (ed.),

Political Science: The State of the Discipline (Washington, DC: American Political Science Association, 1983).

—— 'The Heresthetics of Constitution-Making: The Presidency in 1787, with Comments on Determinism and Rational Choice', *American Political Science Review*, 78 (1984), 1–16.

—— *The Art of Political Manipulation* (New Haven, Conn.: Yale University Press, 1986).

—— and ORDESHOOK, P. C., *Introduction to Positive Political Theory* (Englewood Cliffs, NJ: Prentice-Hall, 1973).

ROBERTS, J., *Decision Making During International Crisis* (London: Macmillan, 1988).

ROCK, E., 'The Logic and (Uncertain) Significance of Institutional Shareholder Activism, *Georgetown Law Journal*, 79 (191), 445–78.

ROE, M., 'Political and Legal Restraints on Ownership and Control of Public Companies', *Journal of Financial Economics*, 27 (1990), 7–41.

ROEMER, J., ' "Rational Choice" Marxism', in J. Roemer (ed.), *Analytical Marxism* (Cambridge: Cambridge University Press, 1986).

RORTY, R., *Contingency, Irony and Solidarity* (Cambridge: Cambridge University Press, 1989).

ROTHENBERG, L. S., *Linking Citizens to Government* New York: Cambridge University Press, 1992).

RUNCIMAN, W. G., *A Treatise on Social Theory*, ii. *Substantive Social Theory* (Cambridge: Cambridge University Press, 1989).

RUSSEL, A., 'Olsonian Age Versus Militarism: The Case Against Olson's Account of Relative Economic Decline', MA thesis (Essex, 1989).

SALOP, S. C., 'Practices that (Credibly) Facilitate Oligopoly Co-ordination', in J. F. Stiglitz and G. F. Mathewson (eds.), *New Developments in the Analysis of Market Structure* (Cambridge, Mass.: MIT Press, 1986).

SAMETZ, A. W. (ed.), *Institutional Investing: The Challenges and Responsibilities of the 21st Century* (New York: Business One Irwin, 1991).

SAVAGE, L. J., *Foundations of Statistics* (New York: Dover, 1972).

SCHELLING, T., 'Hockey Helmets, Daylight Saving and Other Binary Choices', in his *Micromotives and Macrobehaviour* (New York: Norton, 1978).

SCHMIDT, M. G., 'The Welfare State and the Economy in Periods of Economic Crisis: A Comparative Study of Twenty-Three OECD Nations', *European Journal of Political Research*, 11 (1983), 1–26.

SCHOFIELD, N., 'Instability of Simple Dynamic Games', *Review of Economic Studies*, 45 (1978), 575–94.

—— 'Generic Instability of Majority Rule', *Review of Economic Studies*, 50 (1983), 695–705.

—— 'Anarchy, Altruism and Cooperation: A Review', *Social Choice and Welfare* 2 (1985).

SCHOFIELD, N., 'Stability of Coalition Governments in Western Europe: 1945–86', *European Journal of Political Economy*, 3 (1987), 555–91.

—— 'Political Competition and Multiparty Coalition Government', *European Journal of Political Research*, 23 (1993), 1–33.

SCHONDHART-BAILEY, C., 'A Model of Trade Policy Liberalization: Looking Inside the British "Hegemon" of the Nineteenth Century', Ph.D. thesis (UCLA, 1991).

—— 'Specific Factors, Capital Markets, Portfolio Diversification, and Free Trade: Domestic Determinants of the Repeal of the Corn Laws', *World Politics*, 43 (1991).

SCHORR, A. L., *Common Decency* (New Haven, Conn.: Yale University Press, 1986).

SCHUMPETER, J., *Capitalism, Socialism and Democracy* (London: Unwin, 1943).

SCOTT, J., *The Moral Economy of the Peasant* (New Haven, Conn.: Yale University Press, 1976).

SEN, A., 'Isolation, Assurance and the Social Rate of Discount', *Quarterly Journal of Economics*, 81 (1967), 112–24.

—— *Choice, Welfare and Measurement* (Oxford: Blackwell, 1982).

SHAPLEY, L. S. and SHUBIK, M., 'A Method for Evaluating the Distribution of Power in a Committee System', in R. Bell, D. V. Edwards, and R. H. Wagner (eds.), *Political Power: A Reader* (London: Collier-Macmillan, 1969).

SHAW, W. 'Marxism, Revolution, and Rationality', in T. Ball and J. Farr (eds.), *After Marx* (Cambridge: Cambridge University Press, 1984).

SHEPSLE, K. A., 'Institutional Foundations of Committee Power', *American Political Science Review*, 81 (1987), 85–104.

—— and WEINGAST, B. R., 'Structure-Induced Equilibrium and Legislative Choice', *Public Choice*, 37 (1981), 503–19.

—— —— 'Political Preferences for the Pork Barrel: A Generalization', *American Journal of Political Science*, 25 (1981), 96–111.

Smith, G., *Democracy in Western Germany* (Aldershot: Gower, 3rd edn., 1985).

SMITH, R., 'Military Expenditure and Investment in OECD Countries', *Journal of Comparative Economics*, 4 (1980), 19–32.

STEEDMAN, I., *From Exploitation to Altruism* (Cambridge: Polity Press, 1989).

STEINMO, S., THELEN, K., and LONGSTRETH, F., (eds.), *Structuring Politics: Historical Institutionalism in Comparative Analysis* (Cambridge: Cambridge University Press, 1992).

STIGLER, G. J., 'A Theory of Oligopoly', in G. J. Stigler, *The Organization of Industry* (Homewood, Ill., 1968).

STIGLITZ, J. E., 'Principal and Agent', in J. Eatwell, M. Milgate, and P. Newton, *The New Palgrave: A Dictionary of Economics*, iii (London: Macmillan, 1987).

STROM, K., *Minority Government and Majority Rule* (Cambridge: Cambridge University Press, 1990).

DE SWAAN, A., *In Care of the State* (Oxford: Polity Press, 1988).

SWEDBERG, A., *Economics and Sociology* (Princeton, NJ: Princeton University Press, 1990).

SYLOS-LABINI, P., *Oligopoly and Technical Progress* (Cambridge, Mass: Harvard University Press, 1962).

TAAGEPERA, R. and SHUGART, M. S., *Seats and Votes: The Effects and Determinants of Electoral Systems* (New Haven, Conn.: Yale University Press, 1989).

TAYLOR, C., *Sources of the Self* (Cambridge: Cambridge University, 1982).

TAYLOR, M., *Community, Anarchy and Liberty* (Cambridge: Cambridge University Press, 1982).

—— *The Possibility of Cooperation* (Cambridge: Cambridge University Press, 1987).

—— 'Rationality and Revolutionary Collective Action', in M. Taylor (ed.), *Rationality and Revolution* (Cambridge: Cambridge University Press, 1988).

—— 'Structure, Culture and Action in the Explanation of Social Change', *Politics and Society*, 17 (1989), 115–62.

—— and LAVER, M., 'Government Coalitions in Western Europe', *European Journal of Political Research*, 1 (1973), 205–48.

THUROW, L. C., *The Zero-Sum Society* (Harmondsworth: Penguin, 1981).

—— *Head to Head* (New York: William Morrow, 1992).

TONG, J., *Disorder Under Heaven* (Stanford, Calif.: Stanford University Press, 1992).

TOWNSEND, R. M., 'Optimal Contracts and Competitive Markets with Costly State Verification', *Journal of Economic Theory*, 21 (1979): 265–93.

TSEBELIS, G., *Nested Games: Rational Choice in Comparative Politics*, (Berkeley, Calif.: University of California Press, 1990).

TULLOCK, G., *Towards a Mathematics of Politics* (Ann Arbor, Mich.: University of Michigan Press, 1967).

UNGER, R., *Plasticity into Power: Comparative-Historical Studies on the Institutional Conditions of Economic and Military Success* (Cambridge: Cambridge University Press, 1987).

VROOM, W. H., *Work and Motivation* (New York: Wiley, 1964).

WAGNER, R. H., 'The Theory of Games and the Balance of Power', *World Politics*, 38 (1985/6): 546–75.

WALLACE, S. and TURNER, J. T., 'Explaining Differences in State Growth: Catching up Versus Olson', *Public Choice*, 51 (1990), 201–13.

WEEDE, E., 'Catch-Up, Distributional Coalitions and Governments as Determinants of Economic Growth or Decline in Industrialised Democracies', *British Journal of Sociology*, 37 (1986), 194–220.

WEISS, F. D., 'Domestic Dimensions of the Uruguay Round: The Case of West Germany in the European Communities', in H. R. Nau (ed.), *Domestic Trade Politics and the Uruguay Round* (New York: Columbia University Press, 1989).

WEITZMAN, M. L. and XU, C., 'Chinese Township Village Enterprises as Vaguely Defined Cooperatives', *Journal of Comparative Economics* (forthcoming).

WHEELER, D., 'Revolution by the Weak, Discursive Warfare, Symbolic Combat and the Palestinian Intifada', paper presented to the American Political Science Association (1992).

WHITE, J., 'Rational Rioters: Leaders, Followers and Popular Unrest in Early Modern Japan', *Politics and Society*, 16 (1988), 35–69.

WHITELEY, P., 'The Political Economy of Economic Growth', *European Journal of Political Science*, 11 (1983), 197–213.

WIKELEY, N., 'Unemployment Benefit, the State and the Labour Market', *Journal of Law and Society*, 16 (1989), 291–309.

WILLIAMS, P. M., 'Public Opinion and the Railway Rates Question in 1886', *English Historical Review*, 67 (1952), 37–73.

WISHAW, F., *Wishaw's Railways of Great Britain and Ireland* (London: John Weale, 1842), 430–71.

YOUNG, I., 'Polity and Group Difference: A Critique of the Ideal of Universal Citizenship', *Ethics*, 99 (1989), 250–74.

ZUSMAN, J., *Governments, Markets and Growth: Financial Systems and the Politics of Industrial Change* (Ithaca, NY: Cornell University Press, 1983).

INDEX